Christian Mortalism from Tyndale to Milton

Christian Mortalism
from
Tyndale to Milton

Norman T. Burns

Harvard University Press
Cambridge, Massachusetts
1972

Permission to quote has been obtained for *Luther's Works*, Volume I,
edited by Jaroslav Pelikan, Copyright 1958 by Concordia Publishing House;
The Pursuit of the Millennium, by Norman Cohn, Copyright ©1961, 1970,
by the author, and published by Oxford University Press; *Religio Medici
and Other Works*, by Sir Thomas Browne, edited by L. C. Martin, published 1964 by The Clarendon Press, Oxford.

To my parents, John J. and Elizabeth Burns;
their love and their guidance have nourished me.

"Any attempt to determine the filiation of the lesser sects in seventeenth-century England must be content to reach uncertain and provisional results."

Ronald A. Knox, *Enthusiasm*

Acknowledgments

This study began some years ago as a doctoral dissertation, and I shall always be grateful to Professor Warner G. Rice, then Chairman of the Department of English Language and Literature at the University of Michigan, who encouraged me at the critical stages of a study that (as he must have known far better than I) was not likely to be free of errors. Professor Frank L. Huntley was the kind and loyal chairman of my doctoral committee. Professor Rune L. Evaldson and Mr. Claude H. Orr, both of the University of Michigan's Willow Run Laboratories, were most kind and understanding as I tried to be both student and publications manager; Mrs. LaVerna Arnett and Miss Charmayne Hall gave almost daily assistance in this matter. Professor Myron Simon offered valuable counsel, and Donald E. Thackrey generously assisted me when I was far from the books I needed.

The work of revising the manuscript for publication has been greatly aided by the suggestions of the readers and staff of the Harvard University Press. My colleague Professor Arthur L. Clements gave a draft of the manuscript the benefit of a discerning critical reading. My work in the summer of 1969 was assisted by a Faculty Research Fellowship from the Research Foundation of the State University of New York; through the good offices of Hugh E. Hunter, Assistant Vice-President for Graduate Studies and Research at my university, some of the costs of manuscript preparation and publication were borne by the Foundation of the State University of New York at Binghamton, Inc. For all that, errors and infelicities doubtless remain in the book; for them only I am responsible.

My wife Dorothy assumed many burdens throughout the years required for this study; her generosity never failed.

State University of New York at Binghamton   N.T.B.

Contents

Introduction

When in the *Christian Doctrine* Milton maintained that the soul dies with the body and is resurrected with the body on the Last Day, "mortalism" was a thoroughly unorthodox but quite unoriginal idea. He had been anticipated in the the heresy by a host of his contemporaries, the most notable of whom were the young Sir Thomas Browne, Thomas Hobbes, and Richard Overton, the author of the notorious *Mans Mortalitie*.[1] It is, on the face of it, strange that such an odd idea could be agreed upon by such a heterogeneous group:[2] the Cromwellian and independent Milton, the Royalist and devout Anglican Browne, the absolutist, "atheistic" Hobbes, and the Leveller and Baptist Overton, three of them splendid representatives of seventeenth-century university education, the fourth a self-educated printer. One would expect such men to agree on very little, but the appeal of Christian mortalism was sufficient to reach across religious, philosophical, social, and political boundaries despite the fact that the idea contradicted a doctrine that had been long

---

[1] The Christian mortalist ideas of these men may be found in the following works: "The Christian Doctrine," in *The Works of John Milton*, gen. ed. Frank A. Patterson, 18 vols. (New York: Columbia University Press, 1931–1938), XV, 37–53, 215–251, Bk. I, Chaps. 7, 13; "An Answer to Bishop Bramhall's Book, Called 'The Catching of the Leviathan,'" *The English Works of Thomas Hobbes*, ed. William Molesworth, 11 vols. (London, 1839–1845), IV, 349–355; Thomas Hobbes, *Leviathan* (London: J. M. Dent, 1965), pp. 240–247, 336–349, 367–371, Chaps. 38, 44, 46; Sir Thomas Browne, *Religio Medici and Other Works*, ed. L. C. Martin (Oxford: Clarendon Press, 1964), pp. 7–8 (Pt. I, Sects. 6–7 of *Religio Medici*); Richard Overton, *Mans Mortalitie*, ed. Harold Fisch (Liverpool: Liverpool University Press, 1968) [hereafter cited as *MM*]. In quotations from older works I have aligned all superscript letters and, with few exceptions, I have not used *sic* to denote irregularities in spelling.

[2] That is, a "group" as we may conceive them. There is no reason to believe that these mortalists were drawn into association by their heresy. Denis Saurat's view that Milton and Overton were intimately associated is thoroughly conjectural: *Milton: Man and Thinker* (London: J. M. Dent, 1944), pp. 268–269, 273–282. In the absence of clear evidence to the contrary, Haller's observation that Milton was virtually unknown to the gossiping Presbyterian heresiographers must be considered a strong argument against Masson's (and later Saurat's) speculation that Milton was personally acquainted with the sectaries. See David Masson, *The Life of John Milton*, 7 vols. (London, 1859–1880), III, 188, 262–263; *Tracts on Liberty in the Puritan Revolution: 1638–1647*, ed. William Haller, 3 vols. (New York: Columbia University Press, 1933–1934), I, 132–134.

cherished by almost all Christians as a fundamental article of their faith.

An inquiry into the circumstances in which these men arrived at their conclusion about the nature of the soul will raise some difficult questions. Why did they think their doctrine was more truly Christian than the received doctrine of the soul's immortality, which continued to get the support of the Roman, Swiss, and English churches? Was their belief in the soul's mortality related to the growing interest of their contemporaries in Epicurean thought? Were these mortalists in some sense proto-Deists? How original were their ideas on the state of the soul between death and resurrection? To what extent, if any, did they influence each other? Did they take their inspiration, as Browne suggests he took his, from the third-century Arabian mortalists mentioned by Eusebius? How radical was their position in relation to Reformation Protestantism? These are pertinent questions for the literary historian who wishes to form some estimate of the significance of mortalism in the thought of Browne, Hobbes, and Milton and to discover what their heresy tells us about their religious attitudes and their relation to the seventeenth-century English intellectual milieu.

Even tentative answers to such questions cannot be formulated with any confidence unless one studies the works of the Interregnum mortalists in historical perspective. In Interregnum England there were men and women who denied personal immortality altogether because they believed that the personal soul was annihilated with the body and that neither soul nor body would be resurrected. There were others who, like Milton, young Browne, Hobbes, and Overton, believed that the soul died temporarily until God at the end of time restored life and immortality to the bodies of the dead. Others, still more moderate, thought the soul was immortal but unconscious until the Last Day. All these unorthodox people were perfectly sure that they were good Christians who understood the true message of Holy Scripture. Most of them were poor and ignorant, many of them we might consider religious fanatics, and none had the stature of Milton, Browne, or Hobbes. They were, in fact, part of a radical Christian theological tradition whose representatives had, mostly orally, taught Englishmen these strange ideas about the sleep or annihilation of the soul from the earliest days of the English Reformation. Without a good understanding of this elusive radical tradition, one is likely to misapprehend the significance and perhaps even the meaning of Interregnum mortalism.

For lack of a satisfactory history of English Christian mortalism, those who have studied the prominent Interregnum mortalists have generally placed them in a false light. (A brief survey of the scholarship on English mortalism appears an an appendix.) Having little or no knowledge of the popularity of all forms of mortalism in the English sects, scholars have, variously, both overestimated the novelty of the heresy in mid-seventeenth-century England and mistaken it for a contribution to the secularization of English life and thought that would culminate in Deism by the end of the century.

I hope to show that the English Christian mortalists, both annihilationists and soul sleepers, looked backward to the earliest days of the Reformation rather than forward to the Enlightenment. It is as wrong to see these mortalists as precursors of secularism as it would be to suppose that the twentieth-century Christian mortalism of such literal biblical exegetes as the Jehovah's Witnesses, the Seventh-day Adventists, and the Christadelphians represents an effort to accommodate the views of scientific positivism, or even to suppose that their mortalist creed makes it easier for their members to accept positivism.[3] The epistemology of the seventeenth-century mortalists, like that of their twentieth-century counterparts, was based on a wholehearted belief in

---

[3] For the Christian mortalist views of these millenarian sects, see Marley Cole, *Jehovah's Witnesses: The New World Society* (New York: Vantage Press, 1955), pp. 156–157; Arthur W. Spalding, *Origin and History of Seventh-day Adventists*, 4 vols. (Washington, D.C.: Review and Herald, 1961), I, 239; for Christadelphian belief, see Bryan R. Wilson, *Sects and Society* (Berkeley and Los Angeles: University of California Press, 1961), pp. 226–227; and Saurat, *Milton*, pp. 282–287. Support for Christian mortalism among modern Protestant theologians is sketched in the Epilogue to this present study.

the Word of God, as it was set down in the Holy Scriptures or (among the annihilationists) communicated by the Holy Spirit. Arguments from reason, if they entered the question at all, were doubtless used as Overton used them, to convince those whose religion was so weak that scriptural proof alone was not sufficient to win their assent.[4] Philip de Mornay, in a parallel case, had once attempted to prove the truth of Christianity, including the immortality of the soul, by rational arguments alone, not because he thought that the Holy Scriptures did not make the best case, but because he assumed an audience that lacked faith in divine revelation.[5]

If the learned discoursed of Pomponazzi, Epicurus, Lucretius, and Aristotle, Protestant England's poor and ignorant sectaries were tutored in mortalism from the Scriptures by the fanatic Edward Wightman, the scandalous Mistress Attaway, the chiliastic William Bowling of Kent, the "arch-Heretique" Clement Wrighter, the Dipper Crab, the Independent John Goodwin, the mystical Thomas Webbe, the libertine and Ranter Laurence Clarkson, and the grand heresiarch Lodowick Muggleton. Thousands of others who held the heresy in England were too lowly to be noticed as individuals, but as Familists, millenarians, Ranters, and General Baptists they testify to mortalism's appeal among the common people. Since the beginnings of the English Reformation,

---

[4] Belief in the General Resurrection is not, of course, rational; since soul sleeping made all hope of immortality rest on belief in the resurrection of the body according to the promise of Christ, Overton's argument (if we grant its sincerity) turns on faith, not reason. Archdeacon Francis Blackburne, in his *An Historical View of the Controversy concerning an Intermediate State and the Separate Existence of the Soul between Death and the General Resurrection . . .* , 2d ed. (London, 1772), p. lxi, urged Christians to accept the sleep of the soul partly because it would destroy the Deists, whose hope for immortal life was based on rational arguments for the natural immortality of the soul.

[5] Philip de Mornay, *A Worke concerning the Trewnesse of Christian Religion,* tr. Sir Philip Sidney and Arthur Golding (London, 1592). Mornay attempted to persuade atheists, Jews, Moslems, and pagans; in a similar effort, Richard Baxter *(The Reasons of the Christian Religion* [London, 1667]) limited himself to rational grounds in an appendix (pp. 489–604) that defends the natural immortality of the soul against "Somatists" or Epicureans." One need not conclude that the author of *Saints Everlasting Rest* lacked confidence in the Gospel message; like Overton, Baxter accommodated that message to his audience.

whenever it was reasonably safe to do so, Christian mortalism had been preached to the people. The pagan mortalism of Epicurus and Lucretius, which alone denied all hope of eternal life, did not contribute to the development of Christian mortalism in England; even the ideas of the more philosophical Interregnum Christian mortalists stand well apart from Epicurean mortalism.

The close study of Christian mortalism in its proper social and theological setting will yield a better understanding of the nature and genesis of the mortalist ideas of Milton, Hobbes, Browne, and Richard Overton (who, being a Baptist, best represents the sectarian origins of the heresy). Opinions about the sleep, death, and even the irrevocable annihilation of the personal soul were part of their Protestant heritage, but until they took up the heresy, records of even the most moderate branch of English mortalism were scanty. In the century after Tyndale attacked the orthodox view of the soul's immortality, no Englishman set down a coherent argument for Christian mortalism until formidable defenses of the heresy were prepared by Overton, Milton, and Hobbes. These prominent Interregnum mortalists articulated and gave permanent form to some of the views of those generations of obscure radical Protestants who, though vocal enough in their day, left us no account of their beliefs. It is the duty of scholarship to give those now silent generations their voice again, to recover their vision of man and his destiny. As the rest of this study will demonstrate, theirs was not a secular but a religious, indeed a Christian, vision, however unorthodox.

One / The Appeal of Christian Mortalism in Reformed England

From the beginning of the English Reformation, Christian mortalism had to struggle against both the traditional Catholicism of England and the influence of the Reformed Church of Switzerland. English Christians traditionally believed that the soul was a spiritual substance that, when freed by death from the body, took up an enlivened, immortal existence in a spiritual world where, in heaven, hell, or purgatory, it awaited the General Judgment at the Last Day. John Calvin, Henry Bullinger, and the reformed Church of England confirmed this doctrine, excising only the offensive idea of purgatory, which savored of salvation by good works, and denying that the saints had any role as intercessors for divine favor. Yet despite this formidable league of the old and the reformed religions, many Englishmen abandoned the idea that the soul after death retains its identity as a conscious and immortal substance. A heresy to traditionalists and most reformers, Christian mortalism was nevertheless established as a minor tradition in Reformation and post-Reformation England. Even a small success against such opposition calls for some account of how a doctrine repugnant to most Englishmen could appeal to Christians at all.

The moderate reforms of the English Church, aimed primarily at removing the most offensive features of Roman Christianity, left much of Roman doctrine intact. The doctrine of a soul immortal from the moment it was infused by God into the embryo was accepted by almost all the English reformers as the teaching of Holy Scripture; thus this Roman doctrine continued to be the received doctrine of Protestant Christianity. Like Thomas More's Utopians, most Englishmen thought that belief in man's dignity required belief in the immortality of his soul. Man's place at the apex of mundane creation was based on the idea that he had a rational, immortal soul, a substance whose vitality was independent of the life of the body. To doubt the existence of this substance would be to doubt the moral nature of the universe, for on the certainty of a life after death depended the whole system of rewards and punishments by which God's justice was vindicated. Epicurean philosophers, standing apart from Christian thought and feeling, might argue that the soul ceases to exist when the body dies, but how could a man claim to be a Christian and yet deny that his soul is immortal? To orthodox Christians such men were plainly Epicureans, atheists disguised as Christians.

But from the Reformation to the Restoration most of England's mortalists were not pagans or atheists but Christians. Some followed the soul-sleeping ideas that Luther had found in Scripture, but most sprang from Anabaptist seed blown over from the Continent. Their strength was among the semiliterate and illiterate poor. Seldom led by regularly ordained ministers and never by secular philosophers, these Englishmen believed mortalism to be the doctrine of the Bible; even the "spiritual" branch of the mortalists was convinced that its belief was based on the revealed Word of God interpreted "spiritually," that is to say, allegorically. After fifteen centuries of biblical commentary by the leaders of a church that was always concerned with integrating faith and reason, it was, of course, not possible even for the ignorant to perceive the Word of God free of the accretions of human philosophy. Throughout this study there will repeatedly be heard in the mortalists' opinions echoes of Aristotle, Plato, Epicurus, and the Scholastics; particularly in the messages of those popular mystics who taught the annihilation of the individual soul and the merging of the soul's divine essence with God will be heard Averroës' contention that the intellectual component of the individual soul leads an impersonal, immortal existence as part of the universal intellect. Christian tradition, oral as well as written, had assimilated many of the terms and ideas of philosophy, and even the least sophisticated mortalists sometimes dealt with ideas whose philosophical origins were obscure to them. The influence of philosophical ideas on the English doctrines of Christian mortalism was, nevertheless, indirect, mediated in some cases perhaps by continental Libertinism and the German mysticism of Meister Eckhart, Johann Tauler, and Heinrich Suso. Most English mortalists of all types seem quite unaware that their analyses of Scripture commonly had something of philosophy in them. Milton, Hobbes, Browne, and Overton were, on the whole, accomplished in philosophy, and the last three were pleased to note that immortality could not be successfuly defended on philosophical grounds, but like their more naïve brethren they believed in mortalism not because it was the doctrine of Aristotle, Averroës, Epicurus, or Pomponazzi, but primarily because they believed it had the authority of Holy Scripture behind it.

Thoroughly Protestant in their acceptance of revelation as the only source of Christian doctrine, the Christian mortalists did not, however, maintain their belief about the soul as a peculiar doctrine isolated from the rest of their faith; mortalism complemented and sanctioned other articles of their creed. Mortalism was frequently held in association with other doctrines and attitudes that were more broadly supported among English Protestants: the belief that the resurrection of the body was central to the faith of Christians; the expectation that Christ would establish his millennial kingdom on earth; the dislike for the Roman doctrines of purgatory and the invocation of saints; and the confidence that heaven could in some sense be enjoyed in this life. To be sure, many of those attracted to these positions were not ready to abandon the traditional belief about the soul in order to direct attention to the importance of the General Resurrection and the Second Coming, to add force to their arguments against the Church of Rome, or to stress the necessity for personal union with Christ in this life; nevertheless, some of the more daring spirits among them saw mortalism not only as a scriptural doctrine, but also as part of a coherent Christian creed.

Before we inquire further into how mortalism appealed to English Christians or into the nature of the Protestant position that mortalism opposed, it will be necessary to clarify what the doctrines of English Christian mortalism were and to establish the meaning of the terms used to describe them. Christian mortalism was never a unified or even a coherent movement in England, and there is no agreement among scholars about either the nature of Christian mortalism or the proper terminology to be used in discussing the various positions encompassed by the term "Christian mortalism."[1]

When scholars speak of the "mortalism" of Milton, Hobbes, and the young Browne, they follow the hyperbolic title of Overton's *Mans Mortalitie.* Despite the fact that "mortalism" suggests opposition to human immortality in any form, an idea far from the minds of these Interregnum soul sleepers, the currency of the term for three centuries makes it seem wiser and more useful to clarify its meaning rather than to introduce a wholly new term for the idea that the personal soul is not in a conscious state between death and resurrection.

The problem will be simplified if we eliminate at the outset some types of belief in the natural mortality of the soul that frequently confuse discussions of Christian mortalism. We must keep in mind that we are speaking of what most Reformation Christians considered a *heresy;* to come within the scope of this study, a mortalist idea must not only be repugnant to what most members of the Roman, Reformed, Lutheran, and English churches conceived to be their true Christian heritage, but it must be derived from the Word of God by Christians who obstinately profess it, thereby hoping to clarify the divine revelation, to show the harmony of mortalism with the other essential doctrines drawn from Holy Scripture, and to establish mortalism as the restored doctrine of Christianity. Like all heresies, Christian mortalism was a threat to the orthodox position chiefly because it was developed and supported by Christians within the framework of Christian thought and feeling; had it been so foreign to Christianity and so great a perversion of the truth as its orthodox opponents liked to claim, Christian mortalism would not have been so difficult to purge from Reformation and post-Reformation Protestantism.

[1] George H. Williams *(The Radical Reformation* [Philadelphia: Westminster Press, 1962], pp. 582–583) complains of the "ineptness of nomenclature" with which discussion of the heresy has been burdened. My attempt to clarify the terms is indebted to Williams' exposition (pp. 21–24, 104–106, 581–586, *et passim*) although I have not completely adopted his terminology. The other scholars who have studied Christian mortalism are not sufficiently aware of the complexity of the heresy to be helpful in clarifying the nomenclature (see Appendix).

We therefore need not consider those who, like the Epicureans Farinata and Cavalcante in Canto X of the *Inferno*,
derived their denial of immortality from pagan philosophers;
such men not only avoided scriptural argument, but they did
not declare themselves to be attempting the restoration of
the true doctrine of Christ. The Epicureans of the Reformation, with whom the enemies of the Christian mortalists were
happy to confuse them, are in this class, as are certain Italian
Aristotelians who flourished at the beginning of the sixteenth
century. These Italians, the most notable of whom was Pietro
Pomponazzi (1462–1524), maintained (or said that Aristotle
maintained) that the immortality of the individual human
soul could not be demonstrated by philosophy. Their philosophical interests and not their piety led them to their conclusion; so far were they from being Christian mortalists that
they granted that divine revelation proved the immortality of
the soul.[2] In 1513 the Fifth Lateran Council under Leo X,
needlessly citing appropriate proofs from Scripture, denounced those who raised even philosophical doubts about
the immortality of the soul.[3] When Sir John Davies wrote
Nosce Teipsum (1599), his spirited defense of the soul's immortality was grounded in philosophy, thereby answering
the doubters in their own terms.

[2] The doctrines of the Italian Aristotelians are ably summarized by
Williams *(Radical Reformation,* pp. 20–24) and in *The Renaissance Philosophy of Man,* ed. Ernst Cassirer *et al.* (Chicago: University of Chicago
Press, 1948), pp. 257–279. Williams, however, makes Pomponazzi more of
a Christian mortalist than he was by saying that Pomponazzi thought
revelation taught us to expect immortality only at the resurrection (pp.
22–23). But Pomponazzi, in the fifteenth chapter of his *Tractus de Im-
mortalitate Animae* (1516), repudiates his philosophical views as inferior
to the more certain truths of Holy Scripture as interpreted by the Fathers.
He nowhere limits his acceptance of immortality to anything less than
the Roman dogma of the soul's uninterrupted, conscious life. See Pietro
Pomponazzi, *On the Immortality of the Soul,* tr. William H. Hay II, in
Renaissance Philosophy of Man, ed. Cassirer *et al.,* pp. 280–381. For an
account of rationally grounded skepticism about the immortality of the
soul during the Renaissance, see Don Cameron Allen, *Doubt's Boundless
Sea* (Baltimore: Johns Hopkins Press, 1964), pp. 150–185.

[3] The relevant passage of the decree is quoted in Williams, *Radical
Reformation,* p. 23. Rome was, of course, more likely than the reformers
to consider a modification of the traditional understanding of Aristotle a
threat to Christian truth.

Nor does Christian mortalism include the whole of the belief that the soul is by its nature destined to die with the
body, for in one sense that belief was among the reformers
a pious view intended to express man's humble position relative to God and to provide an orthodox gloss on 1 Tim.
6: 16, which refers to God "who only hath immortality."
Many of the Fathers believed that the soul of man was by
nature mortal, and immortal only by the grace of God.[4] Calvin, in a tract expressly written to refute Christian mortalism,
nevertheless denies the *natural* immortality of the soul.

> When we say that the spirit of man is immortal, we do
> not affirm that it can stand against the hand of God, or sub-
> sist without his agency. Far from us be such blasphemy!
> But we say that it is sustained by his hand and blessing.
> Thus Irenaeus, who with us asserts the immortality of the
> spirit, (Irenaeus adv. Haeres. lib. 5,) wishes us, however, to
> learn that by nature we are mortal, and God alone immor-
> tal. And in the same place he says, "Let us not be inflated
> and raise ourselves up against God, as if we had life of
> ourselves; and let us learn by experience that we have
> endurance for eternity through his goodness, and not from
> our nature."[5]

Even with the scope of this study thus limited to the
heresy, the question of nomenclature remains vexing. "Christian mortalism" is itself but a convenient term for referring
to a variety of incongruous opinions, heresies that had in
common only the belief that the soul does not lead a conscious existence between death and the General Resurrection.
The disparate "schools" of Christian mortalism had no common origin except possibly among the amorphous "Ana-

[4] For an illuminating discussion of this distinction between the Platonic and Patristic views of immortality, see Harry A. Wolfson, *Religious
Philosophy* (Cambridge, Mass.: Belknap Press of Harvard University Press,
1961), pp. 69–103.

[5] John Calvin, *Psychopannychia* (1542), in *Calvin's Tracts*, tr. Henry
Beveridge, 3 vols. (Edinburgh, 1851), III, 478; all citations are from this
edition. For a commentary on this belief of Calvin, see François Wendel,
Calvin, tr. Philip Mairet (New York: Harper and Row, 1963), pp. 174–175.
Williams slips when he says that the Protestant opponents of the Christian
mortalists believed in natural immortality (*Radical Reformation*, pp.
24, 583).

baptists" whose own movement resists sharp definition; the mortalist "schools" never made common cause, and no leader of sufficient stature and purpose arose to forge them into a weapon for the reform of Christian doctrine. It is likely that the task of reconciling their views would have been impossible even if it had been attempted, for the Christian mortalists through the Restoration did not agree on the nature of the soul or even on its ultimate destiny.

Any historical account of Christian mortalism, however, is in continual danger of leaving the impression that these heretics were more unified than in fact they were. Historical exposition demands an orderly and structured presentation of even the chaotic and frequently "spiritual" ideas of the Reformation sects. Like the historian who freely uses the term "Puritan" even while he insists on the irreconcilable factionalism of a "movement" that must somehow be conceived of broadly enough to embrace both a William Prynne and a Roger Williams, I shall refer to "Christian mortalism" and its "branches" as if it were a coherent "movement" even while I insist that the mortalist sects perceived no such coherence in their own ranks. The following schematic, somewhat artificial account of the "branches" of Christian mortalism is offered merely as a guide through the tangle of the mortalists' actual thoughts, beliefs, hopes, and attitudes, which will be presented in sufficent detail and in their appropriate contexts in the succeeding chapters of this study; those chapters will duly correct any impression of a coherent movement that this analysis may leave.

"Christian mortalism" is the generic term for the belief that according to divine revelation the soul does not exist as an independent, conscious substance after the death of the body. Two branches of Christian mortalism may be sharply distinguished. Since all Christian mortalists agreed that the destinies of the personal soul and the body were inextricably linked, they may be distinguished quite as easily by their beliefs about the ultimate destiny of the body as by their beliefs about the nature of the soul: the "annihilationists," who denied there would ever be a resurrection of the body, believed that the personal soul suffers irrevocable dissolution with the body, while the "soul sleepers," who believed in the ultimate resurrection of the body on the Last Day, also believed that the personal soul will share in that resurrection to immortality. Although these two types of Christian mortalists, resurrectionists and antiresurrectionists, hold clearly incompatible doctrines, they have not heretofore been clearly distinguished in any discussion of English mortalism; modern scholars as well as the mortalists' contemporaries have confused the two.[6]

The annihilationists were part of a group of enthusiasts, most often called "Libertines" or "Familists" by their contemporaries, that was often accused of denying the resurrection of the body. In the next chapter I shall suggest the name "experimental Christians" for these enthusiasts and trace their historical and doctrinal development in England from their sparse documentary remains. It must suffice at this point to say that many of these enthusiasts became pantheists who envisioned immortality only for the "divine essence" in man, an impersonal eternal existence as an undifferentiated part of God. For them the Gospel message of resurrection referred only to the spiritual rising from the bonds of sin in this life; at death the immortal essence of the soul was dissolved in God while the body and personality, by which man had been individualized, underwent complete and final annihilation. The annihilationists struck at the roots of orthodox Chris-

---

[6] Williams *(Radical Reformation)* comes closest to identifying the full range of mortalist beliefs (p. 21), but his discussion of continental annihilationists (pp. 351–353) is brief and, at least for English annihilationism, misleading. He notes a relationship between the Averroistic idea of the absorption of the rational soul into the universal Intellect and the Libertine denial of personal immortality; the English annihilationists were sustained more by their variety of mysticism than by pagan philosophy. Among the mortalists' contemporaries, Alexander Gill the elder touched upon the complexity of the movement. Thomas Edwards *(Gangraena,* 2d ed. [London, 1647]) included all varieties of Christian mortalism in his catalogue of heresies, but gave no coherent account of any Interregnum sect. Robert Baillie, the Scottish Commissioner to the Westminster Assembly, thought that the annihilationists were simply soul sleepers grown bolder; see *Anabaptism, the Trve Fovntaine of Independency, Brownisme, Antinomy,* [and] *Familisme* (London, 1647), p. 99.

tianity, for their views could not be reconciled with the traditional doctrine of an afterlife in which discrete souls are personally judged in their individuality as fit either for eternal bliss or eternal pain. Their mortalism thus destroyed the traditional sanctions that supported the Christian moral system. Although the more moderate annihilationists tried to replace the older sanctions with exhortations on the joys of sanctity and the horrors of alienation from God in this life, in 1648 the conservative majority in Parliament recognized the danger and prescribed the death penalty for those who obstinately denied the General Resurrection or a day of Judgment after death.[7]

The soul sleepers, since they merely insisted that personal, conscious immortality did not begin until the resurrection of the body, offered a milder challenge to traditional Christianity. To be sure, some of their contemporaries doubtless joined Sir Thomas More in maintaining that punishment deferred until the Last Day is an incitement to sin, and others may have agreed with Henry More that memory and personality could not survive so long a sleep.[8] Although neither of these objections is very weighty, both men understood the soul sleepers' position and addressed the problem fairly. The soul sleepers were more seriously threatened by those who assumed that they meant to cast doubt on the certainty of an afterlife; to these the soul sleepers constituted a social danger. Many people had more excuse than Henry Bullinger, an able theologian, to make such a gross error. "If as yet there be any light-headed men to whom the immortality of the soul seemeth doubtful, or which utterly deny the same, these truly are unworthy to have the name of men; for they are plagues of the commonwealth, and very beasts, worthy to be hissed and driven out of the company of men. For he lacketh a bridle to

---

[7] *Acts and Ordinances of the Interregnum, 1642–1660,* ed. C. H. Firth and R. S. Rait, 3 vols. (London: His Majesty's Stationery Office, 1911), I, 1134.

[8] Sir Thomas More, *The Dialogue concerning Tyndale,* ed. W. E. Campbell (London: Eyre and Spottiswoode, 1927), pp. 276, 279, of the modern text; Henry More, "Antipsychopannychia," *Psychodia Platonica* (Cambridge, 1642), stanzas 2–14.

restrain him, and hath cast away all honesty and shame, and
is prepared in all points to commit any mischief, whosoever
believeth that the soul of man is mortal."[9] Despite such pious
slanders, in its 1648 ordinance against blasphemy Parliament
seemed to recognize that the sleepers were less dangerous
than the annihilationists when it prescribed imprisonment
rather than death for those who obstinately maintained that
"the soul of man dieth or sleepeth when the body is dead"
(*Acts and Ordinances,* ed. Firth and Rait, I, 1135).

Parliament's proscription of the "death" as well as the
"sleep" of the soul follows the traditional formula of the reformed creeds that, under the influence of Calvin and Bullinger, first attempted the suppresion of the soul sleepers. As
the formula suggests, the soul sleepers were divided into two
distinct camps. Alexander Gill the elder, High Master of St.
Paul's School from 1608 to 1635, identified the Christian mortalist positions of his own day and provided a useful set of
distinctive names for them: "if . . . the soule immediately
after it is departed, is a partaker of joy or paine: How shall we
hearken to that doctrine of the *Sadduces, Act.* 23.8. or to that
Arabian errour of the *Thnetopsychitoe,* that the soule doth
die with the body? Or to our late dreamers the *Prychopenny-
chitoe* [*sic*], who affirme, that the soule sleepes in the grave
till it bee awaked againe with the body at the generall resurrection?"[10] The annihilationists were commonly called "Sadducees" at the time because they denied the resurrection of
the body: the scriptural citation refers to the verse "For the
Sadducees say that there is no resurrection, neither angel, nor
spirit." Gill's reference to the Arabian error recalls the pas-

---

[9] Henry Bullinger, "Of the Reasonable Soul of Man; and of His Most
Certain Salvation after the Death of His Body: The Tenth Sermon," *The
Decades of Henry Bullinger: The Fourth Decade,* tr. H. I., ed. Thomas
Harding, Parker Society (Cambridge, 1851), p. 386. Calvin, no less ready
than Bullinger to suppress the soul sleepers, did not descend to such a
scandalous misrepresentation as this. Bullinger's *Decades* (first published
in England as *Fiftie Godlie Sermons,* tr. H. I., 3 vols. (London: 1577), was
exceedingly popular; new editions were issued in 1584 and 1587.

[10] Alexander Gill, *The Sacred Philosophie of Holy Scripture* (London,
1635), pp. 90–91, cited in C. A. Patrides, " 'Paradise Lost' and the Mortalist
Heresy," *Notes and Queries,* CCII (1957), 250 n.

sage in Eusebius that describes a mortalist sect that flourished in Arabia about the middle of the third century: "About the same time others arose in Arabia, putting forward a doctrine foreign to the truth. They said that during the present time the human soul dies and perishes with the body, but that at the time of the resurrection they will be renewed together. And at that time also a synod of considerable size assembled, and Origen, being again invited thither, spoke publicly on the question with such effect that the opinions of those who had formerly fallen were changed." Scant as this account is, it formed the sole basis for St. Augustine's condemnation of the heresy, and probably St. John Damascene referred to these Arabians when he gave the heretics a name that reflects their error: "The *Thnetopsychites* introduce the doctrine that the human soul is similar to that of beasts and that it perishes with the body."[11] Those who granted that the soul lives after the death of the body, but argued that it is unconscious until the General Resurrection Gill calls the "psychopannychists," a term introduced by Calvin and used extensively by Henry More.[12]

Although the thnetopsychists did not believe that the soul was an immortal substance that slept when separated from

[11] Eusebeius, *Church History*, tr. Arthur C. McGiffert, in *A Select Library of Nicene and Post-Nicene Fathers*, ed. Philip Schaff and Henry Wace, 2d Ser., 14 vols. (New York: 1890–1900), I, 279 (Bk. VI, Chap. 37); *The De Haeresibus of Saint Augustine*, tr. Liguori G. Müller (Washington, D.C.: Catholic University of America Press, 1956), p. 117 (Chap. 83); *Saint John of Damascus: Writings*, tr. Frederic H. Chase Jr. (New York: Fathers of the Church, 1958), p. 150. In the *Dialogue of Origen with Heraclides*, which was not found until 1941, Origen defends at length the soul's immortality on scriptural grounds alone; see *Alexandrian Christianity*, tr. John Oulton and Henry Chadwick (Philadelphia: Westminster Press, 1954), pp. 444–454. Origen considers the point abstruse and the argument is involved, but presumably he took a similar approach at the (earlier?) synod that Eusebius refers to.

[12] *The Oxford English Dictionary*, ed. James A. H. Murray *et al.*, 13 vols. (Oxford: Clarendon Press, 1933), defines "psychopannychy" as the "all-night sleep of the soul" and lists Calvin's *Psychopannychia* as the first use. Calvin attacked thnetopsychists as well as psychopannychists in his tract. More refuted the thnetopsychists only indirectly in his philosophical poem "Antipsychopannychia" and in *An Explanation of the Grand Mystery of Godliness* (London, 1660), in *The Theological Works of . . . Henry More* (London, 1708), pp. 11–21 (Bk. I, Chaps. 6–10).

the body, but rather maintained that "soul" was merely a name for the insubstantial "breath of life" that, of course, could not exist without the body, they may still properly be called soul sleepers because they had a lively expectation of the future resurrection of both soul and body to immortal life. Like Christians who since New Testament times have referred to the death of the body as a "sleep" because they are confident of its resurrection, the thnetopsychists may well have said that the soul "sleeps" whenever they wanted to emphasize their faith that the soul will be raised to immortality on the Last Day. Milton, having revealed himself as a thorough thnetopsychist in Book I, Chapter 13, of the *Christian Doctrine*, yet refers to that chapter as his proof "that the soul as well as the body *sleeps* till the day of resurrection."[13] The psychopannychists believed that the immortal substance called soul literally slept until the resurrection of the body; the thnetopsychists, denying that the soul was an immortal substance, believed that the soul slept after death only in a figurative sense. Both groups of soul sleepers believed in the personal immortality of the individual after the resurrection of the body, and so they should not be confused with the annihilationists.

A nation committed to Protestantism had, in fact, little to fear from the soul sleepers of either type. The reformed religion had eschewed purgatory and the invocation of saints; thus, unlike the Church of Rome, it defined no practical relationship between the faithful departed and the faithful on earth. Milton's judgment that the question of whether the whole man, body and soul, dies may be discussed "without endangering our faith or devotion, whichever side of the controversy we espouse" seems a sober and balanced view (*CM*, XV, 219; Bk. I, Chap. 13). Nevertheless, the English Church,

---

[13] *The Works of John Milton*, gen. ed. Frank A. Patterson, 18 vols. (New York: Columbia University Press, 1931–1938), XV, 341; Bk. I, Chap. 16 [italics mine]. This edition will hereafter be cited as *CM* (for "Columbia Milton"), with references to book and chapter numbers in the *Christian Doctrine* following the reference to volume and page in *CM*.

the bishops and most of their Puritan critics as well, firmly opposed the sleepers.

With the exception of some early Lutherans and Anabaptists and later the Muggletonians and some Familists, General Baptists, and Independents, English Christians stayed with the traditional view of the soul. Then as now, belief that spirit is incorruptible, possessed of its own vitality, superior to and independent of matter, seemed to most men the obvious and necessary consequence of being a Christian. If doubt was cast on the received opinion of the nature and destiny of the soul, they thought the question could be easily settled by reference to Holy Scripture. One did not have to be skilled in hermeneutics to know that the Good Thief entered Paradise on the first Good Friday and that Dives saw Lazarus in the bosom of Abraham; if some radical argued that Paradise is not Heaven and that the Dives and Lazarus story is but a parable, not history, then one could turn to that great exegete John Calvin, who had attacked the sleepers on scriptural grounds alone in his *Psychopannychia* and *The Institutes of the Christian Religion.*

Calvin's attacks on the soul sleepers ensured that not even the English Puritans would discard the doctrine of the continuous, conscious immortality of the soul as a Roman innovation comparable to the doctrines of purgatory and the invocation of saints. Calvin's dispute with the continental mortalists in the early years of the Reformation remained remarkably pertinent for more than a century after the beginning of the English Reformation because the stand of both sides in the dispute underwent no essential change. Calvin, like the leaders of the English Church, struggled chiefly against the mortalism preached by members of what George Williams has called the "Radical Reformation," that branch of the reform movement which was impatient with the moderate views and polities of the Lutheran, Zwinglian, and Calvinist churches; although these radical congregations rarely attempted to establish common doctrines, they largely agreed about the need for personal regeneration, even deification, in Christ and for establishing a community after the apostolic model, independent of the state (Williams, *Radical Reformation*, pp. xxiv–xxv). English orthodoxy usually referred to these radicals as "Anabaptists" (although many did not insist on believer's baptism)[14] and delighted in associating them all with the violent, chiliastic Anabaptists who governed Münster in polygamous misrule from 1534 to 1535. In addition to attacking them as a threat to civil order, the orthodox constantly derided the Anabaptists, in England and the Continent, for their lack of unanimity in doctrine. Ready to discard as corrupt and merely human the traditions of more than a thousand years of Christianity, the Anabaptists could look only to Holy Scripture for guidance in their beliefs; being, for the most part, unschooled in philosophy, theology, and the niceties of exegesis, they had to depend on their own often circumscribed resources for their doctrinal interpretations; refusing on principle to coerce in matters of doctrine, they were ready to tolerate a considerable variety of opinions about doctrine.[15] Although some of these radicals were not so ignorant as their opponents liked to think, the common opinion of them as an uneducated people, "men of one book," seems on the whole to have been just.

Such, certainly, was Calvin's judgment when he wrote *Psychopannychia* (1542), the most significant early attack

[14] Franklin H. Littell deals with the problem of defining "Anabaptist" throughout his *The Anabaptist View of the Church*, 2d ed. (Boston: Starr King Press, 1958), and concludes that the central feature of the movement was a church polity based on voluntary membership in a disciplined, gathered congregation whose membership was limited to the elect. Although the word "Anabaptist" is debased coin suggesting a coherence in doctrine and worship that the radicals did not exhibit, it is not without value. It is a simple term for a complex movement and, conscious of its lack of precision, I shall use it as a convenient synonym for "radical reformer," much as it was used in the period.

[15] Anabaptist belief in toleration was well-known and much criticized in England. The more organized Anabaptist congregations, like Menno Simons', reluctantly used "the ban" to enforce discipline (following Christ's injunction, Matt. 18: 15–17), but even then it was used chiefly to reprove sinners, not to gain uniformity of doctrine; see Littell, *Anabaptist View*, pp. 86–89. The "spiritualizers" (to whom the annihilationists were closely related) were, of course, opposed to all forms of compulsion, including "the ban" (*ibid.*, p. 22).

upon the Anabaptist soul sleepers.[16] Calvin argues exclusively from Scripture because Scripture was the basis of the sleepers' argument. Unlike the Jews of Berea who first humbly received the message of Paul and Silas and only then sought to verify it out of Scripture (Acts 17:11), according to Calvin the proud Anabaptists listen to no authority and, lacking guidance, search out strange meanings in Scripture.

> Such was not the conduct of those who, when they had received the word, searched the Scriptures to see whether these things were so (Acts xvii.11)—a noble example, if we would imitate it; but we, I know not from what sloth, or rather contempt, receive the word of God in such a way that when we have learned three syllables, we immediately swell up with an opinion of wisdom, and think ourselves rich men and kings! Hence, you see so many who, unlearned themselves, keep tragically bawling out about the ignorance of the age! But what can you do? They are called, and would wish to be thought Christians, because they have got a slight knowledge of some commonplaces; and as they would be ashamed to be ignorant of anything, they with the greatest confidence, as if from a tripod, give forth decisions upon all things. Hence so many schisms, so many errors, so many stumblingblocks to our faith, through which the name and word of God are blasphemed among

---

[16] The tract was probably written in 1534. It includes two prefaces, one written in Orléans in 1534, the other written in Basel in 1536. Williams (*Radical Reformation,* pp. 580–591) gives an account of Calvin's vacillations in deciding to publish his draft of *Psychopannychia* and argues that the earliest extant version (1542) is the first edition. According to Williams, the prefaces were not part of two earlier, lost editions, as is frequently supposed, but were drafted when Calvin very nearly sent his manuscript to the printer (see particularly p. 583, n. 5). It is, nevertheless, an early work of Calvin. Among attacks against the soul sleepers, it is anticipated in composition and publication only by Henry Bullinger's *Von dem unverschämten Frevel* (Zürich, 1531); see Williams, *Radical Reformation,* p. 201. Bullinger's book was published in English as *An Holsome Antidotus or Counterpoysen, agaynst the Pestylent Heresye and Secte of the Anabaptistes,* tr. John Veron (London, 1548). John Calvin, *A Short Instruction for to Arme All Good Christian People agaynst the Pestiferous Errours of the Common Secte of Anabaptistes* (London, 1549), published five years after the French edition, contains an abbreviated version of *Psychopannychia.* The complete text was not made available in English until the time when the English Familists, often considered to be mortalists, were being suppressed: John Calvin, *An Excellent Treatise of the Immortalytie of the Soule,* tr. T. Stocker (London, 1581).

the ungodly. At length, (this is the head of the evil!) while they proceed obstinately to defend whatever they have once rashly babbled, they begin to consult the oracles of God, in order that they may there find support to their errors [*Tracts*, tr. Beveridge, III, 417].

Calvin's treatise confirmed Holy Scripture as the ground on which the mortalist debate was to be conducted among Christians for the next century. Had Pomponazzi never written his daring analysis of Aristotle's view of the soul, Calvin would still have been compelled to oppose the Christian mortalists, who (as they thought) derived their view from Holy Scripture alone.

In the *Psychopannychia* Calvin conveniently cites and discusses most of the scriptural texts used by both sides in the next century of dispute.[17] It would be tedious to recount the numerous texts at issue and the different constructions each side put on them, but Calvin's description of the two opposed views, the sleepers' and his own, will serve to define for us the nature of the quarrel in the early years of the Reformation.[18]

Calvin distinguishes two opinions among the soul sleepers: "Some, while admitting it [the human soul] to have a real existence, imagine that it sleeps in a state of insensibility from Death to The Judgment-day, when it will awake from its sleep; while others will sooner admit anything than its real existence, maintaining that it is merely a vital power which is derived from arterial spirit on the action of the lungs, and being unable to exist without body, perishes along with the body, and vanishes away and becomes evanescent

[17] Leonard N. Wright, "Christian Mortalism in England (1643–1713)," unpub. diss., University of Texas, 1939, pp. 48, 58, says that Calvin's citation of the texts in dispute and his account of how the sleepers used them preserved mortalism until Overton revived it; this irony is less attractive when one is aware, as Wright is not, of the vital mortalist tradition in England that spanned the years between Calvin and Overton.

[18] Calvin also treats the question of the immortality of the soul in his *Institutes of the Christian Religion*, tr. John Allen, 7th American ed., 2 vols. (Philadelphia: Presbyterian Board of Christian Education, 1936), I, 202–216; Bk. I, Chap. XV. He summarizes his reasons for opposing the mortalists in *Institutes*, II, 251–253; Bk. III, Chap. XXV, Sect. vi, but adds nothing to his thorough attack in *Psychopannychia*.

till the period when the whole man shall be raised again" (*Tracts,* tr. Beveridge, III, 419). The first position, psychopannychism, evidently grants that the soul is substantial (has a "real existence") and does not depend on the body for its being. As we shall see, psychopannychism seems to have been the opinion of Luther (at least in his early career) and his English disciples William Tyndale and John Frith. Calvin is impatient with psychopannychism, partly for what he sees as its dishonesty and partly because it constitutes an unnecessary and unscriptural break with Christian tradition: "For those who admit that the soul lives, and yet deprive it of all sense, feign a soul which has none of the properties of soul, or dissever the soul from itself, seeing that its nature, without which it cannot possibly exist, is to move, to feel, to be vigorous, to understand. As Tertullian says, 'The soul of the soul is perception' " (*Tracts,* tr. Beveridge, III, 427). Calvin recognizes, nevertheless, that psychopannychism is the milder of the two opinions: although he would not tolerate the errors of the psychopannychists, he thinks that the "madness" of those who deny that the soul is a substance "ought to be severely repressed" (*Tracts,* tr. Beveridge, III, 414). These thnetopsychists deny that the soul can be said to exist at all, at least not as an entity separable from the body; to them soul is but the "vital power" of the body, a phenomenon that is really the expression of the organized, material constituents of the body. To the thnetopsychists the human soul can not be distinguished in kind from that of the beasts; be it called "life" or "breath," the soul is an abstraction that signifies the activities of certain material bodies. Since they know by the promise of God that the material body at least of man will be raised to immortal life, it follows that the thnetopsychists believe in the ultimate immortality of the human soul because every living body by definition has "soul." In my last chapter I shall discuss how closely Overton, Milton, Hobbes, and young Browne may be identified with the thnetopsychist position, a radical opinion that was, however, far more conservative than that of the true revolutionaries, the annihilationist enthusiasts, of whom Calvin here takes no notice.

Calvin's own position on the state of the soul between death and resurrection is subtly and carefully drawn. He studiously avoids the pitfalls of Romanism while trying to preserve the traditional belief in an alert, active soul. In Calvin's view, at death the souls of the reprobate go directly to their punishment while the souls of the elect go directly to their reward, each state being but a foretaste of what will follow the Last Day.

> In the mean while, as the Scripture uniformly commands us to look forward with eager expectation to the coming of Christ, and defers the crown of glory which awaits us till that period, let us be content within these limits which God prescribes to us—that the souls of pious men, after finishing their laborious warfare, depart into a state of blessed rest, where they wait with joy and pleasure for the fruition of the promised glory; and so, that all things remain in suspense till Christ appears as the Redeemer. And there is no doubt that the condition of the reprobate is the same as Jude assigns to the devils, who are confined and bound in chains till they are brought forth to the punishment to which they are doomed [*Institutes*, II, 253; Bk. III, Chap. XXV, Sect. vi].

Calvin is careful to insist that the state of the elect souls is imperfect, though joyous and peaceful, for Resurrection and Judgment must keep a role even while the sleepers are being refuted; the imperfect state is, however, always represented as static, lest the papist ideas of purgation and spiritual development beyond the grave creep in.

> Now, when they wait for something which they see not, and desire what they have not, it is evident that their peace is imperfect. On the other hand, while they confidently expect what they do expect, and in faith desire what they desire, it is clear that their desire is tranquil. This peace is increased and advanced by death, which, freeing, and as it were discharging them from the warfare of this world, leads them into the place of peace, where, while wholly intent on beholding God, they have nothing better to which they can turn their eyes or direct their desire. Still, something is wanting which they desire to see, namely,

the complete and perfect glory of God, to which they always aspire. . . . But if the eyes of the elect look to the supreme glory of God as their final good, their desire is always moving onward till the glory of God is complete, and this completion awaits the judgment day [*Tracts*, tr. Beveridge, III, 435–436].

Calvin was assisted in his dispute with the sleepers by another tireless writer, Henry Bullinger (1504–1575), pastor of Zürich. Although he added nothing substantial to Calvin's argument, Bullinger spoke from an influential pulpit; he was particularly popular in England, where much of his work was published in the native tongue, and where many of the Marian exiles remembered him affectionately for the hospitality he showed them in Zürich. Although his controversial works against the soul sleepers were doubtless effective, he struck his most powerful blow against the mortalists when he condemned them in *The Second Helvetic Confession* (1566):

> We say, also, that man doth consist of two, and those diverse substances in one person; of a soul immortal (as that which being separated from his body doth neither sleep nor die), and a body mortal, which, notwithstanding, at the last judgment shall be raised again from the dead, that from henceforth the whole man may continue forever in life or in death.
> We condemn all those who mock at, or by subtle disputations call into doubt, the immortality of the soul, or say that the soul sleeps, or that it is part of God.[19]

Bullinger's was not the first Protestant creedal statement against the Christian mortalists, being preceded by both the English Edwardine Articles of 1553[20] and *The Confession of*

---

[19] *The Creeds of Christendom*, ed. Philip Schaff, 4th ed., 3 vols. (New York: Harper, 1919), III, 842. Schaff says (I, 392) that Bullinger was the sole author of this creed.

[20] "XL. *The soulles of them that departe this life doe neither die with the bodies, nor sleep idlie.*

"Thei whiche saie, that the soulles of suche as departe hens doe sleepe, being without al sence, fealing, or perceiuing, vntil the daie of iudgement, or affirme that the soulles die with the bodies, and at the laste daie shalbe raised vp with the same, doe vtterlie dissent from the right beliefe declared to vs in holie Scripture." Charles Hardwick, *A History of the Articles of Religion*, 3d ed. (London, 1884), p. 348.

the Faith and Doctrine, Belevit and Professit be the Protes-
tantis of Scotland (1560),[21] but it was the most important,
since his creed became an international standard for Protestantism.[22]

With the formulation of these creeds, the face of Reformed
Protestantism was officially turned against the Christian mortalists. Those churches under Swiss influence, particularly
those that felt themselves menaced by the sectaries, defined
their belief and repudiated the mortalists.[23] Thus the opposition to mortalism quickly moved from reliance on polemics
to an appeal to regulation and church unity. The nature of
the intermediate state of the soul could no longer be considered among the adiaphora; the Swiss Reformation, at least,
had closed its mind on the subject. Calvin thought the question easily resolved and expressed his vexation with those
who wanted to continue the discussion. "Over-curious inquiry respecting their [the departed souls'] intermediate state
is neither lawful nor useful. Many persons exceedingly per-
plex themselves by discussing what place they occupy, and

[21] "The Elect departed are in peace and rest fra their labours: Not that
they sleep, and come to a certaine oblivion, as some Phantastickes do
affirme; bot that they are delivered fra all feare and torment, and all
temptatioun, to quhilk we and all Goddis Elect are subject in this life,
and therfore do beare the name of the *Kirk Militant:* As contrariwise, the
reprobate and unfaithfull departed have anguish, torment, and paine,
that cannot be expressed. Sa that nouther are the ane nor the uther in
sik sleepe that they feele not joy or torment, as the Parable of *Christ
Jesus* in the 16th of *Luke,* his words to the thief, and thir wordes of the
saules crying under the Altar, *O Lord, thou that are righteous and just,
How lang sall thou not revenge our blude upon thir that dwellis in the
Eird?* dois testifie." *Creeds of Christendom,* ed. Schaff, III, 459–460; I have
omitted the many marginal references to Scripture.

[22] "The Helvetic Confession is the most widely adopted, and hence
the most authoritative of all the Continental Reformed symbols, with the
exception of the Heidelberg Catechism." *Ibid.,* I, 394.

[23] The English Church at the time the Edwardine Articles were promulgated clearly falls in this category. Fifteen of the Forty-two Articles
were aimed, at least in part, against the Anabaptists. Calvin and Bullinger
were known in England as eminent hammers against the soul sleepers.
The *Institutes* was available in a number of Latin and French editions
from the Continent. A Latin edition of *Psychopannychia* (1542) had been
published in Strassburg, and an abbreviated version of that tract formed
a part of Calvin's *A Short Instruction* (1549). The tenth dialogue of Bullinger's *An Holsome Antidotus* (1548) made his argument against the soul
sleepers available to an English audience.

whether they already enjoy the glory of heaven, or not. But it is folly and presumption to push our inquiries on unknown things beyond what God permits us to know. The Scripture declares that Christ is present with them, and receives them into paradise, where they enjoy consolation, and that the souls of the reprobate endure the torments which they have deserved; but it proceeds no further. Now, what teacher or doctor shall discover to us that which God has concealed?" (*Institutes*, II, 253; Bk. III, Chap. XXV, Sect. vi.)

Despite Calvin's obscurantism, despite creeds and the opposition of Reformation leaders, the radicals continued to produce teachers who were not satisfied that the true, scriptural doctrine of the soul was yet generally understood. They objected to Calvin's opinion of the soul chiefly, of course, because they thought it did not agree with Scripture, but they were not insensitive to the fact that, compared to soul sleeping, Calvin's was an inferior weapon to use against so formidable an enemy as Roman Christianity. Calvin's view of the intermediate state did not sufficiently protect Protestant Christianity from the Roman abuses of purgatory and the invocation of saints. If the elect are with Christ, is it not a short step to asking that they intercede with him in behalf of human petitions? If the departed souls are alive but not yet judged at the General Judgment, might they not be capable of spiritual development? Might they not even be said to be progressively purged of imperfection? To many of those struggling against the power of Rome, faced by a subtle and dreaded Counter-Reformation that continually probed weaknesses in the Protestant defenses, Calvin's doctrine of the soul's life in the time between death and resurrection left the gate open for a Roman assault.[24]

Always sensitive to the appeal the Roman doctrines about the faithful departed had to a populace raised with the Roman rituals and liturgy, Martin Luther used psychopannychism to bar the gate against Rome's practices. Although one must

---

[24] Luther, Tyndale, Overton, Hobbes, Milton, and the Socinian Joachim Stegmann were, as we shall see, alert to the way soul sleeping destroyed all possibility of purgatory and the intercession of saints.

be slow to suggest that a reformer of Luther's stature and conservative temper shared the heresy of the Anabaptists he hated, there are sufficient reasons for believing that he was a soul sleeper. The heresy he enunciated, and perhaps originated, was, if one may use the word, the most conservative of the Christian mortalist positions. He entertained none of the thnetopsychist ideas of some Anabaptists, but always maintained that the soul was an incorporeal and immortal substance that lived (although unconscious) when separated from the body. It might be better said, moreover, that the psychopannychist Anabaptists shared his heresy, for it is likely that Luther's thoughts on the intermediate state were formed before the Zwickau prophets (Nicolas Storch, Mark Stübner, and Thomas Münzer) had even come to the public's attention (after 1521) or the Anabaptist radicals had begun troubling Europe.

When, in 1520, he answered the bull ordering him to submit to papal authority, Luther expressed his impatience with the Roman habit of basing the doctrines of immortality on philosophy as if Holy Scripture were not a sufficient guide. First citing texts (such as Col. 2:8 and 2 Peter 2:1) that warn of the false doctrine that develops out of philosophy and merely human wisdom, Luther objects with heavy sarcasm to the decree of the Fifth Lateran Council. "Hence the experts in Rome have recently pronounced a holy decree which establishes that the soul of man is immortal, acting as if we did not all say in our common Creed, 'I believe in the life everlasting.' And, with the assistance of the mastermind Aristotle, they decreed further that the soul is 'essentially the form of the human body,' and many other splendid articles of a similar nature. These decrees are, indeed, most appropriate to the papal church, for they make it possible for them to hold fast to human dreams and the doctrines of devils while they trample upon and destroy faith and the teaching of Christ."[25] Although the passage does not make clear exactly

[25] Martin Luther, "Defense and Explanation of All the Articles of Dr. Martin Luther Which Were Unjustly Condemned by the Roman Bull," tr. Charles M. Jacobs, *Luther's Works*, ed. Jaroslav Pelikan and Helmut T.

what Luther's attitude toward the dogma of immortality is, it is certain that he considers the elements drawn out of Aristotle to be irrelevant to, and probably contrary to, Christ's teaching. We cannot be sure that Luther considered the continuous consciousness of the soul after death to be a false conclusion of unreliable philosophy, but the passage does suggest that he thought that in this matter Christians were bound not by philosophy or conciliar decree, but only by the simple declaration of the Apostles' Creed: "I believe in the life everlasting." In common with the other early creeds of the church, the Apostles' Creed makes no mention of a soul, mortal or immortal, nor does it fix belief about when everlasting life is to begin.[26]

In 1532, in a commentary on Ecclesiastes, Luther's psychopannychism is most clearly stated.[27] He first establishes his opposition to the thnetopsychists in his exposition of Eccles. 3:19. The text was doubtless a favorite with those who denied the immortality of the soul; it served as Overton's epigraph for *Mans Mortalitie:* "For that which befalleth the sons of

---

Lehmann, 55 vols. (St. Louis: Concordia Publishing House; Philadelphia: Fortress Press, 1955–   ), XXXII, 77–78 (Article 27). The German makes clearer Luther's subordination of philosophy to the authority of the Word. What is here translated as "with the assistance of the mastermind Aristotle" reads "durch hillf Aristoteles, des grossen liechts der natur": *D. Martin Luthers Werke* (Weimar: Hermann Böhlau, 1883–   ), VII, 425 [hereafter cited as *WA*].

[26] The early creeds are conveniently available in *Creeds of the Churches*, ed. John H. Leith (Garden City, N.Y.: Doubleday Anchor, 1963), pp. 23–33. I refer particularly to the creeds of Hippolytus (ca. A.D. 215), Marcellus (340), (Rufinus (ca. 404), Caesarea (325), Nicaea (325), and Constantinople (381). The present form of the Apostles' Creed was established about 700.

[27] Luther's psychopannychism was evident much earlier. Williams (*Radical Reformation*, p. 104) reports that in a sermon given in 1524, Luther declared that the soul sleeps until the Last Judgment. In 1528 Sir Thomas More detected and attacked Luther's psychopannychism in *The Dialogue concerning Tyndale*, pp. 261, 270, 276, 279 of the modern text. Tyndale answered More in 1531, defending Luther's psychopannychism: William Tyndale, *An Answer to Sir Thomas More's Dialogue*, ed. Henry Walter, Parker Society (Cambridge, 1850), pp. 180–181, 188–189. For a thorough discussion of Luther's psychopannychism, see Paul Althaus, *The Theology of Martin Luther*, tr. Robert C. Schultz (Philadelphia: Fortress Press, 1966), pp. 410–417.

men befalleth beasts; even one thing befalleth them: as the
one dieth, so dieth the other; yea, they have all one breath;
so that a man hath no preeminence above a beast: for all is
vanity." Luther turns this pessimism into a declaration of
the inadequacy of natural philosophy, a statement of the
superiority of revelation to "Aristotle, the great light of nature": "This place can not be wrested to the mortalitie of the
soule, because he speaketh of things under the sunne. Certes
the world can not perceaue, nor beleue that the soule is immortal . . . . For the immortalitie thereof cā be proued by no
reason of man, because it is a thing beyond the sunne, to
beleue the soule is immortall. In the world it is not seene, nor
understanded for a certeinty, that ye minde of mā is immortall."[28] Although he there denies the death of the soul, Luther,
in his reading of Eccles. 9:5 ("the dead know not any thing,
neither have they any more a reward"), discards the traditional idea of a soul whose nature it is to be conscious and
alert in understanding: ". . . I thinke there is not a place in
the scripture of more force for the dead that are fallen in
sleepe, vnderstanding naught of our state and condition,
against the inuocation of Saintes and fiction of Purgatory"
(*Salomons Booke*, p. 148 r, v; *WA*, XX, 160). It cannot be
argued that Luther here says merely that the souls of the
dead are not aware of the activities of the living, for unless
he thought the scriptural text taught the total unconscious-
ness of the dead he would have no cause to use it as a proof
that purgatory is a "fiction."

Any lingering doubt that Luther's view of the soul could
have been similar to an Anabaptist opinion will be dispelled
by Luther's commentary on Eccles. 9:10 ("there is no work,
nor device, nor knowledge, nor wisdom, in the grave, whither
thou goest").

---

[28] [Martin Luther,] *An Exposition of Salomons Booke, Called Ecclesiastes or the Preacher* (London, 1573), p. 60r, v (*WA*, XX, 70). This is the
first translation into English. At Luther's request the Latin commentary
was compiled by several editors, with a preface by Luther, using notes of
Luther's 1526 lectures on Ecclesiastes and supplementary material not
written by Luther (*WA*, XX, 2–3).

An other place, prouing that the dead haue no perseuer-
aunce or feeling. There is (saith he) no deuise, no science,
no knowledge, no wisedome there. Salomon iudgeth that
the dead are a sleepe, and feele nothing at all. For the dead
lye there accompting neyther dayes nor yeares, but when
they are awaked, they shall seeme to have slept scarce
one minute.

Hell signifieth a pit or graue, but properly (as I iudge) that
secret withdrawing place, where the dead sleepe out of this
lyfe, whence the soule goeth to her place (whatsoeuer it be,
for corporall it is not) so that thou mayst understād hell to
be that place where the soules be kept, being a certayne
graue (as it were) of ye soule, without this corporall worlde,
as the earth is the sepulchre of ye body. But what maner
of place it is, we know not. . . . For they that truely are holy,
goe not into hell to suffer any thing there. The dead therefore are out of all place. For whatsoeuer is out of this lyfe,
is out of place. Euen as after the resurrection, we shall be
cleare from place and tyme [*Salomons Booke,* pp. 151v–
152r; *WA,* XX, 162–163].

This doctrinal agreement between the great German reformer, the friend of princes, and the troublesome Anabaptists was not publicly noticed during the sixteenth century,
when such notice would have been certain to hurt the cause
of reformation by dignifying the divisive Anabaptist movement and causing additional strife between the Swiss and
German reformers.[29] Although his *Psychopannychia* attacks
by name only the Anabaptists, Calvin was persuaded to post-
pone its publication lest the book offend Luther.[30] Bullinger
blamed only the Anabaptists for the heresy.[31] George Joye

[29] Although Sir Thomas More would have felt no reticence in the
matter, he does not seem to have known that the Anabaptists were also
spreading psychopannychism.

[30] Williams, *Radical Reformation,* p. 586. Williams elucidates the philosophical differences reflected in the opposition of Luther and Calvin
in the matter of immortality (pp. 581–583). In his 1536 preface to *Psychopannychia,* Calvin harshly condemns the Anabaptists as the originators
of soul sleeping, but grants that "some good men," to whom he does not
want to give offense, have fallen into the error (*Tracts,* tr. Beveridge, III,
416); since he clearly means to distinguish them from the malicious Anabaptists, Calvin may well be referring to Lutheran soul sleepers.

[31] *An Holsome Antidotus,* sigs. N5v–P3v. He does not identify the
soul sleepers in "Of the Reasonable Soul of Man," *Decades of Henry
Bullinger: The Fourth Decade,* pp. 365–408.

charged both Luther and the Anabaptists with the heresy, but in a private letter to Hugh Latimer in 1533.[32]

It is likely that Luther considered the intermediate state of the soul to be a suitable subject for discussion among Protestants as long as Roman doctrines did not intrude. No Lutheran confession or catechism of the Reformation pays any attention to the matter.[33] On the question of the soul, Calvin was charged, perhaps by Lutherans, "with stirring up fierce contests about nothing, and making trifling differences the source of violent dissensions . . ." (*Tracts*, tr. Beveridge, III, 418). However useful a weapon against Rome Luther may have found psychopannychism to be, he does not seem to have insisted on it. Probably some Lutheran ministers promulgated the doctrine in the early days of the Reformation, but shrank from it as the Anabaptists acquired title to it in the public mind. Although Lutheran psychopannychism was not the important source of the belief in England, it was responsible for the first recorded expressions of Christian mortalism in English religious life, for William Tyndale, John Frith, and perhaps William Tracy supported psychopannychism shortly before Anabaptism was introduced into England.

When the Lutheran reformers failed to give vigorous support to psychopannychism, soul sleeping lost what small chance it might have had to be considered a debatable doctrine, a thing indifferent. Once it was identified solely with the Anabaptists, there was no hope for a hearing before respectable Protestants, ministers who believed God was reforming his Church but who did not want to be discharged from their livings, laymen who felt that not all of the Word of God had yet been clearly understood, but who were not prepared to attend irregular meetings and risk imprisonment and exile. Unchallenged by the doctrine of a Reformation

[32] The letter is quoted in Charles C. Butterworth and Allan G. Chester, *George Joye* (Philadelphia: University of Pennsylvania Press, 1962), pp. 95–96.

[33] See Luther's Small Catechism (1529), the Augsburg Confession (1530), the Heidelberg Catechism (1563), and the Formula of Concord (1576). All of these may be found in *Creeds of Christendom*, ed. Schaff.

church of comparable stature, the view of the churches of Geneva and Zürich (and of Rome) on the nature of the soul had to prevail in England. Calvin and Bullinger, after all, did not try to overthrow the traditional understanding of the nature of the soul. Against such potent opposition in a realm in which even much of Genevan doctrine and discipline was considered radical, the English Anabaptists could not expect to convert many to Christian mortalism.

The mortalist radicals had, nevertheless, surprising success in being heard in England, even if most refused to be persuaded by their arguments. Probably, like most radical groups, they were more vocal than their number warranted, but their success in establishing a viable, if minor, Protestant doctrine in a generally hostile society suggests that they spoke to some of the concerns of English Protestantism. It will be evident throughout Chapter Three that although soul sleeping was believed only because it was thought to be the true doctrine of Scripture, it was also appreciated as a powerful instrument in polemics. Apart from those who would be interested in any doctrine that could be proved by Scripture, many Englishmen must have realized that soul sleeping could be used to buttress other doctrines that they cherished. We have already seen how soul sleeping could be effective in argument against prayer for the dead, purgatory, and the invocation of saints, but the appeal of soul sleeping was broader than that: it could also be used to support the idea that the resurrection of the body had a vital role in the Christian hope of immortality, and the chiliast could argue from it that Christ's promises could not be fulfilled until he established his earthly kingdom in the last days. Thus soul sleeping would not have been rejected out of hand by some of those who were sympathetic with these rather common Protestant ideas and attitudes.

To those Protestants who wanted to hear the Word of God unalloyed with human philosophy, the radicals could point out that God never spoke of an "incorporeal substance," and they could put a mortalist construction on the texts commonly cited by the orthodox as proof that "incorporeal substance" is the implicit biblical doctrine. Among men who thought that to be a Protestant was to be an exegete, the mortalists could hope for an attentive audience. Even the annihilationists, who scorned the literalism of the "Scripture-learned," insisted that the irrevocable death of the soul was a truth of Scripture "spiritually" rather than "carnally" understood; if their allegorizing temper seemed to take them far from Scripture as a historical record, they nevertheless could cite the "dead letter" of the texts they were expounding in their significance as a living message of salvation.

Christian mortalism, then, appealed to the more radical temperaments among those who feared the return of Roman superstition or who were convinced that Holy Scripture contained yet undiscovered truths that must be searched out diligently without human prejudgments. The orthodox compromise with the Roman doctrine of immortality not only left these Christians restive, but it seemed to some of them that the compromise denied to the resurrection of the body the central importance it seemed to have for St. Paul. If the souls of the departed were already in joy or misery, how could the resurrection of the body be important to eternal life? For those caught up in St. Paul's rapture in 1 Cor. 15, the General Resurrection seemed to be of the greatest significance to the Christian experience; surely, they thought, the Apostle was not speaking of the mere addition of a "crown of glory" to the just who are already with Christ in heaven when he said: "For if the dead rise not, then is not Christ raised: And if Christ be not raised, your faith is vain: ye are yet in your sins. Then they also which are fallen asleep in Christ are perished" (1 Cor. 15:16-18). Men like Tyndale, who believed that ideas of blissful immortality before the resurrection of the body threatened Christian belief in the promised drama of the conquest of death on the Last Day, were prepared to discover that soul sleeping is the doctrine of Scripture.

Still more were the chiliasts, who studied the apocalyptic scriptures and impatiently awaited the Kingdom, prepared to believe that immortal life was deferred until the bodies of the just were resurrected and formed into the people of God. If the soul slept or died until Christ returned in his power, all attention could be given to preparing for the advent of the messianic Kingdom. Like their counterparts in our time, the Seventh-day Adventists and Jehovah's Witnesses, the chiliasts were alienated from the orthodox majority by the millennial heresy itself; soul sleeping added little to their burden. Although belief in the millennial Kingdom had been condemned by the Council of Ephesus (431) and, during the English Reformation, by the Edwardine Articles of 1553, it persisted in popular religion, ready for a resurgence in times of social upheaval. The conditions for a renewed interest in the earthly Kingdom were present in mid-seventeenth-century England, and with millennial sentiment rose increased talk of the sleep of the soul.

As we examine the history of the English soul sleepers in Chapter Three we shall see in some detail how soul sleeping fitted in with these various Christian beliefs. First, however, we must study in the next chapter the history of the English annihilationists, for only when we understand the thought and feeling of these revolutionaries, who not only denied immortality to the human personality but fell easily into antinomianism and pantheism, shall we be able to place the soul-sleeping heretics in the context of Christian mortalism.

The annihilationist enthusiasts were commonly called "Epicureans" by their enemies, and the epithet was not completely off the mark. Like Epicurus, the annihilationists denied the eternal persistence of human personality; like Epicurus, they insisted on the consequence of that belief—that human aims had to be fulfilled in this life or not at all; like Epicurus, they sought to maximize pleasure and minimize pain; and, like Epicurus, they were slandered because the multitude (including, if we are to believe the testimony of their enemies, many of their own announced followers) thought they advocated a life of gross and sensual pleasure. So far the comparison holds, but at bottom the epithet must be judged misleading and unfair, for the annihilationists among the "experimental Christians," those who experienced Christ in their hearts, used the language of Christian

mysticism and piety, not the language of atheistic materialism. They sought not so much pleasure as joy: they called for
the union of man and God in this life, for the promised joys
of heaven to be experienced now, before the human personality at death is dissolved in the eternal sea of the Divine.
They were tutored not by pagan philosophy but, more likely,
by that German mysticism that has never been far from the
surface of Protestant piety, a mysticism that had thoroughly
assimilated many Neoplatonic concepts and transmuted a
pagan into a Christian tradition.

Mysticism has long been suspect within Christian communities because of its tendency to view religious experience
as an individual rather than a communal matter, to stress a
direct personal relationship with God more than a relationship mediated by a church of believers. Not all mystics are, of
course, enthusiastic heretics, for many participate so fully in
the life of a Christian community, with its sacraments and
common doctrines, that their individual experiences do not
lead them to challenge the traditions and doctrines of the
community. But when the mystic is not rooted in a community, or feels that the traditions and doctrines of an unsettled
community are of uncertain authority, his private experiences of God are liable to yield spiritual insights that have
doctrinal implications; thus mysticism that lacks the counter-
balancing influence of an authoritative community and
tradition more frequently falls into heresy. When the doctrinal quarrels of the first century of the Reformation drove
many people back on their own spiritual resources and per-
spectives without the guidance of a settled religious community, the notorious enthusiastic heresies of some "spirituals"
could not be contained.

The dearth of surviving works actually written by English
enthusiasts themselves makes it difficult to judge how far
they departed from Lutheran and Calvinist doctrines. We
have few reliable records of the words the enthusiasts used
to describe their experiences, and in the absence of those
words we must draw tentative conclusions about their ideas.
Like the traditional Christian mystics, they had to express

extraordinary experiences through the medium of ordinary language, and when one is trying to communicate one's perception of the unity of man and God and of a state in which one is free from sin, carnality, and selfhood, one needs both a subtle command of language and a sympathetic audience to avoid being charged with a blasphemous arrogance (if either the language or the audience's comprehension is gross) for saying that one is the equal of the Eternal God and that one is incapable of sinning. Even Meister Eckhart had to defend himself against the charge of Church authorities that he claimed full identity with God.[34]

It is probable that some enthusiasts were not misunderstood and actually thought that they could not be distinguished from God; they took the language and concepts of St. Paul and German pietism and twisted them but a quarter-turn into heretical doctrine. German mysticism had long been plagued by those who perverted its meaning. The fourteenth-century monk who wrote *Theologia Germanica* does not shrink from referring to the "deified man" (a phrase he uses to describe one whose will is almost perfectly replaced by God's will), but he repeatedly attacks those who go too far in identifying themselves with God. The spirit that follows the False Light has not purged itself of selfhood and fails to recognize that it is a creature, not the Creator:

> it imagines itself to be that which it is not, for it imagines that it is God, and yet it is nothing but nature. And because it imagines that it is God, it arrogates to itself what belongs to God; and not that which is God in so far as He is man and dwells in a deified man, but it dares to arrogate to itself that which is of God, and belongs to Him, so far as He is God, without the creature, in eternity. For, as it is said, God is without needs, free, actionless, apart, above all things, and so forth (which is all true); and God is immovable and takes part in nothing, He is without conscience, and what He does, that is well done; "So will I be," says the False Light, "for the liker to God, the better; therefore

[34] W. T. Stace, *Mysticism and Philosophy* (Philadelphia: Lippincott, 1960), pp. 224–226.

I will be like God and will be God, and will sit and go and stand beside God." Just as Lucifer the Devil did! God in eternity is without pain, suffering, and trouble, and lets nothing of all that is or befalls, grieve or hurt Him at all. But where God is man, and dwells in a deified man, it is otherwise.[35]

The "False Lights" were outspoken enough in Reformation England to bring much of the German tradition of piety under suspicion. As we have seen, the *Theologia Germanica* is hostile to irresponsible "enthusiasm," and yet this book, which was frequently reissued under Luther's direction, was denounced by Samuel Rutherford (1600–1661), the Scottish Presbyterian, as a "Familist" work that denies the life to come, and by John Strype (1643–1737), the church historian, who even thought it was written by Henry Nicholas, the spiritual father of the English annihilationists.[36]

The demands for doctrinal soundness and personal piety were, of course, not thought to be in irreconcilable conflict. Among the English Puritans the Elect were expected to be both sound and pious; even those vigorous advocates of purity in doctrine, the Presbyterians, were not afraid of an emotional element in their religion that often verged on enthusiasm, as accounts of the conversion experience attest. But the orthodox man did not confuse zeal with enthusiasm: zeal supported established doctrines; enthusiasm imagined new heresies. The line between piety and heresy was not well defined. Even Ralph Cudworth's *A Sermon Preached before the Honourable House of Commons at Westminster, March 31, 1647* (Cambridge, 1647)[37] comes so dangerously close to the thought and language of the hated enthusiasts that, had Giles Randall, the notorious Familist, delivered it, the sermon might have earned him imprisonment rather than the approbation that Cudworth received from the grate-

[35] *Theologia Germanica*, tr. Susanna Winkworth, ed. Willard Trask (London: Victor Gollancz, 1951), pp. 185–186; Chap. XL.

[36] Samuel Rutherford, *A Survey of the Spirituall Antichrist*, 2 vols. in 1 (London, 1648), I, 167; John Strype, *Annals of the Reformation*, 7 vols. (Oxford, 1824), II, i, 563–564.

[37] Reprint, New York: Facsimile Text Society, 1930.

ful Commons. What in Randall would have been thought antinomianism and perfectionism was judged in Cudworth a pious expression of the joys of regeneracy: "Every true Saint, carrieth his Heaven about with him, in his own heart; and Hell that is without him, can have no power over him. He might safely wade through Hell itself, and like the *Three children*, passe through the midst of that *fiery Furnace*, and yet not be scorched with the flames of it: he might walk though the *Valley of the shadow of death*, and *yet fear no evil*" (*A Sermon*, p. 51).

To be sure, Cudworth believed that heaven is primarily a place where the souls of the just reside, and he was far from antinomianism, but his language skirts the edge of the perfectionist heresy of the enthusiasts. A preacher like Randall who had repudiated the doctrinal authority of the community or an ignorant laborer who had always been alienated from that community could not be expected to maintain the fine balance of a philosopher like Cudworth. Attracted by the image of the joys of sainthood attainable by those yet living, anxious to persuade their fellows of the importance of having Christ formed within, some enthusiasts found it but a short step from saying that this regenerate state was the beginning of the salvation spoken of in the Gospel to saying that it was the *only* salvation. The birth, Crucifixion, and Resurrection of Christ that took place inwardly in each regenerate man put him in a state that was not just *like* heaven, but one that was the *actual* heaven promised in the Gospel. Those who were in bondage to the "outward Law" and the "dead and killing Letter" of Scripture were in hell, in thrall to sin, knowing not the liberty of the Spirit; heaping their sins on a Christ by whose historical sacrifice they shall be reckoned righteous, these carnal men expect their reward after death and therefore miss the only resurrection and heaven the Gospel promises.

The English annihilationists and the enthusiastic religious movement of which they were a part have been neglected by historians since the Scottish Presbyterian Rutherford wrote his tendentious *A Survey of the Spirituall Antichrist* (1648), a

work that presents the views of the annihilationists chaot-
ically and inadequately.[38] The reasons for this neglect are not
far to seek. Unlike the soul sleepers, the annihilationists
had no champion of Milton's stature; instead, our knowledge
of their doctrines must be drawn almost entirely from the
works of their acknowledged enemies, a situation in which
no historian can be entirely comfortable. Their doctrines are
dark, often secret, and, like the ideas of all radical enthusiasts, beyond reason. It is rarely possible to identify names
and places with this shadowy movement. Finally, from a
modern perspective, the annihilationists and their ideas are
not important, for the movement went into a sharp decline
after the Restoration, while soul sleeping, assisted by John
Locke, remained a subject of controversy throughout the
eighteenth century.[39]

[38] Many historians of English religious thought, of course, touch briefly
on the Family of Love, but they view it as a curiosity brought over from
Holland and fail to recognize the force and vitality the Familist ideas had
until the Restoration. Rutherford at least sensed that the "spiritual" movement was a vast and complex phenomenon with a history. The work of
Rufus M. Jones is chiefly valuable for its sympathic portrayal of the
English "spiritual reformers" and for its demonstration that their ideas
helped bring about the Quakers. A student of English religious thought
must acknowledge vast indebtedness to this Quaker scholar. His studies
are, however, overly general and, finally, not significantly less tendentious than the work of Rutherford. Jones too readily dismisses the less
attractive features of the spiritual movement, such as Ranterism and
pantheism, as aberrations, insignificant departures from the true line of
spiritual reform which culminated in George Fox and the Society of
Friends. See Rufus M. Jones, *Spiritual Reformers in the 16th and 17th Centuries* (Boston: Beacon Press, 1959), first published in 1914; *Studies in
Mystical Religion* (London: Macmillan, 1909); and *Mysticism and Democracy in the English Commonwealth* (Cambridge, Mass.: Harvard University Press, 1932).
[39] John Locke, *The Reasonableness of Christianity,* ed. George W.
Ewing (Chicago: Regnery, 1965), pp. 2–7, 129–135. Locke's work, first published in 1695, presents soul sleeping without elaboration. Henry Layton
was an indefatigable controversialist in behalf of soul sleeping, having
provoked the dispute in 1692 by publishing an answer to Richard Bentley's
sermon on immortality. Layton was aided in the quarrel by William
Coward. The controversy raged until the second decade of the next century. A bibliography of the controversy may be gleaned from pp. 691–692
in Ezra Abbot's bibliography "The Literature of the Doctrine of a Future
Life," published as an appendix to William R. Alger, *A Critical History
of the Doctrine of a Future Life,* 10th ed. (New York, 1878). Near the end
of the eighteenth century the controversy again flared up with the publication of Joseph Priestley's formidable *Disquisitions relating to Matter and*

If historians have chosen to ignore some of the wilder ideas of the more ephemeral English sects, they have perhaps chosen judiciously, for our understanding of other features of the sixteenth and seventeenth centuries has benefited from their work. But it should be observed that they have chosen to ignore what Milton and his contemporaries could not ignore: the power and influence of the enthusiasts in their society. Unless we understand the thought and feeling of those Christians who denied man a personal immortality, those Christians whom Bullinger in the *Second Helvetic Confession* condemned for blasphemously daring to say that the soul is "part of God," we shall remain the poorer in our comprehension of the theological context in which Milton, Hobbes, Overton, and young Browne stated their more moderate views of the destiny of man's soul.

Spirit, 2d ed., 2 vols. (Birmingham, 1782), which defended soul sleeping and materialism as the scriptural doctrine; see Abbot's bibliography, pp. 696–697. For a detailed account of documents advocating soul sleeping since the Reformation, see LeRoy Edwin Froom, *The Conditionalist Faith of Our Fathers*, 2 vols. (Washington, D.C.: Review and Herald, 1965), II; for a brief notice of the status of soul sleeping in contemporary theology, see the Epilogue to the present volume.

Two / Epicurus Turned Enthusiast

It might be said that St. Paul's dictum, "the letter killeth, but the spirit giveth life" (2 Cor. 3:6), insofar as it was taken by many Protestant radicals as an injunction permitting loose interpretation of the letter of Scripture (even encouraging the transmission of utterly new messages from God), defined an approach to the Word that contributed to the fragmentation of Reformation Christianity into innumerable sects. To be sure, most of those in orthodox Protestant congregations to some degree believed in the priesthood of all believers and in the active operation of the Holy Spirit upon the spirits of individual men, but the radical individualism inherent in those doctrines was checked by the respect the orthodox continued to show for such "outward" institutions as a church with an ordained clergy, the sacraments, and the Holy Scripture viewed in its "plain meaning." Luther and Calvin considered the outward ordinances of God, such as baptism and preaching, to be the bridge by which the Holy Spirit comes to individuals. Although both reformers saw typological relationships between the Old Testament and the New, neither was entirely comfortable when he ventured away from literal exegesis. In his mature *Lectures on Genesis* Luther repudiates the allegorizing habit that he had as a youth learned from Origen and Jerome.

> Ever since I began to adhere to the historical meaning, I myself have always had a strong dislike for allegories and did not make use of them unless the text itself indicated them or the interpretations could be drawn from the New Testament.
> But it was very difficult for me to break away from my habitual zeal for allegory; and yet I was aware that allegories were empty speculations and the froth, as it were, of the Holy Scriptures. It is the historical sense alone which supplies the true and sound doctrine. After this has been treated and correctly understood, then one may also employ allegories as an adornment and flowers to embellish or illuminate the account. The bare allegories, which stand in no relation to the account and do not illuminate it, should simply be disapproved as empty dreams. This is the kind which Origen and those who followed him employ....
> Therefore let those who want to make use of allegories

base them on the historical account itself. The historical account is like logic in that it teaches what is certainly true; the allegory, on the other hand, is like rhetoric in that it ought to illustrate the historical account but has no value at all for giving proof.[1]

For those who saw such a view of exegesis as a threat to their newfound spiritual liberty the road to separation lay open. Those sectarians who believed they were living under the Third Dispensation, the Age of the Spirit, recognized no earthly authority in spiritual matters; scrutinized by their spiritual eye, the Holy Scripture became a source of a great variety of revolutionary ideas, and those who opposed their interpretations on traditional grounds they dismissed as "legalists." They refused to be intimidated by the learning of their orthodox opponents. What need was there for schooling in the ancient languages, logic, and philosophy? Had not the Apostles been ignorant men, yet chosen to preach the Word by Christ himself? What was needed to understand the will of God was not Pharisaical university training or the discipline of an established church, but spiritual insight. Had not St. Paul said as much?

Biblical exegesis was, of course, a commonplace activity in Reformation England. No serious disputant failed to propose his reading of Scripture against that of his opponent. Among the orthodox, however, neither disputant suggested that the text could not be made to yield God's single meaning to the faithful exegete who used properly such rational tools as logic, historical knowledge, and languages. Luther insisted that each text had, at bottom, a single, plain sense that was obvious.[2] Those who held that the letter of the text concealed its true meaning until it was illuminated by the Holy Spirit through an inspired exegete destroyed all possibility of rational discourse and joined in the anarchy of "enthusiasm."

[1] "Lectures on Genesis," tr. George V. Schick, *Luther's Works*, ed. Pelikan and Lehmann, I, 232–233; *WA*, XLII, 173–174. For Calvin's denunciation of those who think their private illuminations replace the literal message of Scripture, see *Institutes*, I, 105–109; Bk. I, Ch. IX.

[2] *What Luther Says*, ed. Ewald M. Plass, 3 vols. (St. Louis: Concordia Publishing House, 1959), I, 91–92 (*WA*, VII, 650).

The anti-intellectual and anticlerical attitudes of the enthusiasts are well expressed by Gerrard Winstanley (1609-ca. 1660),
the tradesman who found a communistic message in Scripture and led the Diggers during the Commonwealth. "Nay
let me tel you, That the poorest man, that sees his maker, and
lives in the light, though he could never read a letter in the
book, dares throw the glove to al the humane learning in the
world, and declare the deceit of it, how it doth bewitch &
delude man-kinde in spiritual things, yet it is that great
Dragon, that hath deceived all the world, for it draws men
from knowing the Spirit, to own bare letters, words and his-
tories for spirit: The light and life of Christ within the heart,
discovers all darknesse, and delivers mankind from bondage;
And besides him there is no Saviour."[3]

It is understandable, therefore, that the enthusiastic sects
earned the contempt and hatred of the educated classes, even
of those who were themselves separated from the established
church. It is just as understandable that the enthusiastic sects
flourished in the face of this opposition, for these sects provided a spiritual home for those members of the ill-educated
masses, rural as well as urban, who refused to accept the authority of the ordained clergy. Filled with a new interest in
religion by Puritan preaching against many traditional ideas
and by Puritan emphasis on the individual, and emboldened
by the years of attack on the authority of the episcopacy,
many of the poor eagerly joined those sects in which their
spiritual independence was respected and their religious opinions sought. Those who were not equipped to compete with
the learned in rational discourse about religion could, nevertheless, to their own satisfaction surpass them in spiritual
understanding. Some enthusiasts even went so far as to deny
the "legalists" their text, for we hear "of those who deny the
Scriptures to be the Word of God."[4]

[3] Gerrard Winstanley, *The New Law of Righteousnes* (London, 1649),
pp. 80–81, in *The Works of Gerrard Winstanley*, ed. George H. Sabine
(Ithaca: Cornell University Press, 1941), p. 214. Sabine's introduction on
Winstanley's religion, political theory, and movement is excellent.
[4] Edwards, *Gangraena*, I, 114; cf. *A Relation of Severall Heresies* (London, 1646), pp. 10, 14.

In such a setting it is not surprising that Thomas Edwards, the greatest of the Presbyterian heresiographers, could, with only a little straining and a commonplace narrowness of mind, catalogue 267 errors current among the sects in the years 1645–1646.[5] Although *Mans Mortalitie* made a great stir among the Presbyterians when it appeared in late 1643 or early 1644, its doctrine was by then commonplace enough among many sectaries. To some in the English enthusiastic sects, Overton's soul sleeping must even have seemed "carnal," for there were sectaries who believed in the utter and final extinction of the personal soul, with no hope of the resurrection of the body to eternal life.

It is possible to trace to the reign of Edward VI a group of enthusiasts so unworldly, so spiritual, so dedicated to achieving an unheard of perfection in their lives in this world through a mystical union with the deity that many of them refused to believe in a personal immortality for man either as soul alone or as soul in a resurrected body. Through the reign of James I these pietists seem to have joined in organized communities that offered spiritual guidance to those who, often outwardly conforming to the established church, sought the way to a direct knowledge of God through the mystical experience. Newcomers to this "Family of Love" were given the guidance of the sect's books and spiritual counselors, illuminati who progressively revealed the secret doctrines of the sect as the novice developed in spiritual understanding. By the time of the Long Parliament these enthusiasts no longer appear to have gathered into organized communities.[6]

---

[5] Edwards' "Catalogue" is actually a disorderly enumeration of sectarian errors. The errors are listed in five different places in the three parts of *Gangraena*; each of the parts has a primary list, prominently displayed, but the first two parts each have an additional, smaller list. The matter is further confused because Edwards did not number the errors in the five lists consecutively and because in Part II (as he noted) he repeated a heresy from Part I. In sum, Part I contains a total of 180 heresies, Part II, 34 (not counting the repeated one), and Part III, 53.

[6] The Family of Love seems to have been an organized body in 1622, when it was attacked in print by a Baptist congregation. After that, only Edwards' description of the Independent Churches in Somersetshire (*Gangraena*, I, 217–219, falsely numbered 117–119 in my copy) suggests the enthusiasts were organized. A pious slander published in 1641, which

Since they had never been much concerned about such "externals" as sacraments and polity, and since there was no longer much need to conceal their doctrines from persecuting authorities, the enthusiasts preferred to hear the public sermons of such spiritual preachers as Thomas Webbe, Giles Randall, and Samuel Gorton without organizing their own church. Many doubtless retained membership in General Baptist and Independent congregations while they sought the way to personal union with God.[7]

Modern scholars have named these radicals "spiritual reformers," "popular mystics," and "spiritualists."[8] Their orthodox contemporaries who looked to their origins called them "Anabaptists," "Familists," and "followers of David George"; those contemporaries who fastened upon some single aspect or tendency of their doctrines gave them a host of other names: "Libertines," "Antinomians," "Perfectionists," "Anti-scripturists," "Sadducees," and "Anti-resurrectionists." Their most distinctive characteristic, however, was their view of salvation as a mystical union with God in this life which transformed a man into Christ (that is, God incarnate), made him a being incapable of sinning, and rewarded him in this life with the fullness of those joys of heaven which the orthodox reserved for the life hereafter. This intensely personal relationship of the saved man and

---

describes a group that worships Priapus in a forest, must be dismissed as worthless: "A Description of the Sect Called 'The Family of Love,'" in *The Harleian Miscellany*, ed. William Oldys and Thomas Park, 10 vols. (London, 1808–1813), III, 568–570. [Thomas Middleton,] *The Famelie of Love* (London, 1608) is a play that reveals that the Familists have passwords and secret meetings, but Middleton does not seem to have been well informed about the sect. He apparently felt a play about the sect could draw a crowd in London. About 1604 John Marston associates the sect with London brothel life: *The Dutch Courtesan*, ed. M. L. Wine (Lincoln: University of Nebraska Press, 1965), I, i, 139–140, ii, 17; III, iii, 48–50.

[7] The tendency of such mystics to avoid organizing their own sects is analyzed in Ernst Troeltsch, *The Social Teaching of the Christian Churches*, tr. Olive Wyon, 2 vols. (London: Allen & Unwin, 1950), II, 741–746. Throughout this chapter I am indebted to Troeltsch's discussion of Protestant sects and mysticism (II, 691–820).

[8] *Ibid.*, 741; Jones, *Spiritual Reformers*, and *Mysticism and Democracy*, p. 130; Williams, *Radical Reformation*, *passim*.

God was incompatible with what the radicals would call the "legal" concept of salvation by imputed righteousness,[9] and ultimately it could not respect external religious authority of any kind, be it prince, clergy, church, or Holy Scripture.[10] Winstanley heaps contempt upon the ordained ministers because they preach the Word without knowing it in their hearts: "That man that cannot speak the testimony of the Father, no other way, but from his book as he reads, or from the mouth of another what he heares: as the publike teachers doe, speakes by hearsay and not from experience, and so declares himself to be a false Christ, a false prophet, that runs to teach others, before he have any discovery of God within himself."[11] The Holy Scripture, for Winstanley, is not the direct Word of God, but a record of the religious experiences of inspired men, and true understanding of the record requires a repetition of those experiences in one's own soul and a readiness to transmit new messages from the Father; the Scriptures, then, need to be properly understood:

> First, they are, or may be kept as a record of such truths as were writ not from imagination of flesh, but from pure experience, and teachings of the Father. Secondly, we are taught thereby to waite upon the Father with a meek and obedient spirit, till he teach us, and feed us with sincere

[9] One of their Puritan critics saw the Familist moral view as a "doctrine of works": "By this doctrine, we suffer the death of the Crosse for our own sinnes, & make the purchase thereof by our selues. By this doctrine wee are released of our sinnes by imitation, but not not [sic] by imputation." John Knewstub, *A Confutation of Monstrous and Horrible Heresies, Taught by H. N. and Embraced of a Number, Who Call Themselues the Familie of Loue* (London, 1579), p. 45.

[10] "For if it shoulde but suddenly come into the giddie pate of one of their perfites, that there ought to be no Magistrate, or that none ought to bee better than other, or possesse more then other: it must bee by and by holden for so resolute a doctrine amongst them as if it had beene ripely debated and decreed by all the Vniuersities in Europe: yea (a horrible thing) as if it hadde proceeded from the sacred mouth of GOD" (Knewstub, *A Confutation*, pp. **3–**4). Although its enemies tried tirelessly to associate the Family of Love with the revolutionary Anabaptists of the Münster Kingdom, the Familists seem to have been aggressively conformist in social and political affairs. Knewstub was, nevertheless, quite right about their tendency in principle.

[11] Gerrard Winstanley, *Truth Lifting Up Its Head above Scandals* (London, 1649), p. 41, in *Works*, ed. Sabine, p. 127.

milk, as he taught them, that wrote these Scriptures.

Thirdly, when I look into that record of experimentall testimony, and finde a sutable agreement betweene them, and the feeling of light within my own soule, now my joy is fulfilled. And every man and woman may declare what they have received, and so become preachers one to another.

For the Scriptures doth but declare the sending down of the spirit and how he shall rule in the earth in the latter dayes: but they doe not declare every particular measure and beame of the spirits ruling, for this the sons and daughters are to declare, by their particular experiences, as they are drawn up [*Truth Lifting*, pp. 42–43, in *Works*, ed. Sabine, p. 128].

Since enthusiasts such as Winstanley recognized only the authority of their personal experience of God, they can best be distinguished from their more conventional contemporaries by giving them a name that would, I think, be acceptable to Dr. John Everard (1575?–1650?), their most learned and articulate spokesman: "Experimental Christians." The *Oxford English Dictionary* records from as early as 1521 the use of "experimental" in the sense of "based on or derived from experience as opposed to mere testimony or conjecture." To avoid the almost exclusively scientific connotations the word now has, we should today probably say "experiential," but the sectaries might have liked the associations "experimental" now has with "knowledge directly evident to the senses," provided an intuitive or religious sense was recognized in addition to the other five.

Ronald Knox has observed that "perhaps the leading characteristic of seventeenth-century English enthusiasm was the distinction . . . between the Christ of history and the Christ of experience."[12] John Everard forcefully stated this distinction in his sermon "The Star in the East, Leading unto the true Messiah."

They that would have any Benefit by Jesus Christ, they must have him in their Hearts, born within them; not only to know that Christ was born at *Bethlehem*, but *born In*

12 Ronald A. Knox, *Enthusiasm* (New York: Oxford University Press, 1950), p. 175.

Them, and not to know only that Christ dyed at such a
Time, so many Years ago; this will do you no good, except
you experimentally find and feel, how he is arraigned; crucified, dead and buried Within You.

I charge you, let no Man (whatever he be) delude you,
and make you believe, that any other Christ will save you.
Let no Man upon Pain of the Salvation and Damnation of
his Soul, once dare to think, that any other Christ will do
him any good; but that he experimentally feel Jesus Christ
buried and risen again within him; . . . as St. *Paul* saith Gal.
4,19. *My Beloved! Of whom I travel in Birth, till Christ be
formed in You;* Not Christ divided, and a Christ by halves,
here a Patch and there a Piece of him, to pick and chuse,
take and refuse what you like or not like of him, but *whole
Christ formed in You.*[13]

Luther, too, was sure that saving faith involved a change of
heart and was not a matter only of gaining historical knowledge, but he, along with Calvin, placed great importance on
belief in the historical person of Jesus who, as the incarnate
Son of God, redeemed the human race, reconciling humanity
and the Father by living a life of perfect obedience in history
and by sacrificing himself on a particular cross. It was a delicate matter to describe vividly the experience of regeneration
without communicating a Gnostic scorn for the historical
testimony of Scripture and thereby undermining belief in the
historicity of the Incarnation. Everard was not wholly successful. Not only was he harassed by the bishops and, in 1636,
charged before High Commission with Familism, antinomianism, and anabaptism, but the compiler of the posthumous
volume of his sermons says that Everard himself complained
that "some of his acquaintance and followers abused the
precious truths he taught, insomuch that he was constrained
to threaten prosecution of them to punishment, and forbade
their following or hearing him."[14]

[13] John Everard, *Some Gospel Treasures* (Germantown, Pa., 1757), p. 41.
This collection of Everard's sermons was first published in London in 1653.
Cf. Gal. 2:20–21.

[14]*The Dictionary of National Biography,* ed. Sir Leslie Stephen and
Sir Sidney Lee, 27 vols. (London: Oxford University Press, 1937–   ),
s. v. "Everard, John"; Eironnach, "Notes on Certain Theosophists and
Mystics," *Notes and Queries,* 4th Ser., I (1868), 598.

Despite his way of concentrating on the spiritual or allegorical meaning of the Holy Scriptures, Everard is at pains to
make clear that he does not deny the historical or literal truth
of the record. In his sermon "The Spiritual Crucifying of the
true Messiah," Everard says that the vital meaning of Scripture is that Christ is crucified daily by our lusts and reason,
but he hastens to curse those who make of Scripture a "mere
Fable" (*Some Gospel Treasures*, pp. 66-67). Nevertheless,
many Protestants who were convinced that God acts in history to redeem man would not be satisfied with Everard's
warning. Everard says unequivocally that the events recorded in Holy Scripture really occurred in history, but they
appear to have no meaning for him until they are viewed
spiritually, as allegorical representations of spiritual reality.
Indeed, the events of the Passion took place *in order to provide a basis for the allegory:* "Friends, bear me Record; I say:
They were All Actually and Really done in the Flesh; but yet
I also say: They were to teach us, that the same Things are
always in doing . . ." (*Some Gospel Treasures*, p. 67). One who
believed that the Christ of history offered himself in expia-
tion for the sins of mankind on a particular day on Calvary,
after which the spiritual history of the race changed, could be
forgiven if he suspected that Everard's view of the letter of
Scripture drained the record of meaning even while it granted
its truth as history. Since Everard habitually subordinates the
literal truth of Holy Scripture to its allegorical meaning, it is
not surprising that many Protestants associated him with
those who denied the letter.

Other experimental Christians, both before and after Everard, were less careful than he to assert their belief in the historical validity of Scripture. Their emphasis on Scripture as
spiritual metaphor was such that many accused them of
denying its historical truth. As we have seen, Everard himself
was troubled by those who handled his spiritual instruction
irresponsibly. From their beginnings in England about the
middle of the sixteenth century, many experimental Christians so ignored the literal sense of Scripture that they were
perilously close to denying it. To be sure, the spiritual father
of the English experimentalists and founder of the Family of

Love, the Dutchman Henry Nicholas, concedes that Jesus was "borne of the Seede of *Dauid* after the Fleash,"[15] but, like Everard, when he seeks the meaning of the scriptural narrative he habitually reads the text allegorically, as an illustration of a spiritual state in man or of a spiritual idea. Knewstub thought the Familists scorned Scripture even while they claimed to emphasize it: "What can bee a more shamefull abasing of Christ, then to make him but vsher, and their Spirite in place aboue him, chiefe Schoolemaister? . . . They will not denie the woorde, but in trueth, they make it a matter of nothing. For they will allowe no sence unto it, but suche as their Spirite shall sette vppon it. So that in verie deede howe so euer they woulde bee thought to leade vs to the woorde, they doe leade their Disciples, onely to the dreames and deuises of their owne heade" ("A Sermon Preached at Paules Crosse," in Knewstub, *A Confutation*, sig. R4). What was habit in Nicholas became habit in experimental Christians, for his voluminous writings were the textbooks of the enthusiasts, particularly in the sixteenth century, when the Family of Love may even have substituted them for the Bible.[16]

Nicholas' books are notoriously cloudy, full of the "monstruous new kind of speach neuer found in the Scriptures, nor in ancient father or writer of Christs Church" that Queen Elizabeth denounced in the preachers of the Family of Love who used it, she thought, to get simple people to marvel at them.[17] Though Nicholas' books are difficult, the main drift of his religious ideas is reasonably apparent. He considers his religious knowledge certain beyond doubt because it springs

[15] [Henry Nicholas,] *Evangelivm Regni: A Joyfull Message of the Kingdom* (Amsterdam? 1575?), p. 45r.

[16] William Wilkinson, *A Confutation of Certaine Articles Deliuered unto the Familye of Loue* (London, 1579), p. 52. Wilkinson was told by some members of the sect that the Elders took the Scriptures away from new members and left them with the books of Nicholas only. Some members of the Family of Love thought that Nicholas' books were easier to understand than Holy Scripture.

[17] *A Proclamation against the Sectaries of the Family of Loue* (London, 1580). Wilkinson (*Confutation of Certaine Articles*, pp. 32–33) says that members of the sect can be identified by their unusual manner of speaking; he remarks that he himself, having read so much of Nicholas, has fallen into the jargon and has been mistaken for a Familist.

from his direct experience of God in a mystical union. God heard the prayers of the poor who yearned to understand the Will of God in Scripture, so God "through the heartie Mercifulnes of his Loue, wrought a great and wonderfull Worke upon Earth, out of his holie heauen, and raised-upp Mee *HN*, the Least among the holyons of God (which laye altogether dead and, without Breath and Life, among the Dead) from the Death and made me aliue, through *Christ*, as also annointed mee with his godlie Beeing, manned himself with Mee and godded Mee with Him to a liuing Tabernacle or Howse for his Dwelling and to a Seate of his *Christ*, the Seede of *Dauid*, To-thend that his Wonderful-woorkes mought now in the last time, be knowen . . . ."[18]

Just as Christ's disciples did not understand the "Cleernes of *Christ*" until Pentecost, so those "Scripture-learned" will not understand the Scripture "which haue not kept or passed-thorowe with *Christ* after ye Fleash, the Passe-ouer from Death into Life and from Fleash into Spirit" (Nicholas, *Evangelivm Regni*, p. 53v).

These passages suggest why, even in an age so full of competing enthusiasts as seventeenth-century England, Nicholas and the experimental Christians who absorbed his doctrines were considered to be the preeminent enthusiasts. Most Protestants admitted, at least in theory, the possibility that the Holy Spirit might occasionally illuminate the mind of an individual, but they insisted that the purported message of the Spirit be tested, usually by the Holy Scripture in its literal sense.[19] Nicholas and many subsequent experimental Christians, since they felt that their inspiration was a necessary consequence of their union with God, would admit of no test except, perhaps, the Holy Scripture interpreted in their own spiritual sense (which, of course, begged the question). In *An Explanation of the Grand Mystery of Godliness* (1660), Henry More noted that Nicholas would allow no test of his Spirit:

[18] Nicholas, *Evangelivm Regni*, p. 81v. In this and other citations from this book, I have left out the marginal references to biblical texts and made minor changes in the punctuation without notice.

[19] Geoffrey F. Nuttall, *The Holy Spirit in Puritan Faith and Experience* (Oxford: Blackwell, 1946), pp. 34–47.

"in his *Revelatio Dei* . . . he plainly forbids to try the Spirits by *Reason,* or *Knowledge,* or *Scripture-learning,* but by the *true Being of the living Godhead.* Which are high Words, but signifie nothing but that we never attain to the living Godhead till we think as he thinks . . . ."[20]

The passages also show Nicholas' characteristic way of allegorizing those events which most Christians were sure happened and took their meaning within the context of past or future history. To Nicholas' spiritual understanding the past and future have meaning only in the present. For Nicholas the Crucifixion has meaning chiefly as an allegory signifying the death of the flesh, the mortification of men's sinful nature that must precede the rising of the spiritual man (Nicholas, *Evangelivm Regni,* p. 56r, v). In a similar way, the significance of the Last Supper is not that it happened in history and established a Christian sacrament, but that it symbolizes the way to the spiritual life for men living now. "Beholde This is the right Passe-ouer with *Christ,* or the right Supper which the vpright Beleeuers and Disciples of *Christ,* keepe with *Christ:* to-wit, that they depart euenso with *Christ,* out of the Fleash into the Spirit and out of the Death or Mortalitie, into the eternall Life of euerlasting Immortalitie wherthrough the Sinne and all Destruction becometh vanquished" (Nicholas, *Evangelivm Regni,* p. 51r). Henry More interprets this passage as an injunction to forget the historical Christ (the Flesh or Letter) and accept him as a spiritual mystery. He adds that the immortality promised does not refer to the individual, but to the sect (Henry More, *Theological Works,* p. 182). Knewstub (*A Confutation,* pp. 74–75) also puts this construction on Nicholas' use of the phrase "eternal life." Edmond Jessop, who almost joined the sect about 1620, says that they believed that the Family of Love would inhabit the earth forever, but he also says they thought their souls would go to heaven after their bodies die.[21]

---

[20] More, *Theological Works,* p. 188. More discusses Nicholas' doctrines on pp. 171–188.

[21] Edmond Jessop, *A Discovery of the Errors of the English Anabaptists* (London, 1623), p. 89.

The mystical impulse in Nicholas, then, leads him to view the events of sacred history as symbols of the mystical experience that must be attained in the present day because it is the Last Day, the Day of the Love of God the Father. The Last Trump, which is Nicholas' call to join his mystical sect, has already sounded: "For this Sound of the last Trompet [namelie this Voyce or Testimonie of the Grace of the holie Spirit of Loue] shall be heard in all the Worlde" (Nicholas, *Evangelivm Regni*, pp. 55r, 96r). Nicholas and many later experimental Christians had no interest in traditional eschatology because for them the Christian drama of salvation was complete in this life, in the mystical union with God. Death, Resurrection, Heaven, and Hell were not "last things" but "present things," the spiritual states of the regenerate and unregenerate in this life.[22] Holy Scripture describes these states allegorically in largely physical terms, and carnal readers mistakenly see them as future physical states. To some experimental Christians, Death and Hell represented the state of misery of those who were still in thrall to sin and carnal views (that is, those who were outside the sect), and Resurrection and Heaven represented the joyous state of those who, under the guidance of the mystical doctrines of the sect, had achieved perfection in this life, being released not only from the guilt of sin, but from its power. Winstanley does not equivocate in asserting the truth of his idea of heaven and the falsity of the view preached by the ordained ministers.

> Some there are, nay almost every one, wonders after the Beast, or fleshly man; they seek for new *Jerusalem*, the City of *Sion*, or Heaven, to be above the skies, in a locall place, wherein there is all glory, and the beholding of all excellent beauty, like the seeking of a show or a mask before a

---

[22] The idea that heaven and hell are states present in this life was, when stated with caution, not necessarily heretical. Benjamin Whichcote said "Heaven is a temper of spirit, before it is a place" (Aphorism 464, quoted in Jones, *Spiritual Reformers*, p. 301), but he did not forget that it is a place. Chapter XI of the *Theologia Germanica* (p. 132) dwells on heaven and hell as spiritual states, but the author makes clear the joy of this heaven is but a "foretaste" of a future joy.

man: And this not to be seen neither by the eies of the body till the body be dead: A strange conceit.

But, poor Creatures, you are deceived; this expectation of glory without you, will vanish, you shall never see it; this outward heaven is not the durable Heaven; this is a fancy which your false Teachers put into your heads to please you with, while they pick your purses, and betray your Christ into the hands of flesh, and hold *Jacob* under to be a servant still to Lord *Esau.*

Wel, what a man sees or hears to day, may be gone to morrow; all outward glory that is at a distance from the five senses, and taken in by a representation, is of a transient nature; and so is the Heaven that your Preachers tell you of.

But when the second *Adam* rises up in the heart, he makes a man to see Heaven within himself, and to judge all things that are below him: He makes many bodies to be the declarers of him, who is the power of righteousnesse that rules therein: And this is Heaven that will not fail us, endurable riches, treasures that shall not wax old, and where moth and rust cannot corrupt, nor thieves break through and steal: This Christ is within you, your everlasting rest and glory [*New Law of Righteousnes,* p. 97, in *Works,* ed. Sabine, pp. 226–227].

Henry More, in his *An Explanation of the Grand Mystery of Godliness,* denounced Nicholas as but *"Epicurus* turned *Enthusiast"* because he detected a certain equivocation in Nicholas' books whenever he dealt with scriptural passages usually thought to support belief in the immortality of the soul. More's evidence that Nicholas believed the soul to be mortal is largely his own allegorical interpretation of Nicholas' words (Henry More, *Theological Works,* pp. 185–188). The evidence is not, therefore, thoroughly convincing although, given Nicholas' cast of mind, the assumption that his words have an allegorical as well as a literal meaning is not unreasonable. Indeed, there is reason to believe that the construction More puts on Nicholas' words is similar to the interpretation one of the Elders might have given to a novice of the Family of Love as he gradually revealed the secret doctrines of the sect.

That the Family of Love had secret doctrines is quite cer-

tain. In public the Familists claimed to be harmlessly orthodox, obedient members of the Established Church: in their
confession of 1575[23] and their supplication addressed to King
James[24] in 1604 it is difficult to find any unorthodox views.
Their protestations of conformity did not save them from
persecution, however, for it was well known that the sect
encouraged equivocation on principle. Although Queen
Elizabeth declared the sect illegal in 1580, her proclamation
is notably vague about the precise nature of its pernicious
doctrines; of the two stated reasons for the ban, however, the
sect's teaching that a member may deny anything before an
outsider, even when under oath, must have been the more
infuriating to the Queen and her government, for she complains that her magistrates cannot get confessions even from
known teachers.[25] When the charge of equivocation was
made against Nicholas, it was answered by one of the sect's
Elders, who grants the truth of the charge, but argues that
equivocation is justified in a hostile society. The Elder says
of Nicholas: "He biddeth them confesse their beliefe among
the sinfull generations and false hartes of the Scripture
learned &c, and not to reueile the secretes of God . . . to the
bloud thirstie ones, and aduersaries to all truth, which lye in
wayte to deuoure thē: more then a true man is bound to
confesse his treasures to a theefe or a murtherer."[26] John
Rogers complained that he was unable to examine many of
the sect's books because the sectarians would let only sym-

[23] This confession is quoted at length in Strype, *Annals*, II, i, 557–559.
The title of the confession is given there as *A Brief Rehearsal of the Belief of the Good-willing in England, Which Are Named the Family of
Love; with the Confession of Their Upright Christian Religion, against
the False Accusation of Their Against-speakers* (1575).

[24] *A Svpplication of the Family of Loue* (Cambridge, 1606).

[25] *Proclamation against . . . the Family of Loue*. The other charge was
that the Family of Love believed there was no salvation outside their
sect. Nicholas, at least, was clearly guilty of the charge *(Evangelivm
Regni*, p. 76).

[26] Wilkinson, *Confutation of Certaine Articles*, p. 61. I have omitted
the reference to Matthew 7:6: "Give not that which is holy unto the
dogs, neither cast your pearls before the swine, lest haply they trample
them under their feet, and turn and rend you." In order to allow rebuttal,
Wilkinson submitted a copy of his charges to the Family of Love before
he went to press; he was answered by an Elder who called himself
"Theophilus."

pathizers have them, neither would they discuss their doctrines with him.[27] A commentator on the supplication to
King James complained that the sect kept its confession of
1575 to "wave about," although these sectaries admittedly
had many secret rituals and doctrines as well as the heresies
in Nicholas' books (*Svpplication*, p. 64). In 1622 the Baptists
attacked the deceit of the Familists, citing "M.P.," one of
their leading Elders, who wrote, " 'Hide secrets from the
vnbeleeuers' "; in 1648 Winstanley counseled his followers
to keep their manner of worship secret from the world.[28]

Despite such injunctions, the secret doctrines leaked out.
The preceding pages of this chapter show in general outline
those doctrines and attitudes which formed the essence of
experimental Christianity; its enemies supply details in considerable abundance. The rest of the chapter will focus on
the mortalism of the experimental Christians as it was publicly revealed before the Restoration. It will be seen that from
their early days as an organized sect, the experimental Christians were accused of secretly espousing mortalism and of
falsely disavowing the heresy in their public confessions;
later, during the relative freedom of the Interregnum, they
amazed their enemies with bold declarations that the personal soul dies with the body while only the divine essence
of the soul survives as an undifferentiated part of God.

The secrecy with which the experimental Christians
shrouded such heretical doctrines as this before the Interregnum makes it necessary to depend almost wholly upon the
accounts written by their enemies for evidence of the sect's
beliefs.[29] Although such a dependence makes it difficult to
write reliable history because the objectivity of such bitter

---

[27] J[ohn] R[ogers], *The Displaying of an Horrible Secte of Grosse and Wicked Heretiques, Naming Themselues the Familie of Loue* (London, 1578), sig. A4r.

[28] *A Discovery of the Abhominable Delusions of Those, Who Call Themselues the Family of Loue* (London? 1622), p. 94; Lewis H. Berens, *The Digger Movement in the Days of the Commonwealth* (London: Simpkin, Marshall, 1906), p. 59.

[29] Many of Nicholas' books were published in English in the decade preceding the suppression of the Family of Love in 1580. A valuable bibliography of these and other works by Nicholas is available: J. H. Hessels, "Henrick Niclaes: The Family of Love," *Notes and Queries*, 4th

enemies of the sect may be doubted, there are two reasons for believing these hostile accounts to be basically factual. First, the attacks, which span two generations, are in surprising agreement about what the chief tenets of the experimental Christians are despite the fact that they were written variously by conformists, Puritans, and even a Baptist. Second, the views ascribed to the early experimental Christians are fundamentally the same as those boldly avowed during the Interregnum by such later experimental Christians as Everard, Winstanley, Giles Randall, and the Ranters; the popularity of the later teaching suggests that it was built on a strong native tradition of enthusiastic religion such as the views ascribed to the earlier experimental Christians could provide. The pronounced tendency of Interregnum critics of the sects to identify as "Familism" any of a great variety of heresies was, I believe, based on a more precise knowledge of English theological history than they have generally been thought to have. Rufus Jones (*Mysticism and Democracy*, p. 126) thought that the name "Familist" was used loosely for any disliked sect and implied only that the members of the sect were a "bad lot." In my studies, I have seen the name used for no one but the advocates of "inward religion," people who appear in Jones's books on "spiritual religion." I would suggest that seventeenth-century critics used "Familism" as a name for what Jones called "spiritual religion" and I call "experimental Christianity." As the following examination of the evidence connecting at least some experimental Christians with belief in the irrevocable annihilation of the personal soul at death will show, Robert Baillie was quite correct in identifying a group of such mortalists as "Familistick Anabaptists."[30]

Before 1550 some Englishmen had begun to deny the ortho-

Ser., IV (1869), 356–358; 404–406; 430–432. Other early Familist works, such as those by "M.P." and "the servant of M.P." (*Abhominable Delusions, passim*), seem to have been lost.

[30] Baillie, *Anabaptism*, p. 99. In an annotation Baillie refers to the description of annihilationism in the Independent Churches of Somersetshire given by Edwards, *Gangraena*, I, 217–219 (falsely numbered 117–119).

dox view of the afterlife. They may have been disciples of the enthusiast Eligius (Loy) Pruystinck, a slater of Antwerp, some of whose followers had fled to England in 1545, a year after Loy was executed (Williams, *Radical Reformation*, pp. 351–353). Roger Hutchinson, however, in his *The Image of God, or Layman's Book* (1550), does not hint that the heretics are anything other than native Englishmen: "there be many late Libertines, and late English Sadducees, which would teach out of scripture, that there is neither place of rest ne pain after this life; that hell is nothing else but a tormenting and desperate conscience; and that a joyful, quiet, and merry conscience is heaven; and that devils are evil thoughts, and good angels good thoughts."[31] These Libertines and Sadducees had strong antinomian tendencies and saw the resurrection spoken of in Scripture only as a spiritual resurrection in this life from the death of sin, not as a promised regeneration of the physical body on the Last Day (*Works of Hutchinson*, ed. Bruce, pp. 79, 138). The Church of England thought the denial of the resurrection of the body a heresy serious enough to be denounced in Article XXXIX of the Forty-two Articles of 1553: "The Resurrection of the dead is not as yet brought to passe, as though it only belonged to the soulle, whiche by the grace of Christe is raised from the death of sinne, but it is to be loked for at the laste daie: for then . . . to all that bee dead their awne bodies, fleshe, and bone shalbe restored . . . ."[32]

Soon after, during the reign of either Edward VI or Queen Mary, the joiner Christopher Vitels and his accomplices from Delft established Henry Nicholas' Family of Love in England,[33] where enthusiastic doctrines were already so prominent that in the Forty-two Articles the Church condemned not only the idea of spiritual resurrection but also the doctrines that a regenerate man lives without sinning (Article XIV) and

[31] *The Works of Roger Hutchinson*, ed. John Bruce, Parker Society (Cambridge, 1842), p. 138.

[32] Hardwick, *History of the Articles*, p. 346.

[33] Wilkinson, *Confutation of Certaine Articles*, p. ☞ 4. Williams (*Radical Reformation*, p. 482) thinks that Nicholas may have visited England in 1552–1553, but the opinion, which is common enough, lacks factual support.

that Christians are freed from the moral as well as the cere-
monial law of Moses (Article XIX). The sect flourished for
more than a generation, adding native converts to what was
probably originally a membership composed largely of Dutch
immigrants and making its name synonymous with "enthusiasm." Their doctrines were spread by itinerant tradesmen
who were primarily successful with the poor and ignorant.
William Wilkinson uses one "W.H.," who fell into Familist
errors, as an example of an ignorant man with some words
who teaches when he should be taught: "And so is it with the
chief *Elders* of our *Louely Fraternitie,* some of them be
Weauers, some Basketmakers, some Musitians, some Botle-
makers" (*Confutation of Certaine Articles,* p. 30). Some of the
clergy, however, took up their doctrines, and the sect also
had adherents in Queen Elizabeth's household and in the
court of James I.[34] After Queen Elizabeth issued *A Proclamation against the Sectaries of the Family of Loue* (1580), which
ordered imprisonment for any who owned, smuggled, or
printed books supporting the heresies of the sect and con-
signed the books themselves to the flames, the Family of Love
as an organized fellowship having meetings, rituals, and officers appears to have gone into a sharp decline until, when
James began his reign, it was reduced virtually to insigni-
ficance: "For we are a people but fewe in number, and yet
most of us very poore in worldly wealth" (*Svpplication,* p.
56). The anonymous critic of the sect's petition to King James
disputes this claim, saying that the sect was large twenty-five
years before and had grown since (*Svpplication,* p. 57). It is
possible that both parties to the dispute were correct, since
the sect could decline even while its cause prospered. Although organized Familism waned, the books survived, and
through them and the remains of the organized sect Familist
ideas were kept alive until they could be preached openly
during the Interregnum. Just as in the modern world far more
people entertain socialist ideas than join socialist societies,

[34] John Strype, *The Life and Acts of John Whitgift, D.D.,* 3 vols. (Oxford, 1822), III, 158–160; *Svpplication,* p. 46; Jessop, *Discovery of the
Errors,* pp. 90–91.

so in Reformation England many people were attracted by Familist ideas without being motivated to join the sect. As the "literal" Christians had reason to know during the Interregnum, the decline of the Family of Love was by no means accompanied by the decline of Familism. There is evidence that the doctrine of the annihilation of the personal soul was secretly cherished for almost a century by at least some Familists until during and following the Interregnum the doctrine was more boldly preached as part of a thoroughly pantheistic message that incorporated the idea of universal restoration and even, in at least one instance, introduced the possibility that the soul will be purified in a series of incarnations.

By 1561 Vitels had evidently formed a sect, for in that year two members of the Family of Love were examined before a magistrate and confessed their beliefs.[35] Among the numerous doctrines recorded in their testimony, two suggest that, even at this early date, at least some members of the Family of Love had adopted a mortalist view more radical than the soul sleeping of the Anabaptists.[36] The two Familists testified that heaven and hell had no existence outside this world and that those who did not belong to their sect would be annihilated at death: "Whosoeuer is not of their sect they accompt him as a beast, that hath no soule, and shal yaelde no account for his doing: but as a beast shall dye, and not rise againe, in bodie or soule" (Rogers, *Displaying*, sigs. I7v–I8v). As we have seen, to conceive of heaven and hell as spiritual states in this life is not necessarily to deny their existence as abodes of souls in an afterlife, but these Familists differ radically from the traditional piety of Whichcote and *Theologia Germanica*. By denying the existence of a heaven or hell outside this life, they took away the traditional residences of immortal human souls; by denying that ungodly men lead an

[35] Rogers (*Displaying*, sigs. I4v–K3v) cites their testimony at length. At the time, the sect was presumably composed of Dutch immigrants, for the witnesses testified that only a few of the sect could read English, and they could not do it well.
[36] William Hugh had attacked soul sleeping fifteen years earlier: *The Troubled Man's Medicine* (1546), in *Writings of Edward the Sixth* (Philadelphia, 1842), pp. 36–38.

immortal life in torment, they opposed the traditional view
that the human soul, elect or reprobate, is immortal. Although the testimony gives no account of Familist doctrine
concerning the eternal state of the godly members of the sect,
later revelations of the secret teachings suggest that the implied contrast here between the future states of the wicked
and the just might not have meant that the godly will enjoy
a personal immortality.

Nicholas seems to offer those who follow his sect the un-
qualified joys of heaven in this life as a necessary consequence of their becoming "new men." Those who with Christ
go through "the Passe-ouer from Death into Life and from
Fleash into Spirit" will find that they "are entred into the
true Beeing of *Christ;* are serued with the spirituall and
heauenlie Goods and with the liuing Woord of Trueth, in
the vpright Beeing of the Loue of *Iesu Christ*" (Nicholas,
Evangelivm Regni, p. 55v). Such is the Family of Love's
heaven on earth. Since there is no other heaven, presumably
man must experience conscious heavenly joy now or never.
If the godly souls are, in contrast with the wicked, to attain
some kind of immortality (as the testimony of the two Familists implies), and if there is no heaven apart from this life,
then the Familists must have conceived of a state or abode for
immortal souls that could be distinguished from the orthodox
Christian view of heaven as a celestial residence of individual
souls conscious of their blessed state. As we have seen,
Knewstub and More thought the Familists believed that only
the sect was destined to immortality. Jessop's opinion, drawn
from a more intimate acquaintance with the sect, that they
believed the soul goes to heaven, is not in itself evidence
that they believed in an orthodox heaven. The testimony of
1561 gives no hint of what conception the Family of Love
might have had of the afterlife awaiting the sect's illuminated
members, but, as we examine later revelations of the secret
doctrine, it will appear that these early enthusiasts might have
believed in a return to the divine essence for the godly only.
Such a belief would make it possible to distinguish between
the spiritual destinies of the godly and the wicked while, at

the same time, it would permit hope in only a depersonalized immortality that could not be considered a substitute for the intensely personal joy of those who lived in the Family of Love's heaven on earth.

By 1575 the Family of Love was frequently being charged with mortalism, for in that year the sect issued its *Apology* in the hope of refuting those who said, among other things, " 'that they denied the resurrection of the flesh, and the immortality of the soul.' "[37] Strype tells of "the spawn and improvements" of the Family of Love that also existed at that time: "The sectaries of the *family of the mount* held all things common, and lived in contemplation altogether; denying all prayers, and the resurrection of the body. They questioned, whether there were an heaven or an hell, but what is in this life. And they said, that what the scriptures spake of, was begun and ended in men's bodies here, as they do live. As heaven was, when they do laugh and are merry; and hell, when they are in sorrow, grief, or pain. And lastly, they believed that all things came by nature."[38] One may only guess whether the responsibility for debasing the ecstatic state of the "godded" Henry Nicholas to a merry mood rests with the Family of the Mount or with a hostile reporter of their beliefs. Experimental Christianity always stood in peril of such debasement in the hands of its followers; thus, before we assume that some contemporary enemy has distorted the Family of the Mount's doctrine of heaven and hell, we should observe that Strype's account of that Familist sect could also serve as a description of some of the Ranters of the Interregnum, whose views we know from their own books.

[37] *An Apology for the Service of Love* (London, 1656), quoted in Strype, *Annals*, II, i, 559.

[38] Strype, *Annals*, II, i, 563. George Mosse traces the "removed God" of English Deism to the influence of French and Italian Deists of the late sixteenth and early seventeenth centuries and to the thought of Interregnum Ranters ("Puritan Radicalism and the Enlightenment," *Church History*, XXIX [1960], 424–439). He is apparently unaware that the Ranters were not the first Puritan radicals to deny a providential God. As early as 1561 the two members of the Family of Love deponed that "they may not say, *God saue any thing*. For they affirme that all thinges are ruled by nature, and not directed by God" (Rogers, *Displaying*, sig. I6v).

The Family of Love's *Apology* failed to turn aside its
enemies. Provoked by the continued success of the sect and
by the challenge of the English translations of Nicholas'
books that appeared throughout the 1570's,[39] moderate Protestants mounted an assault in the press that did not abate
until the Queen suppressed the sect in 1580. The attack was
aimed at the secret doctrines the sectaries learned from Nicholas' books. John Knewstub, a Puritan divine, made a con-
cise summary of Nicholas' major doctrines, most of which
supported the charge of mortalism against the Family of Love.

> Euerlasting life if that we beleeue him, is fully felt & pos-
> sessed in this life: here is our heauen, & here is our hell:
> the resurrection is not corporall of the body, but spirituall
> of the minde: Now is Christ come to judgement, and this
> doctrine is the last trump: they are rysen againe and in
> perfect ioy, who haue perfectly imbraced it, and those haue
> alredy receiued their iudgement & be in hell, who do resist
> it: to be gilty of death by the sinne of an other, or to be
> iustified by the righteousnes of an other, is a doctrine not
> onely not receiued of them, but throughout all their bookes
> impugned: our sinnes by this doctrine, are answeared
> within vs, and no righteousnesse that shall doe vs good is
> without vs [*A Confutation*, p. *4].

Knewstub was quite certain that the followers of Nicholas
did not believe there is a heavenly state beyond this life:
"yf wee shall imbrace his doctrine, then shall we lyue as hee
doeth heere vppon earth. This is all the benefite that our faith
obteyneth by the resurrection of H.N. his Christ from the
dead" (*A Confutation*, p. 63).

The Family of Love's mortalism, then, seems to have developed out of its view of man. According to Knewstub, the
sect denied that man is condemned by original sin. Man is
sinful, the sect admits, but he is capable of attaining moral
perfection by inward and heartfelt repentance, by dying to
the Flesh and rising in the Spirit, by imitating Christ's suffering, death, and resurrection in their spiritual significance

[39] Rogers supposed Christopher Vitels to be the translator (*Displaying*,
sig. B4r).

and becoming a "new man," united with God and great in spiritual understanding. Knewstub voices the objection of orthodox Protestantism: "By this doctrine, we suffer the death of the Crosse for our own sinnes, & make the purchase therof by our selues. By this doctrine wee are released of our sinnes by imitation, but not not [sic] by imputation" (*A Confutation*, p. 45). The mainstream of Reformation Christianity saw man as a creature naturally bound to sin; even though the historical Christ had, by his perfect and free sacrifice, ransomed at least some men from the punishment due to sin, the orthodox Christian believed that man lived under the power of sin because he shared the nature of fallen Adam. Luther and Calvin agreed that the justified man is not *intrinsically* or *inherently* righteous (that is, he is not justified by his works) but he, though guilty, is considered righteous by a merciful God because the righteousness of Christ is *imputed* to him. This view that man is saved by the *extrinsic* righteousness of Christ is, of course, central to the theology of both Luther and Calvin, and the following statements from their works are merely samples of a doctrine frequently reiterated by them. As early as 1515–1516, commenting on Rom. 4:7, Luther said:

> in the sense of Scripture "righteousness" depends more on the imputation of God than on the condition of the guilty; for a man does not have this righteousness if he possesses only the quality in his character. Nay, such a one is rather utterly a sinner and unjust. But that man has righteousness whom God mercifully regards (*reputat*) and will consider righteous in His presence because he has confessed his unrighteousness and has implored the righteousness of God. Thus all of us are born and die in iniquity, that is, in unrighteousness, and we are righteous only because the merciful God considers us righteous through faith in His Word [*What Luther Says*, ed. Plass, III, 1227; WA, LVI, 287].

And Calvin is no less clear that saving righteousness is extrinsic to the justified man: "Justification, therefore, is no other than an acquittal from guilt of him who was accused, as though his innocence had been proved. Since God, therefore, justifies us through the mediation of Christ, he acquits us, not by an admission of our personal innocence, but by an imputation of righteousness; so that we, who are unrighteous in ourselves, are considered righteous in Christ" (*Institutes,* I, 795; Bk. III, Chap. XI, Sect. iii). To the Family of Love, this orthodox view of man made men complacent in their sins. The two Familists in 1561 testified that they and their brethren "scorne all those yt say, *Good Lorde haue mercie vppon vs miserable sinners:* saying, those that so say, declare themselues neuer to amend, but still to be miserable sinners, whereas we doe liue perfectly and sinne not" (Rogers, *Displaying,* sig. I6v). In their view, man could, in a mystical transformation, leave sin and achieve moral perfection: "They teach, that the same perfection of holinesse which *Adam* [had] before he fell, is to be attained here in this life; and affirme, that all their Family of loue are as perfect and innocent as he" (Jessop, *Discovery of the Errors,* p. 89). For those thus regenerated, heaven was revealed in the fullness of God's promises. This was a heaven that man could attain now with the help of God's love by imitating Christ's spiritual development, not a heaven purchased for unworthy man by the sacrificial act of a historical Christ.

But for orthodox Protestants, to claim as the Familists did that "our sinnes ... are answeared within vs, and no righteousnesse that shall doe vs good is without vs" was to overrate man's role in his salvation at the expense of Christ's redeeming sacrifice. Luther and Calvin, as we have seen, are sure that men live by the historical Christ's righteousness, not by their own. The most influential Protestant theologians were not willing to emphasize *personal* righteousness at the price of neglecting the *imputed* righteousness that believers gained from the historical person of Jesus; for them the believer could confidently depend on the efficacy of the righteousness imputed to him by God for Jesus' sake even while he recognized that, despite his best efforts, his personal righteousness fell far short of God's standard. The Familist's concern for personal regeneration led him away from the doctrine of Atonement and its emphasis on the historical sacrifice of Jesus. Indeed, by 1622 at least some Familists seem to have dispensed entirely with a need for a historical Christ, even as a spiritual model, and apparently thought of Christ primarily as the divine spark in every man. The Baptist author of the *Abhominable Delusions* is clearly shocked by the radical spiritualism of Nicholas' progeny:

> His now followers affirme: *That men may bee saued by the workes of the Law; without knowledge or Faith in the blood of the man Christ Jesus:* yea the holde it a meere fable, and speake of it with great contempt, that we looke for justification with God in and through another; that we looke for justification without vs that we speake of imputatiue righteousnes; that wee holde justification by beleeuing; for in truth they doe not hold that *Christs* Death & bloodshed hath purchased any man; but that he was an example to vs and such like; for they holde that those Gentiles, *Rom.* 2. kept the Law, which (say they) *was the Christ within them*, and those by this *Christ*, namely by keeping the Law were justified [sig. A3v].

It may be doubted that the author has correctly stated the position of the Family of Love. The Familists might not have thought of Christ as a synonym for the Law, but as a synonym for the "godded" state in which God took flesh again and man naturally obeyed the Law. At any rate, the complete disregard for the role of Christ's historical sacrifice in salvation that the Baptist complains of here seems a natural development from the earlier position of experimental Christianity.

The Familist contention that heaven is fully attainable in this present life quite naturally contrasts with the commoner view that the experience of heaven begins at death for a saved sinner; if the esoteric doctrine is true, the commonplace doctrine is in some sense false. The polemical position of a proselytizing sect probably heightened the contrast between the two views of heaven: a man will not be content to wait for the heavenly joys of the afterlife if he can be persuaded that he will not retain his identity after death. The Family of Love, like many mystical sects, tended to obscure the traditional distinction between God and his creation. Its Baptist critic challenged the sect to prove its orthodoxy by denying "that which H. N. hath written of God, *That God and Man had one Order, Spirit, Nature and being; that God was all that Man was, and man all that God was*" (*Abhominable Delusions*, p. 97). The pantheistic thrust of Nicholas' theology encouraged at least some members of his sect to conceive of immortality as the soul's eternal existence as an undifferentiated part of God. When the members of the Baptist congregation asked the Familists what became of the bodies of the illuminated Elders after death, "some of their younglings haue answered vs, they conceiue, their iudgement is, that the soule goes into God againe, and so becometh God; and their bodies lye and become as when they were not . . ." (*Abhominable Delusions*, p. 79). Thus the secret doctrine of the annihilation of the personal soul at death, implicit in the testimony of the two Familists in 1561, was stated explicitly sixty years later. The Family of Love, by eliminating personal identity in an afterlife, emphasized that the conscious enjoyment of heaven was possible only in this life and yet distinguished the destiny of the spiritual godly from that of the fleshly wicked. By the mystical route experimental Christians arrived at a position approximating Aristotle's opinion as interpreted by his Averroistic commentators: "The only immortality within the Averroistic context was the impersonal absorption of the individual in the universal Intellect" (Williams, *Radical Reformation*, p. 22).

By the time of Charles I, Nicholas' doctrines were more important for their influence on spiritual sympathizers than they were as the basis for the remnant of a persecuted sect. Whatever discipline the spiritual hierarchy of the Family of Love may have been able to maintain could, of course, have little effect on Nicholas' unaffiliated admirers.[40] Experimental

---

[40] Nicholas (*Evangelivm Regni*, pp. 73–76) describes an elaborate ecclesiastical hierarchy that was to administer ordinances and maintain discicipline in the sect. It is doubtful that the hierarchy existed in England, although the sect did have spiritual leadership in its Elders. See also Allen C. Thomas, "The Family of Love, or the Familists," *Haverford College Studies*, No. 12 (1893), p. 34; and Williams, *Radical Reformation*, pp. 481–482.

Christians had absorbed Nicholas' attitude toward spiritual
enlightenment and the role of the Christ of experience, but
without the influence of a structured sect to impose some
degree of coherence their specific doctrines varied widely.
In this new phase of experimental Christianity most English
experimentalists developed more radical ideas than are known
to have existed in the sect, and during the Interregnum many
of these enthusiasts became Ranters; some experimentalists,
however, like John Everard and Anne Hutchinson, had
opinions that were somewhat more conservative than those
of the sect.

Rufus Jones maintained that the views of Anne Hutchinson should be considered part of the tradition of spiritual
religion that the books of Nicholas spread in England. Just as
William Wilkinson complained that Theophilus, the Familist
Elder, accused him of having "no experimented, but a literall
knowledge" (*Confutation of Certaine Articles*, p. 35), Hugh
Peters charged that Mrs. Hutchinson "spoke out plump that
we ministers were not sealed, that we preached in judgment
but not in experience" (Jones, *Mysticism and Democracy*, p.
131). Under examination by the Massachusetts authorities in
1638, Mrs. Hutchinson revealed other doctrines of a decidedly
experimental cast in addition to her contempt for those who
were merely learned in the Scriptures. The proceedings are
full of the jargon of seventeenth-century biblical theology,
and both sides seem more concerned with jockeying for a
favorable legal position than with communicating clear
meanings, but out of the welter of scriptural citations some
of Mrs. Hutchinson's positions emerge with reasonable definition. Among the numerous charges against her in lists
submitted by two separate pairs of accusers were some that
had long been associated with enthusiasm.

4. That the Resurrection mentioned 1 Cor. 15. is not of our
   Resurrection at the last day, but of our Union to Ch:
   Je: . . .
8. That thear is no Kingdom of Heaven, but Christ
   Jesus . . . .
2. That her Revelations about future Events are to be be-

leeved as well as Scripture because the same holy Ghost
did indite both . . . .
6. That not beinge bound to the Law, no Transgression of
the Law is sinfull.[41]

Only the first of these charges was directly debated, and, as
John Cotton's summary admonition indicates, the authorities
were convinced that she believed the resurrection was spiritual and not physical; on the second day of examination she
acknowledged her error (Dexter, "Report of the Trial," pp.
179, 181).

Although Mrs. Hutchinson was examined at length on the
charge that she believed "that the Soules (Ecl. 3. 18–21) of all
men by nature are mortal" (Dexter, "Report of the Trial," p.
162), she was neither an annihilationist nor a soul sleeper.
After some confused discussion she readily assented to Mr.
Damphord's (John Davenport's) restatement of her idea: "the
*soule cannot have Imortaletie in itself but from God from
whom it hath its beinge*" (Dexter, "Report of the Trial," p.
168). She believed that souls went either to eternal pain or
eternal peace;[42] thus she did not deny the conscious afterlife
as some Familists did. Her opinion on the soul's natural
mortality makes a nice distinction, but it makes no significant
difference in theology or morality. John Donne entertained
a similar opinion without endangering his reputation for
piety: "And for the Immortality of the Soule, It is safelier
said to be immortall, by preservation, then immortall by
nature; That God keepes it from dying, then, that it cannot dye."[43]

Soon after the banishment of Mrs. Hutchinson in 1638,

[41] Franklin B. Dexter, "A Report of the Trial of Mrs. Anne Hutchinson
before the Church in Boston, March, 1638," *Proceedings of the Massachusetts Historical Society*, 2d Ser., IV (1887–1889), 162–163.

[42] [John Winthrop,] *A Short Story of the Rise, Reign, and Ruin of the
Antinomians, Familists & Libertines, That Infected the Churches of New
England* (London, 1644), p. 59.

[43] *The Sermons of John Donne*, ed. George R. Potter and Evelyn M.
Simpson, 10 vols. (Berkeley and Los Angeles: University of California
Press, 1953–1962), II, 201. For the identical view of Calvin, see Chap.
One, above.

the New England authorities began their long travail with troublesome, insolent Samuel Gorton, a bold experimental Christian not given to equivocation and not overly endowed with common discretion. Gorton's quarrel with the magistrates of Massachusetts was intricate and legal, involving as it did a land dispute, and it need not concern us here. Much of the rancor the magistrates felt toward Gorton, however, was certainly caused by his religious opinions. Some thirty years after the quarrel began, Nathaniel Morton's feeling still ran so high that he made a virulent personal attack on Gorton, related Massachusetts' case against him, and denounced his religious doctrines.[44] According to Morton, Gorton and his followers, while imprisoned in Boston awaiting trial,

> spared not blasphemously to fly upon the Lord Jesus himself, his Word and Ordinances, in such a manner as scarce in any Age any Hereticks or Apostates have done the like: . . . belching out errours in their *Familisticall Allegories* (if I may so call them) as (to speak with holy reverence) they rendred the Lord Christ no other then an *Imagination;* shunning not blasphemously to say, *That Christ was but a shadow and resemblance of what is done in every Christian;* That *Christ was incarnate in* Adam, *and was that Image of God wherein* Adam *was created;* and, *That his being born afterwards of the Virgin* Mary, *and suffering, was but a manifestation of his suffering in* Adam; *That Man's losing Gods Image, was the Death of Christ; That Christ is the Covenant properly;* and, *That Faith and Christ are all one . . .* [*New-Englands Memoriall*, pp. 109–110].

Gorton's Familism thus well established, Morton went on to accuse him of leading a sordid life, apparently assuming that Gorton's mortalism necessarily called for a life of gross physical pleasures. "[He] hath not shunned to say and affirm, That all the felicity we are like to have, we must expect in this life, and no more: and therefore advised one with whom he

[44] Nathaniel Morton, *New-Englands Memoriall* (Cambridge, Mass., 1669), pp. 108–110. All citations are taken from the facsimile of this first edition published by The Club of Odd Volumes (Boston, 1903).

had some speech, to *make much of her self for she must expect no more but what she could enjoy in this life* or words to the same effect" (*New-Englands Memoriall*, p. 110).

Gorton defended himself in a long, angry letter to Morton, written shortly after the publication of *New-Englands Memoriall.* The theology in the letter is generally turbid, but it is clear that Gorton meant to defend the truth of the "Familisticall Allegories" attributed to him. He vigorously denied, however, that he had ever "spoken words (or to that effect) that there is no state nor con[dition] of mankind after this present life. . . ."[45] Gorton did not say, however, what he thought the state of mankind would be in the afterlife; given the other views he affirmed, there is little reason to believe that he conformed to the conventional conception of a heaven and hell inhabited by individual personalities. Morton was surely not a reliable witness of Gorton's doctrines, but he may have had some ground for thinking that Gorton taught the annihilation of personality at death. Dr. Lewis Janes, in his *Life of Samuel Gorton,* observes that Gorton conceived of immortality as a prerogative of the righteous only: " 'He . . . taught a conditional immortality wholly dependent on the character of the individual.' "[46] Dr. Janes's summary of Gorton's faith suggests that Gorton may have, in the Familist manner, limited heaven and hell to the spiritual states of the regenerate and sinful in this earthly life: " 'The substance of his teaching is that righteousness *is* life eternal; sin *is* eternal death. There is no arbitrary penalty inflicted at the close of man's earthly career, or on some future day of judgment; it is the intrinsic and natural result of evil action' " (in A. Gorton, *Life*, p. 147). As we have seen, the perfectionist

[45] "Samuel Gorton's Letter to Nathaniel Morton," in *Tracts and Other Papers*, ed. Peter Force, IV, No. 7 (Washington, D.C., 1846), p. 9. The letter was written from Warwick, Rhode Island, and dated June 30, 1669. Gorton, unfortunately, seems not to have had Morton's attack before him when he wrote this part of his defense; elsewhere in the letter, his knowledge of what Morton said is quite exact.

[46] Quoted in Adelos Gorton, *The Life and Times of Samuel Gorton* (Philadelphia: G. S. Ferguson, 1908), p. 147.

views of the Family of Love could receive polemical support from radical mortalism; a Calvinist like Morton would, of course, assume that mortalism could support nothing but a *carpe diem* philosophy.

When Gorton took up his preaching in England late in 1645 or early in 1646,[47] his spiritual views were, he claims, warmly received "by all sorts of people and personages vnder the title of a Bishop or a King" whether he preached in London, its suburbs, or more remote places ("Letter to Morton," p. 14). If he taught the mortality of the soul, he would not have had to seek far for a receptive audience. The Presbyterian party was raging against all forms of mortalism. It is clear that *Mans Mortalitie,* published two years earlier, was not the only sore point. Overton had argued only for the death of the soul until the General Resurrection, but Edmund Calamy the elder discerned that some sectarians had more recently begun to preach the irrevocable annihilation of the soul: "Some believe that the *Soul dyeth with the Body,* and that both shall rise again at the last Day. Others begin to say, they believe that the *Soul* is mortal, as well as the *Body,* and that there is no Resurrection neither of Soul nor Body."[48] More important, Thomas Edwards' popular heresiography, which went into its second edition in 1646, tried to show that mortalism had infected all England, even to the counties remote from London and other ports.

Of the 267 errors Edwards lists as heresies current in 1646, eleven state some form of the doctrine of mortalism. It was to Edwards' interest to multiply the errors of the sects by making fine distinctions where none were called for and then listing the errors at random. If Edwards had chosen to group the mortalist heresies according to Calamy's classifica-

---

[47] Kenneth W. Porter, "Samuell Gorton, New England Firebrand," *New England Quarterly,* VII (1934), p. 433. The article makes no attempt to elucidate Gorton's religious radicalism.

[48] Edmund Calamy, *Sermon Before the Lords on Christmas Day, 1644,* quoted in White Kennet, *A Register and Chronicle Ecclesiastical and Civil . . . from the Restauration of King Charles II* (London, 1728), p. 730.

tion, all but one would have fallen into place.[49] We might then have had the more intelligible structure that follows.

HERESIES THAT TEACH THE SLEEP OF THE SOUL

83. That the soul of man is mortall as the soul of a beast, and dies with the body [I, 26].[50]

84. That the souls of the faithfull after death, do sleep till the day of judgement and are not in a capacity of acting any thing for God, but 'tis with them as 'tis with a man that is in some pleasing dream [I, 26–27].

88. That none of the souls of the Saints go to Heaven where Christ is, but Heaven is empty of the Saints till the resurrection of the dead [I, 27].

173. No man is yet in hell, neither shall any be there untill the judgement; for God doth not hang first, and judge after [I, 36].

10. That it is injustice in God to punish the souls of the wicked in Hell while their bodies lie at rest in their graves, for seeing both were sinners together, both must be sufferers together; if God should punish the soul of *Cain* in Hell five or six thousand yeers before he punisheth the body of *Cain*, he then would show himself partiall in his distribution of justice [III, 8–9].

HERESIES THAT TEACH THE ANNIHILATION OF THE PERSONAL SOUL

15. That man had life before God breathed into him, and that which God breathed into him was part of the divine Essence, and shall return into God again [I, 20].

21. That the soul dies with the body, and all things shall have an end, but God only shall remain forever [I, 20–21].

22. Every creature in the first estate of creation was God, and every creature is God, every creature that hath life and

---

[49] The heresy may be unique since it does not seem to apply to the souls of men in general; it does imply that the souls of infants die with the body: "86. Infants rise not again, because they are not capable of knowing God, and therefore not of enjoying him" (Edwards, *Gangraena*, I, 27).

[50] All bracketed references are to part and page numbers in *Gangraena*. Although error Number 83 makes no reference to a future resurrection of soul and body together, it is probable that its author was actually a thnetopsychist rather than an annihilationist: see in Chap. One, above, the similar language that St. John Damascene and Alexander Gill use to describe Eusebius' Arabian thnetopsychists.

breath being an efflux from God, and shall return into God again, be swallowed up in him as a drop is in the ocean [I, 21].[51]

89. There is no resurrection at all of the bodies of men after this life, nor no heaven nor hell after this life, nor no devils [I, 27].

91. There is no hell, but in this life, and that's the legall terrours and fears which men have in their consciences [I, 27].

Robert Baillie, the Scottish Commissioner, identified both the sleep of the soul and the annihilation of the soul with the "Familistick Anabaptists" and thought they had taught soul sleeping only because they did not dare to advocate the more radical doctrine until discipline in religion failed during the Interregnum *(Anabaptism,* p. 99). Baillie is surely wrong in his opinion. *Mans Mortalitie,* which Baillie mistook for an annihilationist work, appeals to reason and philosophy as well as Scripture in its argument and insists that the soul will receive immortal life along with the body on the Last Day; Overton's thought is therefore far removed from the enthusiasm of the experimental Christians. Annihilationism is not only more radical than soul sleeping; it is quite incompatible with it. As the heresies excerpted from *Gangraena* show, soul sleeping presupposes an eschatology in which individuals dwell in a conventional heaven or hell and considers the resurrection of the body and Judgment to be events that will occur in the indefinite future. Even moderate experimental Christians would have thought such views a barrier to the perception of the present spiritual reality; radical experimentalists would surely have considered the soul sleepers no less carnal than their mutual Presbyterian enemies.

Although Baillie failed to distinguish the separate currents

---

[51] The figure was popular among experimental Christians: Everard used it in a parable (Jones, *Spiritual Reformers,* pp. 248–249) and, as we shall see, the Ranters also liked it. The pantheistic attitude exemplified in the figure is doubtless more Averroistic than scriptural, though the enthusiasts, unaware of their indirect debt to philosophy, would have credited the perception to their "experimental knowledge" and thought it consonant with the "spiritual" sense of Holy Scripture.

of mortalism in his time, he rightly saw annihilationism as a
secret doctrine of the Family of Love. Samuel Rutherford, his
countryman, also associated the heresy with the Familists:
"Familists I know say, *As we came from Gods essence, so
wee and our soules returne to God,* and are made in God
eternall, and turned into his essence, and so spiritualized.
. . . ."[52] If by this time the Family of Love was no longer significant as an organized sect, its chief doctrines had left a
lasting impression on English religious thought. Edwards
noted two doctrines that are unmistakably experimentalist,
even in the characteristic jargon.

> 29. That we did look for great matters from one crucified
> at *Jerusalem* 16 hundred years ago, but that does us no
> good, it must be a Christ formed in us, the deity united to
> our humanity, Christ came into the world to live thirty
> two years, and to do nothing else that he knew, and blessed
> God he never trusted in a crucified Christ [I, 21].[53]
> 50. That there is a perfect way in this life, not by Word,
> Sacraments, Prayer and other Ordinances, but by the ex-
> perience of the spirit in a mans self [I, 24].

Both of these doctrines Knewstub considered central to the
faith of the Family of Love; that experimental Christians of
the Interregnum also preached the death of the personal soul,
which Knewstub thought another key doctrine of the sect,
is evident throughout *Gangraena*. The annihilationist heresy
listed by Edwards as Number 22 suggests the pantheism by
which mystics sometimes express their insights when they
are not under the discipline of a strong theological or ecclesiastical tradition; two other heresies (Numbers 89 and 91)
clearly derive from the experimentalists' stress on salvation
as a drama complete in this life. *Gangraena*'s more extended
discussions of the annihilationists reinforce the identification

---

[52] Rutherford, *Survey of Spirituall Antichrist*, II, 219.

[53] In a marginal note, Edwards associates the error with Thomas
Webbe, the mortalist. Mosse calls Webbe a Ranter ("Puritan Radicalism,"
p. 429), but his definition of that group is too broad. In my view, Ranterism is distinguished most readily from the rest of experimental Christianity by its libertine philosophy and behavior; I have seen no evidence
that Webbe was a brazen libertine.

of experimental Christianity with the doctrine of the extinction of the personal soul.

Edwards indirectly connects Giles Randall, the popular preacher of experimental Christianity during the Interregnum, with annihilationism. "There is one *Marshal* a Bricklayer, a yong man, living at *Hackney* (a great follower of Mr. *Randal*) who infects many with his Errors: . . . this *Marshal* further maintained there was no Hell, but all men should be saved, wicked as well as good, and all other creatures who shall return unto God: again, all the hell that is, is in this life, which is nothing else but the legal terrors and fears men had in their consciences. . . ."[54] One of Edwards' anonymous correspondents told him of a similar universalism in the mortalism of Thomas Webbe, another young experimentalist preacher, who had referred so contemptuously to the crucified Christ of history.[55] "I had some conference with one Mr. *Web,* a man that pretends a New Light . . . . I asked him yet further, of his Opinion concerning the Resurrection of the dead; which he affirmed, there was no more Resurrection of a Man then of a Beast, nor had he any more Soul then the Body; yet he granted a Spirit in both wicked and godly, which he sayes goes again to him that gave it: No difference doth he acknowledge betwixt either, for locall torment more then is upon earth; he denies any locall Hell, or Devills, more then men are Devils in themselves . . . ."[56]

Thus within a century English experimental Christianity had moved far from some of the specific doctrines of the early Family of Love even while it held fast to the sect's insistence that spiritual truth must be experienced inwardly, not learned from the letter. If Edwards cites him accurately, Marshall seems to view hell not as the state of alienation from God, not as the miserable condition of a man who is still in thrall to sin, but as the state of one who is still in

---

[54] Edwards, *Gangraena*, I, 112. Note that Marshall is the author of error Number 91 in Edwards' catalogue.

[55] In 1644 Webbe was between the ages of twenty and twenty-one (*ibid.,* 106); nevertheless "many follow him in City and Country" (*ibid.,* 86).

[56] *Ibid.;* cf. Eccles. 3:19, 12:7.

bondage to the letter, of one who still suffers "legal terrors and fears" that God will punish sinners. The perfectionism of the Family of Love had degenerated into an antinomianism that held that in the Age of the Spirit there is no external Law. Whereas Queen Elizabeth had persecuted the sect partly because it denied that any outside the sect could be saved, Marshall and Webbe preached universal salvation. Eternal life consisted in the return of the divine element in the creation to God; since it would be absurd to think that God would judge his own essence, universalism was a necessary consequence of mystical pantheism. This view that the personal soul is mortal and only that portion of the creation which cannot be distinguished from God is immortal became quite popular in the middle of the seventeenth century. Many experimental Christians had begun to probe the pantheistic, universalist, and even the libertine implications of their mystical tradition.

Edwards describes some of the doctrines of the enthusiastic Independent Churches in Somersetshire. As a group the members denied the divinity of Christ, the validity of infant baptism, and the Trinity; they believed that the utterance of the Spirit through all members replaced the ministry, and condemned Scripture as but a covenant of works, the mere Letter. They also held a view close to the familiar doctrine of experimental Christianity, "that there is no hell, or at least no pain of sence in hell."[57] In addition, even these radical churches had a radical wing.

> These three opinions are most stoutly, though not so generally maintained, yet the number of them that are deluded doth exceedingly increase....
> 1. [That the Creator did] give forth of his divine essence a variety of formes and severall substances which we do call creatures, so that God doth subsist in the Creatures, and

[57] Edwards, *Gangraena*, I, 217–218 (falsely numbered 117 and 118 in my copy). The qualification that there is no sensual pain in hell suggests that the church members believed that the wicked were tortured by the pangs of conscience and spiritual misery only; it is not clear whether they thought that the pains of hell continued after death.

hereafter the whole Creation shall be annihilated and reduced into the Divine essence again.

2. Others affirm that the Word Christ, and the word Saint
doth not signifie any persons but some of the Divine essence infused into severall persons, so that Christ and the
Saints shall be saved, that is the Divin essence in those
persons shall be reduced into God again, but the persons
shall be annihilated, for the soul is mortall and the body
shall never rise from the dead, but was annihilated; the
world shall ever endure by way of generation from time
to time without an end.

3. That the Scriptures are not the Word of God but the
conceipts of men, and that we are not to adhere to them,
but to their Revelations therefore they slight the Word of
God, when it is urged to confirm a truth; for where it is
said this or that was done according to the Scriptures, as
I Cor. 15.4. their reply is, That is according to the vulgar
opinion and conceipt of naturall men [*Gangraena*, I, 219
(falsely numbered 119)].

The opinions of the experimental Christians proved disturbing enough to Parliament to be included in *An Ordinance
for the Punishing of Blasphemies and Heresies* of May 2, 1648.
The ordinance ordered the death penalty for those who obstinately maintained that Christ's death is not meritorious to
believers, that the Holy Scripture is not the Word of God,
that there is no day of Judgment after death, or that the body
shall not rise again after death. Imprisonment was ordered
for those who obstinately maintained that all men shall be
saved or that the workings of the Spirit and not the Ten Com-
mandments are the rule of a Christian life.[58] The ordinance
lacked the support of the Army, where sectarian ideas were
notoriously popular; indeed, Edwards believed "there are
some whole Troops in the Army that hold such desperate
opinions, as denying the Resurrection of the dead, and hell
..." (*Gangraena*, III, 107). Parliament could not enforce the
ordinance against blasphemy, and experimental Christianity
developed among the wilder enthusiasts into Ranterism.

In Gorton, Webbe, Marshall, and the Independents of Som-

[58] *Acts and Ordinances of the Interregnum, 1642–1660*, ed. C. H. Firth
and R. S. Rait (London, 1911), I, 1133–36.

ersetshire there are opinions that are quite similar to those of the libertine Ranters.[59] This similarity should not be surprising, for Ranterism is also part of the continuum of experimental Christianity that reaches back in England to the middle of the sixteenth century. Indeed, the Family of the Mount may well have taught a mild form of Ranter libertinism. The connection of Ranter attitudes with those of earlier experimental Christians was not lost on the Ranters' contemporaries. John Tickell noted the relationship in the title of his book *The Bottomles Pit Smoaking in Familisme* [1651] and denounced the Ranter habit of equivocation and their allegorical interpretation of the historical Christ (Cohn, *Pursuit*, p. 296). Gilbert Roulston, a reformed Ranter and author of *The Ranters Bible* (1650), divided the Ranters into seven sects, one of which he called "The Familists of Love" and another the "Athians," who met at King's Lynn, Norfolk, and "held the doctrine of the sleep of the soul."[60] Even a hasty examination of the tracts of Abiezer Coppe, Jacob

[59] The best available source of Ranter opinions is Cohn's appendix on the group and its literature: Norman Cohn, *The Pursuit of the Millennium*, rev. ed. (New York: Oxford University Press, 1970), pp. 287–330. Cohn reprints a good selection of generous extracts from the writings of both the Ranters' contemporary enemies and the Ranters themselves (Salmon, Bauthumley, Clarkson, and Coppe). Barclay's treatment of the Ranters is chiefly useful for its selections from Salmon and Bauthumley, which are not as severely truncated as those in Cohn: Robert Barclay, *The Inner Life of the Religious Societies of the Commonwealth* (London, 1876), Appendix to Chap. XVII, pp. i–v. C. E. Whiting boldly tries to summarize the doctrines of the minor sects existing at the Restoration. He discusses the Ranters, Salmonists, and Coppinists (after Richard Coppin) with considerable emphasis on their beliefs, but his references to his sources are too often sketchy and vague. His method of presenting the opinions of each sect separately has its virtues, but it makes it difficult to see the relationships among ideas. The difficulty is compounded by Whiting's habit of juxtaposing trivial, merely curious ideas and fundamental concepts in random fashion. Whiting is, nevertheless, an excellent source of names, bibliographical information, and assorted ideas: C. E. Whiting, *Studies in English Puritanism from the Restoration to the Revolution, 1660–1688* (London: Macmillan, 1931), pp. 272–283. A. L. Morton's *The World of the Ranters* (London: Lawrence & Wishart, 1970) emphasizes the social and political background of the movement.

[60] Whiting, *Studies in English Puritanism*, pp. 273–274. Richard Baxter also noted the Ranters' connection with Familist teaching: *The Autobiography of Richard Baxter*, ed. J. M. Lloyd Thomas (London: J. M. Dent, 1925), p. 73.

Bauthumley, Joseph Salmon, and Laurence Clarkson reveals the familiar doctrines of radical experimental Christianity: that Scripture must be read in the Spirit, not the Letter; that Christ is only the divinity in men; that salvation is to achieve mystical union with God; that resurrection occurs in this life; that heaven and hell are nothing more than spiritual states in this life; and that an impersonal existence as part of God is the only immortality possible for men.[61]

With the onset of Ranterism, experimental Christianity entered a new phase. Rufus Jones, looking forward to the more fruitful experimental Christianity of the Quakers, called Ranterism "the backwash of the spiritual movement" *(Spiritual Reformers,* p. 320); it represented, nonetheless, the tendencies of the movement when it developed among people who were not strongly committed to traditional Christian conceptions and lacked the leadership that men of George Fox's stature could provide. The precise doctrinal distinctions between a Ranter like Clarkson and a pious experimentalist like Dr. Everard need not be discussed at length here. The differences are often not readily apparent, for both Clarkson and Everard share the experimental tradition. A reading of Jones's account of Everard's beliefs will suggest the doctrines underlying Ranterism *(Spiritual Reformers,* pp. 244–252), but Everard follows their implications with due regard for traditional Christian conceptions of righteousness and the distinction between God and man. The enthusiasm latent in Everard's contempt for "the dead and killing Letter" is held in check by his learning: Everard's conversion to the experimental view of religion did not occur until approximately his fiftieth year (about 1625), well after his long education in traditional divinity was complete *(Spiritual Reformers,* pp. 239–240). Much of the Ranter teaching and behavior seems a vulgar parody of Everard's comparative sober experimentalism, but it is effective parody

---

[61] Barclay *(Inner Life,* p. 416) could find no immediate English predecessors of the Ranters and suggested that their views may have originated among survivors of the medieval Brethren of the Free Spirit in Holland and Belgium.

because it exaggerates weaknesses in its original. For Everard, for example, the righteous man is guided by the Christ in him and not by the Law; though not bound by the Law, he is not tempted to break it. In the Ranters' hands, freedom from the Law meant that sin had no objective reality; an act became unclean only if an individual thought it unclean. The doctrine of perfectibility degenerated into libertinism as Ranters showed the purity of their hearts by committing acts of gross wickedness, preferably in public.

This notorious antinomianism of the Ranters was based on their idea of the relationship of God and man. In *The Light and Dark Sides of God* (London, 1650), Jacob Bauthumley says, " . . . I see that God is in all Creatures, Man and Beast, Fish and Fowle, and every green thing, from the highest Cedar to the Ivey on the wall; and that God is the life and being of them all, and that God doth really dwell, and if you will personally; if he may admit so low an expression in them all, and hath his Being no where else out of the Creatures" (Cohn, *Pursuit*, p. 304); thus in this short passage the moderate doctrine of divine immanence is carried by enthusiasm into the pantheism of the last clause. Their thoroughgoing pantheism left the Ranters so enrapt by their perception of the unity of all things in God that they denied that any state or action could be an expression of anything but God's will; in such a world, evil obviously existed only in the "vain imaginings" of unregenerate men. The regenerate Ranter did not overcome sin; rather, he perceived that unity only was real, "so that Devil is God, Hell is Heaven, Sin Holiness, Damnation Salvation."[62] Before he became a Ranter, Bauthumley worshipped a mutable God who responded to the behavior of the creature: "[Formerly I] thought that my sins or holy walking did cause [God] to alter his purpose of good or evill to me." After he saw that he was part of God, Bauthumley realized that the divine

[62] Laurence Clarkson, *A Single Eye All Light, No Darkness* (London, 1650), in Cohn, *Pursuit*, p. 315. See also *Acts and Ordinances*, ed. Firth and Rait, II, 409–412, for the Act of August 9, 1650, against the Ranters; this opinion is condemned on p. 411.

unity could admit of no discord: "But now I cannot looke upon any condition or action, but methinks there appears a sweet concurrance of the supreame will in it nothing comes short of it, or goes beyond it, nor any man shall doe or be any thing, but what shall fall in a sweet compliance with it; it being the wombe wherein all things are conceived, and in which all creatures were formed and brought fourth" (*The Light and Dark Sides*, in Cohn, *Pursuit*, p. 304).

The annihilationism of Ranter mortalism also derives from their pantheistic vision, for God will one day choose not to reveal himself in diversity and will allow of no distinctions or parts.

The truth is, there is nothing lives to all eternity but God: every thing below God perisheth and comes to nothing: and as all things had their subsistence and Being in God, before they were ever manifested in the world of Creatures: so in the end, whatsover [*sic*] is of God, or God in the world at the end of it, they shall all be rapt up into God againe. And so as God from all eternity lived in himself and all things in him: so when he shall cease to live in flesh and creatures, he will then live in himself unto all eternity, and will gloriously triumph over Sin, Hell and death; and all Creatures shall give up their Power and Glory unto God backe againe, from whence it Originally came, and so God shall be all [Bauthumley, *The Light and Dark Sides*, in Cohn, *Pursuit*, p. 306].

... God is pleased to live in flesh, and as the Scripture saith, He is made flesh, and He appears in several forms of flesh, in the form of man and beast, and other creatures, and when these have performed the design and will of God, that then as the flesh of man and other creatures come from the earth, and are not capable of knowing God, or partaking of the Divine nature, and God ceasing to live in them, and being gone out of them, that then they all shall return to their first principle of dust, and God shall, as he did from all eternity, live in Himself before there was a world or creatures: so he shall to all eternity live and enjoy Himself in Himself, in such a way as no man can utter; and so I see him yesterday, and to day, and the same for ever—the Alpha and the Omega, the beginning and the end of all things [Bauthumley, *The*

Light and Dark Sides, in Barclay, *Inner Life*, Appendix to
Chap. XVII, p. iv].

This I conceived, as I knew not what I was before I
came into being, so for ever after I should know nothing
after this my being was dissolved; but even as a stream
from the Ocean was distinct in it self while it was a stream,
but when returned to the Ocean, was therein swallowed
and become one with the Ocean; so the spirit of man
while in the body, was distinct from God, but when death
came it returned to God, and so became one with God,
yea God it self ... [Laurence Clarkson, *The Lost Sheep
Found* (London, 1660), in Cohn, *Pursuit*, p. 311].

There is, of course, no place in such a pantheistic view for
heaven and hell as eternal entities. Bauthumley, following
the experimental tradition, considers them spiritual states in
this life:

then men are in Heaven, or Heaven in men, when God
appears in his glorious and pure manifestations of himself, in Love and Grace, in Peace and rest in the Spirit ....
... I find that where God dwells, and is come, and hath
taken men up, and wrapt them up into the Spirit; there
is a new Heaven and a new Earth, and all the Heaven I
look ever to enjoy is to have my earthly and dark appre-
hensions of God to cease, and to live no other life then
what Christ spiritually lives in me.
... I was continually suffering the torment of Hell, and
tossed up and down, being condemned of my self .... And
this is that I found til God appeared spiritually, and shewed
me that he was all the glory and happiness himself, and
that flesh was nothing .... God ... brought me into the
glorious liberty of the Sons of God, whereas I was before
in bondage to sin, law, an accusing Conscience which is
Hell ... [*The Light and Dark Sides*, in Cohn, *Pursuit*, pp.
305–306].

The Ranters virtually disappeared after the Restoration,
many of them having been absorbed by the rising Society of
Friends (Jones, *Mysticism and Democracy*, pp. 138–139).
Baxter pronounced the Quakers to be "but the Ranters
turned from horrid prophaneness and blasphemy to a life of

extreme austerity on the other side" (*Autobiography*, p. 73).
Baxter's statement is untrue, of course, since, as I have indi-
cated, Ranter "prophaneness" was supported by their pantheistic doctrine and was not simply aberrant behavior; the
Ranter refusal, from their pantheistic commitment, to distinguish between good and evil was the characteristic doctrine that set them apart from more moderate experimental
Christians. Baxter's statement suggests, nevertheless, that he
did see doctrinal correspondences between Ranterism and
Quakerism. Common doctrines there were for, as Jones
noted, George Fox also owed much to the tradition that the
Family of Love had begun in England (*Mysticism and
Democracy*, pp. 136–138). It was doubtless because they had
spiritual insights similar to those of the Quakers that the
Ranters joined the newer sect in such large numbers. The
union of the Ranters and the Quakers was not, however, a
happy one for the Quakers, who had their peace disturbed
by Ranter tendencies as late as the nineteenth century.[63]

The continuing struggle of the early Quakers against the
imperfectly assimilated Ranter remnant in their midst is told
in Stephen Crisp's *A Faithful Warning & Exhortation to
Friends: To Beware of Seducing Spirits* (London, 1684). Crisp
does not attack the seducers as unreasonable or even as
unscriptural, for the Quakers were accustomed to permitting
considerable liberty of the Spirit. Rather, Crisp rebukes the
dissidents for trusting in the Spirit before they have learned
to control the impulses of the flesh. These undisciplined
spirits were those that Satan "hath stirred up in several Citys
& Countrys such as he knows are fit for his purpose, who
never knew a real Mortification upon that Earthly Sensual
Wisdom that's from beneath . . . " (*Faithful Warning*, p. 13).
Everard had also warned that the control of the flesh was
necessary for illumination: " 'All the Artillery in the World,

---

[63] About 1797 the Friends in Ireland included members who had
marked Ranter attitudes. In America the revered Quaker leader Elias
Hicks began, in his old age, to preach a vigorous pantheistic doctrine
which, in 1827, led almost half of the American Society of Friends into
schism (Barclay, *Inner Life*, pp. 557–561, 571). Neither movement, however, seems to have been marked by Ranter licentiousness.

were they all discharged together at one clap, could not
more deaf the ears of our bodies than the clamorings of desires in the soul deaf its ears, so you see a man must go into
silence or else he cannot hear God speak' " (quoted in Jones,
Spiritual Reformers, p. 249).

One of the doctrines these seducers used to create schism
among the Quakers is the belief in the death of the personal
soul. The annihilationism and perhaps the universalism of
this Ranter remnant seem to be based, as they were among
some earlier experimentalists, upon pantheism.

> Another starts Questions about the *Mortality* or *Immor-*
> *tality* of the Soul. Another *of the state of the Soul after the*
> *Death of the Body, whether it abides a singular Essence, or*
> *ceaseth to have any singuler Essence or being.* Another
> about the *state of the Body after Death.* Another about
> *How many Bodys one and the same Soul may or must have*
> *at sundry times.* Another *How long the Wicked Men or*
> *Angels must endure the Wrath of God for Rebellion.*
> *If there be Wrath and Judgment to be revealed, it will*
> *be but for a time, and then they shall be restored to Glory*
> *and Happiness, or if they fall short of a due fitting and*
> *preparing for the Kingdom of God on this side the Grave*
> *its no great matter, for they shall have other oppertunitys*
> *even in this World hereafter, when they shall be born in*
> *other Bodys* [Crisp, *Faithful Warning*, pp. 13–15].

To the older heresies these radicals have added reincarnation.[64] From Crisp's sketchy account one can only speculate
on the origins of the idea. It is possible that the seducers
introduced a purgative variety of the reincarnation doctrine
in a clumsy attempt to reconcile their pantheistic universalism with the Christian idea of Judgment. If such was their
aim, they did violence to pantheism and Christianity both.
Pantheism, which sees individual forms as only temporary
manifestations of the eternal God, cannot so easily be fitted

---

[64] Apparently some earlier Ranters thought the soul experiences mul-
tiple incarnations. Barclay, paraphrasing seventeenth-century sources,
says the Ranters believe that "as the sea sends back the same water
again sometimes into one spring, and sometimes into another, so with
the spirits of men in a future state" (*ibid.*, p. 417).

with the raiment of a religion based on the unalterable particularity of individuals.

A more rigorous, if less attractive, heretic offered a purer pantheism that attempted no accommodation with Christian theology or morality. "Another he boulsters himself up with a belief, *That if he doth Evil, his Hell is only here in his own Conscience, but when he leaves the World all things will be as if they had not been, and the Soul shall dye with the Body, and suffer an Annihilation as well as the Body, or shall be swallowed up out of all particularity, as a drop of Water into the Sea, and so then what matter.* And this is the Evil Seeds Man, sowing these cursed Seeds of *Fleshly Liberty* and *Ranterisme . . .*" (Crisp, *Faithful Warning*, p. 16). If we accept Crisp's quotation as accurate, here is Ranterism devoid of virtually all moral content. It burlesques the ideas and values of experimental Christianity because its author apparently learned them by rote instead of by experience. How else can one account for such expressions as "*his Hell is only here in his own Conscience*" and "*so then what matter?*" One can hardly read much of Salmon, Bauthumley, Clarkson, or Coppe without believing that their ideas are expressions of their intense experiences, whatever one may think of their conclusions from them. Their libertinism has an emotional power that must be respected because, one feels, they really felt that their experiences had freed them, that they were "Sons of God." They did not think Hell an inconsequential state: they had experienced it inwardly.

This chapter may appropriately conclude with some observations on the significance of Crisp's "fleshly libertine" in this study of mortalism among the experimental Christians. This libertine does not represent the inevitable conclusion of the spiritual movement, as its enemies would have us believe: the Quakers shunned his amoralism and carried experimental Christianity to a high moral level under a superior leadership. Rather, he reminds us that experimental Christianity placed great demands on the inner discipline of men; those who did not have much self-control, or who were alienated from the controls and traditions of

their society, could easily slip into what even moderate experimental Christians would consider errors. This libertine
also reminds us of what may be too easily overlooked, that
one may learn experimental Christianity "by the Letter."
The movement by its nature could have no agreed way of
testing whether its truths were being repeated in a rote
fashion, and we may be sure that not all those who identified themselves with experimental Christianity really had
illuminating "experiences."

When one reads Rufus Jones's sympathetic accounts of the
spiritual leaders of the movement, one wonders why experimental Christianity so shocked the authorities in church
and state. Jones gives us, however, little idea of what doctrines the leaders' principles might have produced in the
hands of the ordinary people who make up a mass movement. All its contemporary critics agree both that "Familism"
had a large and growing membership and that it recruited
its members chiefly from the poor and ignorant classes of
society. Even if one allows for the alarmist purpose of most
of the critics' attacks, one must still conclude that the numbers in the organized sect were often large and that those in
general sympathy with the movement constituted a much
larger number. As we have seen, even the Quakers, who
worked hard to secure a discipline acceptable to the sect, had
great difficulty in containing the centrifugal forces in experimental Christianity. Through most of its history in England
experimental Christianity had a negligible discipline at a
time when many traditional Christian doctrines were being
reexamined. Orthodox critics of the movement could make
little of the writings of its spiritual elite, but they knew
much more about what doctrines were being taught to the
novices and what the novices, in turn, made of them. The
evidence adduced by the movement's contemporary critics,
together with the statements of experimentalists during and
after the Interregnum, provides a valuable insight into popular religious ideas current during the English Reformation.
The evidence of the critics informs us that the roots of enthusiasm were established in English soil almost a century

before the sects grew so wildly during the Interregnum. Regardless of what Henry Nicholas or John Everard may have thought the ultimate destiny of the personal soul to be, the critics demonstrate that many of the common people, the "swarmes" of the lowly (Knewstub, *A Confutation*, p. **4) who were undisciplined in Christian knowledge and who may have acquired much of their "experimental" knowledge by rote, were moved to deny that the individual human soul is immortal.

Three / Soul Sleepers in the Conventicles

If the orthodox Englishman was appalled by the way the enthusiasts disregarded the literal meaning of Holy Scripture, he had no reason to rejoice as he contemplated the conclusions of some of those who professed the utmost respect for its "plain sense." For a century before the publication of *Mans Mortalitie*, English orthodoxy was frequently troubled by those who asserted that the soul was asleep or dead between death and the General Resurrection. These radicals were the more disturbing because they insisted, as did Richard Overton, that they were Christians who derived their views from the letter of Holy Scripture. The orthodox liked to dismiss them as "Epicureans" or "sectaries" who wanted to divide the Christian Church, but the soul sleepers asked to be judged only by the Holy Scripture literally interpreted, an authority upon which Protestant orthodoxy also relied in matters of faith. It will be my task in this chapter to try to identify these heretical literalists in the first century or so of the English Reformation and to show how these exiles, martyrs, and "sectaries" tried to interpret Scripture in its own terms only, with the biblicist's contempt for those who looked for assistance to human philosophy, traditional commentary, or ecclesiastical decrees. Such views, of course, led to the superabundance of doctrines that various radicals proposed as the true scriptural teachings. Often these doctrines were not compatible with each other, but this fact did not shock all the radicals as it did the orthodox dogmatists. Many of the radicals took comfort in the belief that no doctrine that could not be clearly and simply derived from Scripture alone could be essential to salvation, and some were willing to examine Scripture to see whether a clear doctrine of the intermediate state of the soul was evident there.

The theoretical bases for the idea that the way to Christian union was to reduce the number of essential doctrines had been set forth often enough throughout the Reformation. On the Continent Sebastian Castellian's *De Haereticis* (1554), written in response to the Genevan execution of Michael Servetus, was an early landmark in what was to develop into the "latitudinarian" position. While living in Elizabeth's England Jacobus Acontius published in Basle his plea for the toleration of doctrinal differences, *Satanae Strategemata* (1565), a book that was in its first century frequently reprinted in the original Latin and translated into French, German, Dutch, and English. William Chillingworth (*The Religion of Protestants A Safe Way to Salvation* [1638]) and Jeremy Taylor (*The Liberty of Prophesying* [1647]) were eloquent spokesmen for the latitudinarian cause. Despite these formulations of a theoretical ground for the noncoercive discussion of Christian doctrine, Reformation churches that in practice encouraged a truly unfettered "liberty of prophesying" among their members were rare indeed; quite possibly they did not exist. Nevertheless, as the number of Baptist works discussed in W. K. Jordan's great study suggests,[1] there was a sect, the General (that is, Arminian or Freewill) Baptists, that, among the important congregations in Reformation England, most nearly approached a church that imposed a minimal creedal test on its members and encouraged them to explore together the meaning of Holy Scripture without fear of overstepping the limits of prescribed doctrine.

As we shall see in this chapter, in the century between the death of Tyndale and Frith and the disestablishment of the episcopal Church of England under the Long Parliament, the idea of the sleep or death of the soul was kept alive by those disaffected "Anabaptist" radicals who thrived on discussion of the "plain meaning" of Scripture and therefore allowed each other great latitude in doctrinal inquiries. General Baptists seem to have liked open, Scripture-based discussion of a great many questions that the established church considered both essential and settled. The General Baptists were far less inclined than most English sects to define themselves as believers in a comprehensive and detailed creed; rather, they relied on their individualistic method of apprehending divine

---

[1] W. K. Jordan, *The Development of Religious Toleration in England,* 4 vols. (Cambridge, Mass.: Harvard University Press, 1932–1940).

truth, on fellowship and holiness of life, to give them the unity that other Reformation congregations sought in uniformity of professed doctrine.

In the tolerant fellowship of the General Baptists it was possible to get a hearing for the doctrine of the soul's mortality argued in terms of a strictly biblical theology; like Milton, the Baptists seem to have considered the question of the state of the soul after death to be interesting, but not vital to a man's faith or devotion. Throughout our period, however, representatives of the major state churches did not examine mortalist ideas, but denounced them as destructive of faith and morals. Only radical reformers seem to have noticed that mortalism had its pious uses in destroying the Roman arguments for purgatory and the invocation of saints, in restoring the General Resurrection to a central position in eschatology, and (though millenarian views had an uncertain claim to orthodoxy) in giving additional import to the coming establishment of· Christ's thousand-year kingdom by holding off immortal life until the last days.

Whatever one may think of the substance of the scriptural argument for mortalism, it is, I think, reasonable to say that the issue might have been engaged as a problem in the literal interpretation of Scripture since both the radicals and their moderate opponents were committed to reading Scripture for its literal sense. Christian mortalism throughout this period was not, however, discussed seriously outside the conventicles and therefore was condemned to being a minor phenomenon in Reformation intellectual history. It may be that the idea of a mortal soul was too alien to the Christian tradition for the doctrine to get a real hearing, but the same might have been said about more successful ideas in the Reformation—the doctrine of the bondage of the will, perhaps, or of salvation by faith alone. Numerous reasons may be adduced to account for the failure of mortalist ideas to attract widespread support during the Reformation, but that the literalist argument for mortalism could be dismissed so lightly by moderate churchmen dedicated to literal interpretation suggests that the mortalist argument was rejected out of hand because it was thought to come from a tainted source: the hated Anabaptists. The gulf was too great between Baptist individualism and the attitudes of those who wanted to organize a national church around a uniform body of doctrine. A shared interest in the literal interpretation of a book that both parties agreed was the Word of God was not enough to reconcile those who so deeply disagreed about the requirements for membership in a Christian church. When, soon after the death of Tyndale in 1536, Lutherans abandoned the examination of the scriptural bases for mortalism to the Anabaptists, the doctrine was condemned to be considered only among the scorned and lowly who met in irregular, often illegal congregations.

In an age enchanted by Calvin's formulation of a comprehensive Christian doctrine from Holy Scripture, it could not be expected that Protestant unity could be preserved from doctrinal controversy.[2] Faced with Anabaptist and possibly Lutheran support for soul-sleeping doctrines, Calvin himself vigorously rejected the appeal to consider the matter adiaphorous: "I would here obviate the objections of those who will blame my present undertaking, charging me with stirring up fierce contests about nothing, and making trifling differences the source of violent dissensions: for there are not wanting some who so reproach me. My answer is, that when Divine Truth is avowedly attacked, we must not tolerate the adulteration of one single *iota* of it. It is certainly no trivial matter to see God's light extinguished by the devil's darkness . . . ."[3]

Not all Reformation churches would put the case for preserving the seamless garment of scriptural doctrine so uncompromisingly, but no major Reformation church departed

[2] Reformation disunity cannot, of course, be entirely, perhaps not even mainly, traced to disagreements about the proper interpretation of Scripture. Economic, political, and social conditions admittedly played important roles in the fragmentation of Protestantism, but contemporary discourse about disharmony centered about the meaning of the Word, and this study attempts only to discover how English Protestants in the period looked upon Christian mortalism.

[3] Calvin, *Psychopannychia*, in *Tracts*, tr. Beveridge, III, 418.

significantly from the attitude Calvin expressed here; certainly none approached the General Baptists' willingness to accept diversity in so many doctrinal matters. Even the Church of England, probably the most conciliatory of Europe's three major national churches in matters of doctrine, enforced subscription to its Thirty-nine Articles. Those articles were not only a detailed creed, but they also pointedly excluded doctrines frequently voiced by Roman Catholics and Anabaptist radicals; indeed, the Puritan faction in the English Church frequently objected to the doctrinal content of the articles even though it was precisely this faction that the creed was supposed to reconcile to the state church.[4] Committed as they were to building church unity on uniformity of doctrine, the state churches quite correctly saw that without the guidance of an authoritative church, the vernacular Bible was a divisive force in Christianity; the literal reader no less than the allegorizer was liable to fall into heresy. The conservative state churches therefore commonly appealed to the civil magistrate to make the plain meaning of Scripture yet plainer to those who resisted the official interpretation. If the church was to be unified, the exegete must be taught to know and respect the established doctrines of his Christian community; like the godly Jews of Berea, he would first hear the authoritative view of a messenger ordained by God and only then search the Scriptures to see whether it is supported there.[5]

But many Christians of the Reformation were impatient with the messages brought by the official reformers. These radicals expected revolutionary messages, words that would restore the doctrines and polity of the apostolic church, that would cut away the merely human accretions that had developed during the reign of Antichrist; instead, as they saw it, the leading reformers of Germany, Switzerland, and England offered only minor reforms and imposed the still intact

---

[4] Hardwick, *History of the Articles*, pp. 205–218.
[5] See Chap. One, above, for Calvin's view of the proper use of Holy Scripture.

Antichristian system on the People of God by appealing to the power of popery's unholy ally, the civil magistrate. It was clear to the radicals that if the purity of the primitive church was to be restored they would have to ignore the ordained messengers and themselves search the Holy Scriptures, with only divine guidance; these radical literalists tried to read the Bible with an innocent eye, as if the sacred book were but newly published and had had no previous commentators. In the presence of a long tradition of biblical commentary into which philosophical views had been assimilated, it was, of course, not really possible to read the Bible without philosophical preconceptions, but it was the radicals' unshakable faith that the study of Scripture without reference to human learning and philosophy would yield, ultimately, certain knowledge of the doctrines and polity of the earliest Christian communities, knowledge that could be used to establish the True Church.

In its more immoderate forms it was this radical force of reformation that was commonly, though inexactly, called Anabaptism. The more traditional one's approach to Christian questions, the more likely that one would see Anabaptism in the moderate Reformation parties: William Barlow saw Anabaptism, with Zwinglianism, as a third aspect of Lutheranism,[6] and the Presbyterians thought the moderate Independents were hopelessly tainted with Anabaptism. The Anabaptists were the scandal of Protestantism for, scorning fifteen centuries of tradition, they necessarily recapitulated the history of heresy. Many of the ancient heresies, notably those of Arius and Pelagius, flourished again as the Anabaptists formulated their beliefs with Scripture (and the Holy Spirit) their only guide. Official Protestantism, by no means ready to struggle with the old issues again, encouraged the state to suppress these primitives. The secular powers needed little encouragement. At a time when religious discord was regarded as civil commotion, the Anabaptists were especially

---

[6] William Barlow, *A Dyaloge describing the Orygynall Group of These Lutheran Faccyons* (London, 1531), sig. g 1v.

provocative: they typically denied the state any authority in religious matters, refused to assume civil offices or take oaths, and sometimes held, at least as an ideal, that common ownership of goods was necessary in a true Christian society. Those Anabaptist sects that were not exasperatingly pacifistic could too often be associated, with some justice, with the bloody revolutionary spirit of the Münster Kingdom. Temporal authorities could not tolerate such insubordinate attitudes toward all human authority, and throughout Europe there began a savage persecution that did not abate until late in the seventeenth century.[7]

By the reign of King Charles I, the lovers of Christian unity were confronted with a sad spectacle. After a century of the English Reformation, even if one ignored the papists and enthusiasts as hopelessly corrupt, the cause of those who hoped for a united Protestant church guided by the Word of God had to be judged nearly lost in the turbulence that grew worse daily. Devout Puritans were being driven from their livings, many pious Englishmen had separated from the Established Church and their congregations were worshiping God in exile or in hiding, and the Church of England by law established was reviled by many as a sanctuary of popery. Those active in Christian affairs had become used to being reproached as popish ceremonialists, arrogant enthusiasts, or both, and they willingly reproached other Christians with similar epithets.

To Viscount Falkland's circle, which included William Chillingworth and John Hales, it was clear that simple agreement to interpret the Word of God literally would not unite

[7] Hostility between the state and the radicals is still evident. Jehovah's Witnesses flourish with little public sympathy, and their struggles with secular society therefore present a good paradigm of the Reformation conflict. Particularly in the resurgence of nationalism during the two world wars, the American sect was harassed and persecuted by officials, its members set upon by mobs and jailed for refusing military conscription. The sect was relieved by a series of Supreme Court decisions in cases appealed in its behalf by "unbelieving" civil libertarians; like good Anabaptists, the Witnesses even refuse to seek the protection of a secular judiciary. In Nazi Germany the Witnesses were thrown into concentration camps.

Christians in a common and elaborate creed. Coercion did not seem to be the way to achieve Christian unity; it could only result in insincerity or rebellion. Perhaps Christians expected too much guidance from the Word, expected weak mankind to agree on a single interpretation of Scripture in places where even reasonable men could not agree. The Oxford rationalists therefore proposed that schisms could be healed simply by allowing much more doctrinal latitude in the Church. Reason, they insisted, could perceive in Holy Scripture the essential Christian truths, which were simple, apparent, and few; where Scripture was less clear, doctrines derived therefrom could not be judged essential to salvation, and rational discussion of these texts must be encouraged. In 1647 Jeremy Taylor, writing a few years after the deaths of Falkland and Chillingworth, recommended the Apostles' Creed as a good summary of the beliefs essential to Christianity and observed that to venture beyond such a clearly scriptural confession was to create conditions in which schism and heresy were inevitable: "bodies of confessions and articles do much hurt by becoming instruments of separating and dividing communions, and making unnecessary or uncertain propositions a certain means of schism and disunion."[8]

This latitudinarian philosophy had been anticipated by the Baptists, and, by the middle of the seventeenth century in England, some Independent congregations had also developed the habit of keeping to a minimum the doctrines to which members had to subscribe. Almost all the psychopannychists and thnetopsychists in the period were connected with such radical sects, for the doctrine of the soul's mortality was, among the more radical Reformation congregations, apparently thought to be "a thing indifferent." No Reformation church issued a creed that required its adherents to subscribe to any form of mortalism, but no creedal statements

[8] Jeremy Taylor, *The Liberty of Prophesying* (ed. 1817), p. 376, cited in H. John McLachlan, *Socinianism in Seventeenth-Century England* (London: Oxford University Press, 1951), p. 88. I am indebted to McLachlan's excellent chapter (pp. 63–95) on these rational theologians.

from the radical Protestant sects said anything that conflicted with the soul sleepers' view. The radicals, committed only to the letter of the Word, liked to compose creeds that were little more than conflations of biblical phrases, and in these compositions there was no place for such concepts as "separable spirit" or "incorporeal substance"; the sects were content to state their belief in the resurrection of the body to immortal life. For example, neither the Schleitheim Confession (1527) of the early Swiss Anabaptists nor the Dordrecht (Dort) Confession (1632) of the by then safe and established Dutch Mennonite community mentions the state of the soul between death and resurrection; both documents labor to stay as close as possible to biblical language and avoid discussion of doctrines (such as the Trinity and the two natures of Christ) that so concerned the early councils of the Church.[9]

Although the English soul-sleeping tradition developed primarily in the liberal setting of the radical conventicles, soul-sleeping ideas were first stated in England in the form of Lutheran psychopannychism. Until the last years of Henry VIII's reign it appears that only Luther's followers tried to persuade the English public to doubt the conscious immortality of the soul between death and resurrection. More than a century before Overton, Milton, and Hobbes wrote the first developed arguments for thnetopsychism, Tyndale defended Luther's psychopannychism as an opinion far more conformable to the clearer messages of Holy Scripture than either the Roman traditions of purgatory and the intercession of saints or the Calvinist view that the souls of the dead are in either heaven or hell.

Sir Thomas More opened the dispute in *A Dyaloge of Syr Thomas More Knyghte* (London, 1529), which he had completed in 1528.[10] More accuses Luther of maintaining psycho-

---

[9] The texts of both Anabaptist confessions may be found in *Creeds of the Churches,* ed. Leith, pp. 281–308.

[10] A modern edition of More's work is *Dialogue,* ed. Campbell; this volume also contains a facsimile of the *Dialogue* from William Rastell's edition of More's collected English works (1557). All citations are from Campbell's modern edition.

pannychism for petty motives. What are we to think, More asks, of the constancy of a man who once denounced as heretics those who denied purgatory and who now

> a while after, denieth it himself, saying, in the sermon that he wrote on the rich man and Lazare, that all men's souls lie still and sleep till doomsday?
>
> Mary, quod your friend, then hath some men had a sleep of a fair length. They will, I ween, when they wake forget some of their dreams.
>
> By my faith, quod I, he that believeth Luther that his soul shall sleep so long, shall, when he dieth, sleep in shrewd rest.
>
> I much marvel, quod your friend, what evil ailed him to find out this fond folly.
>
> To this opinion, quod I, or rather to the feigning of this opinion (for I verily think that himself thinketh not as he writeth) he fell for envy and hatred that he bare the priesthood, by the malice of which [in] his ungracious mind he rather were content that all the world lay in the fire of purgatory till doomsday than that there were one penny given to a priest to pray for any soul [*Dialogue*, p. 270].

More also charges Luther with encouraging immorality. "What shall he care how long he live in sin, that believeth Luther, that he shall after this life neither feel well nor ill in body nor soul till the day of doom?" "And if they shall be damned, yet they say it shall be long or they feel it. For Luther saith that all souls shall sleep and feel neither good nor bad after this life till doomsday" (*Dialogue*, pp. 276, 279). More's comments are scarcely more than invective, but they are typical of the orthodox English response to Christian mortalist ideas before the Restoration. The English opponents of the sleep of the soul rarely examined the concept on its theological merits and only occasionally and superficially considered the scriptural arguments on which it was based. Henry More attempted to treat psychopannychism seriously on philosophical grounds in his poem "Antipsychopannychia" (1642), but he too hastily turned the poem into a Neoplatonic song asserting the natural immortality of the soul.[11]

[11] More, *Psychodia Platonica*.

When Tyndale answered *A Dyaloge* from his continental
exile in 1531, he boldly met Thomas More's attack on psychopannychism. Since More had attacked only Luther by
name, Tyndale could easily have ignored the issue, but apparently Tyndale was strongly enough committed to psychopannychism to take More's bolt in his own breast.

> *More:*—"What shall he care how long he live in sin, that
> believeth Luther, that he shall after this life feel neither
> good nor evil, in body or soul, until the day of doom?"
> *Tyndale:*—Christ and his apostles taught no other; but
> warned to look for Christ's coming again every hour:
> which coming again ye believe will never be, therefore
> have ye feigned that other merchandise.[12]

Tyndale was never again to be so dogmatic about the truth
of psychopannychism. Elsewhere in *An Answer* and in his
later work he is uncertain about the precise state of the soul
between death and resurrection. He is certain, of course, like
all the reformers, that purgatory is unscriptural, that it savors
of the doctrine of works, and that it impugns the sufficiency
of Christ's redemptive sacrifice, but he does not think the
biblical evidence on the intermediate state of the soul is adequate to support any article of faith on the question.

Throughout his years of disputing about the intermediate
state of the soul, Tyndale was concerned mainly with resolv-
ing the question in a way that would preserve a central role
for the resurrection of the body. There, Tyndale thought, was
an article of faith that beyond doubt had the clear warrant
of Scripture, yet many men pushed it into the background
because they preferred Greek philosophy. Tyndale's insistence that the Christian hope was in the General Resurrection of the dead often was shrill, and he could as quickly
(and with as little justice) charge the Protestant George Joye
with denying the resurrection as he could make that charge
against the Church of Rome. When More listed Luther's

---

[12] Tyndale, *An Answer*, ed. Walter, pp. 188–189.

heresies, Tyndale was not conciliatory toward those proud men who corrupted the Word with pagan ideas.

> *More:*—"Item, that all souls lie and sleep till doomsday."
> *Tyndale:*—And ye, in putting them in heaven, hell, and purgatory, destroy the arguments wherewith Christ and Paul prove the resurrection. What God doth with them, that shall we know when we come to them. The true faith putteth the resurrection, which we be warned to look for every hour. The heathen philosophers, denying that, did put that the souls did ever live. And the pope joineth the spiritual doctrine of Christ and the fleshly doctrine of philosophers together; things so contrary that they cannot agree, no more than the Spirit and the flesh do in a christian man. And because the fleshly-minded pope consenteth unto heathen doctrine, therefore he corrupteth the scripture to stablish it. Moses saith in Deut. "The secret things pertain unto the Lord, and the things that be opened unto us, that we do all that is written in the book." Wherefore, sir, if we loved the laws of God, and would occupy ourselves to fulfill them, and would on the other side be meek, and let God alone with his secrets, and suffer him to be wiser than we, we should make none article of the faith of this or that. And again, if the souls be in heaven, tell me why they be not in as good case as the angels be? And then what cause is there of the resurrection?[13]

Tyndale was not satisfied with the position of those who, like the Roman Catholics and most reformers, stated their belief in both the conscious immortality of the soul *and* the resurrection of the body: for Tyndale, Christians had to believe that the resurrection was the *central* event in the Christian experience, and he was sure that any doctrine that posited a kind of joy or pain for the living soul before the resurrection diminished the importance of the General Resurrection. If Tyndale thought that the state of man's personality between death and resurrection was one of God's secrets, he was cer-

[13] *Ibid.*, pp. 180–181. More's charge may be found in the *Dialogue,* p. 261. Tyndale, in his *The Exposition of the Fyrst Epistle of Seynt Iohn* (Antwerp? 1531), sig. E3, also made the point that the state of departed souls is God's secret.

tain that God had clearly announced that the resurrection of the body was the beginning of the whole salvation of Christians, not just an additional reward for souls already in joy.

In England the case of William Tracy dramatically focused attention on the question of the state of the soul immediately after death.[14] Tracy, a learned Protestant layman, died shortly after writing his will in October, 1530. The testament was vigorously attacked by the ecclesiastical hierarchy because in it Tracy maintained the sufficiency of faith for salvation and explicitly denied the Church a mortuary to pay for prayers for his soul. Vexed that copies of the testament were being widely circulated privately, the hierarchy excommunicated Tracy in 1532 and ordered his body removed from consecrated ground. When an overzealous official of the Bishop of Worcester illegally burned the body as befitted a heretic, Richard Tracy, the dead man's son, instituted proceedings against the official, who was fined three hundred pounds by the civil court for acting without the King's authority.

Tracy's daring testament elicited expositions of his words from both Tyndale and his associate John Frith. These commentaries, found among Tyndale's papers after both he and Frith had been executed (Tyndale in 1536 and Frith in 1533), were probably written in 1532, during the height of the interest in the celebrated case. In the history of English soul-sleeping ideas, Frith's exposition is by far the more interesting work. Tyndale has temporarily strayed somewhat from his position on "God's secret." In a passage attacking purgatory he admits the possibility that the souls of the just may be conscious, but he is careful to exclude any idea that they are either punished or fully rewarded. "Though it seem not impossible haply, that there might be a place where the souls might be kept for a space, to be taught and instructed; yet that there should be such a jail as they jangle, and such

---

[14] Tracy's celebrated story has frequently been retold. I have used for my brief account Walter's summary of the controversy surrounding Tracy's death (Tyndale, *An Answer*, pp. 269–270); Walter's edition also includes the text of Tracy's testament and Tyndale's commentary upon it (pp. 271–283).

fashions as they feign, is plainly impossible, and repugnant to the scripture."[15] Tyndale's receptacle for just souls is similar to the sort of *limbus patrum* that John Archer and Jeremy Taylor would propose in the next century, with the important difference that Archer and Taylor allow the souls a good measure of their reward before the resurrection.[16] The concept of a waiting place for lively souls outside of heaven falls between Protestant orthodoxy and psychopannychism, but it could appeal to those who, like Tyndale, Archer, and Taylor, wanted only a doctrine that would not rob the resurrection of the body of its proper central role in Christian eschatology.

Frith's exposition reveals a good deal about the controversy over Tracy's idea of the afterlife. Tracy's words are open to either a thnetopsychist or a psychopannychist construction: ". . . I commit me unto God, and to his mercy, trusting . . . that by his grace and the merits of Jesus Christ, and by the virtue of his passion, and of his resurrection, I have and shall have remission of my sins, and resurrection of body and soul, according as it is written, (Job xiv.) 'I believe that my Redeemer liveth, and that in the last day I shall rise out of the earth, and in my flesh shall see my Saviour' " (Tyndale, *An Answer*, p. 272). Since Tracy implicitly denies purgatory and does not speak of his soul's going to be with Christ, it is at least curious that he should neglect to suggest an alternative state for the soul before the General Resurrection; instead, he speaks only of looking forward to the "resurrection of body

---

[15] "The Testament of Master William Tracy . . . Expounded by William Tyndale," *ibid.*, p. 281.

[16] John Archer, *The Personall Reigne of Christ vpon Earth* (London, 1643), p. 23; Jeremy Taylor, *The Great Exemplar of Sanctity and Holy Life* (London, 1653), pp. 556–557, 564–565 (Part III, Sect. xvi). Harold Fisch (*Jerusalem and Albion* [New York: Schocken, 1964], p. 179) mistakenly thinks Bishop Taylor is a mortalist because in the *Great Exemplar* (pp. 564–565) Taylor maintains that neither the soul nor body when separated is the "whole man"; on those very pages, however, Taylor says clearly that the just soul, though it is not in heaven until it is united with the body again, communicates with God and the angels. Calvin's discussion of the soul's state after death is not so different from Archer's and Taylor's (see Chap. One, above), but he is careful not to imply the soul rests outside heaven.

and soul." To be sure, Tracy may not have intended to express a soul-sleeping position at all, but his words left him vulnerable to attack from his enemies.

Frith vigorously defended Tracy against his unfriendly critics who charged him with believing in the soul's mortality; Frith, however, took the charge to mean thnetopsychism, and his interpretation of the testament makes Tracy seem very like a Lutheran psychopannychist.

> But there are some, that gather of hys wordes, that he should recounte the soule to be mortall. Whiche thinge after my iudgement is more suttelly gathered thē eyther truely or charitably, for seynge ther was neuer Christen man that euer so thoughte (not the very pagaynes) what godly zele, or brotherlye loue was there which caused thē so to surmise, for a good mā wolde not once dreame such a thinge; but I pray you why shoulde we not say that the soule doeth verely ryse which thorow Christe rysing from ye fylth of synne, doeth enter wyth the body into a new conuersation of lyfe, which they shall leade together wythout possibilitie of synning, we say also of god (by a certain phrase of scripture) yt he ariseth, whē he openith vnto vs his power, & presēce. And why may we not say ye same thinge of the soule whiche in the meane ceason semeth to lye secret & thē shall expresse vnto vs (thorow Christ) her power and presence, in takynge agayne her natural body [?] Why shoulde ye then codempne these thynges [?] There is no man yt can receyue venom by those wordes, except he haue suche a spyderouse nature that he can turne an hony combe into perelous poyson.[17]

Tracy's phrase "resurrection of body and soul" had apparently implied to some that for Tracy the soul as well as the body was to be revivified "in the last day," and Frith's explication of the phrase cannot have been satisfactory to the orthodox critics. Frith's interpretation only argues against the charge of thnetopsychism; he says that Tracy did not deny that the soul is an immortal substance, but he still represents

[17] From John Frith's exposition of Tracy's testament, in [John Wyclif,] *Wicklieffes Wicket*, (n.p., 1548?), sigs. d4v–d5r.

Tracy as saying that the departed soul "semeth to lye secret" until it rises, not, like the body, from death to life, but from inactivity and rest to liveliness and power. Frith thus links Tracy with Tyndale (and, by implication, with Frith himself) as a person who, professing ignorance about the precise state of departed souls before the General Resurrection, was certain that the soul did not attain its heavenly reward except in union with the body. This view is no great distance from Luther's idea that the soul may be said to "sleep"; if it can be said to differ from psychopannychism at all, it does so only by hesitating to use even a vague term like "sleep" without sufficient support from Scripture. Had Frith meant to denounce psychopannychism as an idea unchristian and unworthy even of pagans, he would consciously have been defending Tracy at the expense of his friend Tyndale. Joye claimed that "Frith wrote tindals answers to More for tindale/ and corrected them in the prynte/ and printed them to at Amelsterdam/ and whether he winked at T[indale's]. opinion as one hauyng experience of Tindals complexion/ or was of the same opinion I cannot tel . . . ."[18] We need not believe that Frith was the author of a large portion of Tyndale's *Answer*, but if he had seen the book through the press, or even had merely read it, he would have known that to call psychopannychism unchristian would be gratuitously to insult his friend Tyndale and the leader of reform, Luther. Frith seems to have maintained his "psychopannychism" until he was executed in 1533 for his opinions about the Real Presence. In his last days in prison, it is reported that "he sayd playnely that he thought no sayntes soule came in heuen

[18] George Joye, *An Apology Made by George Joy, To Satisfy, If It May Be, W. Tindale*, ed. Edward Arber (Birmingham, 1882), p. 33. Clebsch observes that Tyndale's biographers concede only that Frith saw Tyndale's *An Answer* through the press (W. A. Clebsch, *England's Earliest Protestants: 1520–1535* [New Haven: Yale University Press, 1964], p. 95). Clebsch (pp. 95–98) argues on stylistic evidence that Frith actually wrote the part of the *Answer* that refutes More point for point; since that part contains a defense of psychopannychism, Clebsch is not on firm ground when he repeatedly links Frith and Joye as opponents of Tyndale's psychopannychism (e.g., pp. 135, 180, 203, 219).

before the day of dome/ but in the meane season reposed
hym selfe he wiste not where."[19]

Both Frith and Tyndale, then, inclined toward the belief
that the soul slept in the intermediate state, but neither felt
that Scripture justified making an article of faith out of even
so indefinite a doctrine as psychopannychism. But if Tyndale
was willing to consider the precise nature of the intermediate state a thing indifferent, he would not tolerate dogmatism
on the subject from anyone else, particularly if the dogma
threatened to make the resurrection of the body superfluous.
When, in one action, his fellow refugee George Joye dog-
matically asserted that the faithful souls were already enjoying their reward in heaven, tampered with the sacred text
to help support his dogma, and cast doubt on the necessity
of the resurrection of the body, Tyndale was understandably
wrathful. Joye provoked Tyndale in matters that Tyndale
considered vital to Christian belief; that Joye had, without
authorization or acknowledgment, meddled with Tyndale's
translation of the New Testament was of only secondary
concern to Tyndale.

After the publication of Tyndale's *An Answer* in 1531, Joye
had disputed with Tyndale about the psychopannychism he
expressed there. Tyndale remained unpersuaded and treated
Joye disdainfully (Joye, *Apology*, pp. 15–18). By 1533 Joye,
alienated from Tyndale and Frith, was seeking support in the
matter from other reformers. He wrote Hugh Latimer from
Antwerp, asking his opinion of a secret letter Joye had sent
one of the Brethren in which he had proved "that the sowles
dep*a*rtyd slepe not nor lye ydle tyll domes daye as Martin
luther and the Anabaptyst*es* saye and as me thynkythe
ffrythe and Willi*a*m tyndall wolde...."[20] Unfortunately,
both Joye's secret letter and any reply Latimer may have

[19] Germen Gardynare, *A Letter of a Yonge Gentylman...Wherein
May Se the Demeanour & Heresy of John Fryth* (London, 1534), sig.
xiv v. In answering the attack on Lutheran psychopannychism that More
in 1529 included in his *Supplication of Souls* (*The Workes of Sir Thomas
More Knyght...Wrytten by Him in the Englysh Tonge* [London, 1557],
p. 325G), Frith made essentially this point (*A Disputacion of Purgatorye
Made by Ihon Frith* [n.p., 1531?], sigs. I2v–I3r).

[20] The entire letter is quoted in Butterworth and Chester, *George Joye,*
pp. 95–96; the italic letters are theirs.

made are lost, but the letter to Latimer does make clear that Frith was offended by the secret letter and complained to Tyndale that the doctrine in it was likely to cause dissension among the Brethren.

Joye therefore had reason to feel alone in his battle to persuade the English evangelicals to adopt the idea that God would reward the just immediately after death. When, in 1534, he accepted the task of correcting the press proofs for an unauthorized edition of Tyndale's *New Testament*, Joye behaved like a desperate man. In twenty places he silently changed Tyndale's word "resurrection" to "the life to come," "the very life," or some similar phrase. Joye admitted that he made the emendations partly to frustrate the psychopannychists:

> For I did translate thys worde *Resurrectio* in to the lyfe aftir thys/ in certayne placis/ for these two causes principally. First because the latyn worde/ besidis that it signifieth in other places the Resurreccion of the bodye/ yet in these it signifieth the lyfe of the spirits or soulis departed as christis answere vnto the Saduceis/ and John declare. Secondaryly/ because that agenst the Anabaptistis false opinion/ and agenst their errour whom Erasmus reproueth in hys exposicion of the Credo which saye the resurreccion of the soules to be this: that is to weet/ when thei shalbe called out of their preuey lurking places/ in whiche they had ben hyd from the tyme of their departyng vnto the resurreccion of their bodies/ because (I saye) that agenste these erroneouse opinions/ these places thus truely translated make so myche and so planely/ that at thys worde *Resurrectio* the lyfe of the spiritis aftir this/ their false opinion falleth and is vtterly condempned [Joye, *Apology* p. 10].

When Joye's emended text was published in August, 1534, Tyndale was enraged.[21] In his own revision of his *New Testa-*

---

[21] The printing history of the edition corrected by Joye and the whole complex quarrel that resulted are ably set forth in Butterworth and Chester, *George Joye*, pp. 148–182; I am indebted to this account. The same authors (p. 161) name the places (in addition to Matt. 22:23–32) where Joye emended "resurrection." Joye's emendation has not influenced later translators (cf. the Authorized Version or the Revised Standard Version).

ment issued in November, he included an extra preface in
which he denounced Joye and his "corrected" edition. Tyndale probably distorts Joye's view of the resurrection and exaggerates its effect on the Brethren, but his chastisement of
Joye repeatedly shows that for Tyndale the issue was not the
intermediate state of the soul, but the truth and importance
of the promised resurrection of the body.

> George Ioye hath had of a longe tyme marvelouse ymagi-
> nacions aboute this worde resurreccion, that it shuld be
> taken for the state of the soules after their departinge from
> their bodyes, and hath also (though he hath been reasoned
> with therof and desyred to cease) yet sowen his doctryne
> by secret lettres on that syde the see [England], and caused
> great division amonge the brethren. In so moche that Iohn
> Fryth beynge in preson in the toure of London, a lytle be-
> fore his death, wrote that we shuld warne him and desyer
> him to cease, and wolde have then wrytten agaynst him,
> had I not withstonde him. Therto I have been sence in-
> formed that no small nomber thorow his curiosite, vtterly
> denye the resurreccion of the flesshe and bodye, affirminge
> that the soule when she is departed, is the spirituall bodye
> of the resurreccion, and other resurreccion shall there
> none be.[22]

When their friends could not get Joye and Tyndale to reconcile their differences, Joye published the defense of his
views and behavior in February, 1535. Joye had kept public
silence about his disagreement with Tyndale's soul-sleeping
opinions, but now, charged with heterodoxy himself, he both
insists on his orthodox faith in the resurrection of the body
and exposes the heterodoxy of Tyndale. Joye rehearses the
scriptural arguments he used against Tyndale's psychopannychism and is content to think that Tyndale has recanted his
error (Joye, *Apology*, p. 18). A careful reading of Tyndale's
last comments about the intermediate state will show that
Joye is too ready to believe he has won the victory over Tyndale. What Joye takes for recantation is but Tyndale's careful

[22] William Tyndale, tr., *The New Testament*, ed. N. Hardy Wallis
(Cambridge: Cambridge University Press, 1938), p. 16.

restatement of the position he had held since 1531: that Holy
Scripture is silent on the exact nature of the intermediate
state though it is clear that the souls of the just do not yet
have their full reward and that Christians must look forward
to the resurrection of the body.[23]

> And I protest before God and oure savioure Christ and
> all that beleve in him, that I holde of the soules that are
> departed as moche as maye be proved by manifest and
> open scripture, and thinke the soules departed in the fayth
> of Christ and love of the lawe of God, to be in no worse
> case then the soule of Christ was from the tyme that he
> delivered his sprite into the handes of his father, vntyll the
> resurreccion of his bodye in glorie and immortalitie. Nev-
> erthelater, I confesse openly, that I am not persuaded that
> they be all readie in the full glorie that Christ is in, or the
> elect angels of god are in. Nether is it anye article of my
> fayth: for if it so were, I se not but then the preachinge of
> the resurreccion of the flesshe were a thinge in vayne. Not
> withstondinge yet I am readie to beleve it, if it maye be
> proved with open scripture. And I have desyred George
> Ioye to take open textes that seme to make for that pur-
> pose, as this is. To daye thou shalt be with me in Paradise,
> to make therof what he coulde, and to let his dreames
> aboute this word resurreccion goo. For I receave not in the
> scripture the pryvat interpretacion of any mannes brayne,
> without open testimony of eny scriptures agreinge thereto
> [Tyndale, *New Testament*, p. 17].

As evidence of Tyndale's doctrinal shift, Joye cites only
Tyndale's statement that the just souls "be in no worse case
then the soule of Christ was from the tyme that he delivered
his sprite into the handes of his father, vntyll the resurreccion
of his bodye in glorie and immortalitie," but Joye's belief that

---

[23] Tyndale earlier had used 1 Thess. 4:13–18 to good effect to make
this point. There the Apostle comforts the Thessalonians about their
dead brethren by assuring them that at the Parousia the dead, far from
being neglected, will be raised first, and the living will join with them
to meet Christ in the air. "And I marvel that Paul had not comforted
the Thessalonians with that doctrine, if he had wist it, that the souls of
their dead had been in joy; as he did with the resurrection, that their
dead should rise again" (Tyndale, *An Answer*, p. 118).

"christis spirit departed slept not oute of heuen/ but wente
into the fathers handis in heuen" (Joye, *Apology*, p. 18) is not
clearly Tyndale's belief. The condition of Christ's soul between his death and the Resurrection was exceedingly controversial during the Reformation;[24] Joye's opinion departs
from the traditional view, based on 1 Peter 3:19, that Christ
before the Resurrection preached to the spirits in prison. Tyndale's reference to the soul of Christ probably means no more
than that the just, like Christ, are neither glorified nor tormented in purgatory before the resurrection of the body. His
suggestion that Joye try to build a scriptural case for his position out of such promising texts as the words to the Good
Thief further indicates that Tyndale remained unpersuaded
that the souls of the just are in heaven.[25] To the end, Tyndale

[24] Thomas Rogers, *The Catholic Doctrine of the Church of England*,
ed. J. J. S. Perowne, Parker Society (Cambridge, 1854), sheds considerable
light on the uncertainty that prevailed in the English Church about
the exact meaning of the phrase "he went down into hell" in the third
of Elizabeth's articles. Rogers' exposition was, in its earliest form, first
published in 1579; by 1607 (the date of the copy text used by Perowne)
Rogers no longer insisted on Calvin's view that, since Christ's body was
in the grave and his soul was in the hands of his father in Paradise,
"hell" must mean Christ's suffering in body and soul before his death.
Instead, Rogers, who usually calls "errors" those opinions that differ
from his own, grants that there are a number of acceptable views of the
descent into hell (*ibid.*, pp. xii–xiii, 60–61). Edward's article in 1553,
formulated amid controversy, clearly said that Christ's soul left the body
and preached to the spirits in prison, but it did not settle the controversy, and Elizabeth's article ten years later was made less specific in
order to encompass the disputants; see Hardwick, *History of the Articles*,
pp. 97, 135, 292–293, and E. J. Bicknell, *A Theological Introduction to
the Thirty-nine Articles*, 3d ed., rev. H. J. Carpenter (London: Longmans,
1955), p. 94. A valuable summary of the various interpretations of the
descent into hell is in Williams' *Radical Reformation*, pp. 840–842.

[25] Luke 23:43 was a favorite text with those who opposed mortalism.
Joye says he used it against Tyndale in conversation, but that Tyndale
wrested it out of its plain meaning (*Apology*, pp. 15–17). As we shall see,
the mortalists "wrested" the Good Thief passage in a variety of ways
throughout the period. In his exposition of Genesis 2:8, delivered in
1535, Luther comments on 2 Cor. 12:2–4 as well as Luke 23:43 when he
interprets Paradise as the inactive, peaceful, intermediate state of the
soul. "Indeed, I myself, do not hesitate to assert that Christ and the thief
did not enter any physical place . . . . Paradise designates the state in
which Adam was in Paradise, abounding in peace, in freedom from fear,
and in all gifts which exist where there is no sin. It is as if Christ said:
'Today you will be with Me in Paradise, free from sin and safe from
death (except that the Last Day must be awaited, when all this will be

thought the state of souls before the resurrection to be one of God's secrets; to say that they sleep, because it is less definite, is likely to be nearer the truth than to say they are in heaven or purgatory.

About the time Tyndale, Frith, and Joye were quarreling about psychopannychism, English trade with the Low Countries brought Anabaptists and their doctrines to England where, particularly in London and the eastern ports, they settled in separate communities and began to influence a native population whose own radical tradition of Lollardy was not yet dead. Perhaps as early as 1532, six Englishmen and two Flemings were arrested for importing and distributing "the booke of Anabaptist confession"; they had a meeting place in London, and their Flemish leader was called "the bishop & reder of the Anabaptists." Anabaptist immigration increased as a result of the persecutions that followed the Münster debacle of 1535, the abortive rebellion at Amsterdam in the same year, and the activities of the Duke of Alva against all Reformation parties in the Low Countries (1567-1573). Suppressed under Henry VIII, Edward VI, and Mary, most Anabaptists (except for the Pelagian group led by Henry Hart of Kent) do not seem to have separated from the Established Church until the reign of Elizabeth, when they sometimes met in secret conventicles. Anabaptist ideas of church polity, doctrine, and society survived in the seventeenth century mainly among the Baptists and Congregationalists.[26]

Amid repressive conditions, the sixteenth-century Anabap-

---

laid open to view), just as Adam in Paradise was free from sin, death, and every curse, yet lived in the hope of a future and eternal spiritual life.' Thus it is an allegorical Paradise, as it were, just as Scripture also gives the name 'Abraham's bosom' (Luke 16:22), not to Abraham's mantle but, in an allegorical sense, to that life which is in the souls who have departed in the faith. They have peace, and they are at rest; and in that quiet state they await the future life and glory" ("Lectures on Genesis," tr. George V. Schick, *Luther's Works*, ed. Pelikan and Lehmann, I, 88–89; *WA*, XLII, 67).

[26] This paragraph is heavily indebted to Irvin B. Horst's excellent summary of early English Anabaptist activity: "England," *The Mennonite Encyclopedia*, ed. Harold S. Bender and C. Henry Smith, 4 vols. (Scottdale, Pa.: Mennonite Publishing House, 1955–1959), and to Williams' *Radical Reformation*, pp. 778–790.

tists left only slight traces of their beliefs; with no protectors and no charismatic leaders, they spread their opinions orally and left few books. Insofar as we may judge from inadequate records, soul sleeping does not seem to have been one of their major doctrines, on a par with their belief in universal grace and their opposition to paedobaptism and to the use of the civil power to coerce in religious affairs. It is more likely that the radicals considered the intermediate state of the soul a matter not clearly settled by Scripture.

Enough Anabaptists advocated the doctrine of the sleep of the soul, however, to keep the issue before the authorities. In 1546, during the examination of George Wishart, the Scottish reformer, martyr, and friend of John Knox, the Scottish bishops charged him thus: "XVIII. 'Thou, false heretic! hast preached openly, saying, that the soul of man shall sleep till the latter day of judgment, and shall not obtain life immortal until that day.' "[27] Wishart indignantly denied the charge, but the incident suggests that the Scottish authorities saw soul sleeping as a threat well before the triumphant reformers condemned the doctrine in the Scottish Confession of 1560.

In England, in the meantime, the Anabaptists seem to have been the only promulgators of psychopannychism; indeed, after the Tyndale-More controversy, Luther's name was no longer publicly associated with the doctrine. Unsupported by any reformer of stature, psychopannychism could be dismissed out of hand as a pernicious and unchristian concept. When William Hugh published a popular book of Christian consolation in 1546, he was freer than Calvin to heap abuse on the psychopannychists, for a decade earlier on the Continent Calvin had had to consider the feelings of the Lutheran psychopannychists. Although he is dealing only with psychopannychism, Hugh treats the sleepers harshly and tries to depict them as, in reality, annihilationists and antiresurrectionists:

> Truly the error of those is great who persuade themselves that the soul, separate from the body, shall sleep

[27] John Foxe, *The Acts and Monuments of John Foxe*, ed. Josiah Pratt, 4th ed., 8 vols. (London, 1877), V, 634.

unto the last day; and this error is old, and was confuted by Origen, and others of his time. Neither was it ever since received into the church, unto such time as a pestilent kind of men, whose madness is execrable, brought it of late days into the world again. But as all others of their opinions are perverse, abhorrent from the truth, and devilish, so is this. Declaring its patrons not to be taught in Christ's school, but in Galen's rather, who affirmed the death of the soul necessarily to follow the death of the body.

Therefore, I say, believe not these false deceivers, who endeavour not only to persuade the sleep of souls, but also to make vain the resurrection of the dead, and so to abolish an article of our faith, and to make our religion vain.[28]

Although Hugh does not expressly identify the sleepers as Anabaptists, it is difficult to believe he would have heaped such abuse on Lutheran psychopannychists. There is, however, no reason to believe that Hugh is aware of the thnetopsychism of some Anabaptists or the annihilationism of some experimental Christians; his claim that soul sleepers deny the resurrection is, of course, absurd, part of his clumsy attempt to slander the psychopannychists by wildly extrapolating from their position one that utterly denies a life to come. In his attempt to refute the sleeper's error from philosophy and Holy Scripture, Hugh argues only against psychopannychism. His refutation is of little interest, consisting as it does merely of the assertion that the soul is naturally vital and alert, and of a pedestrian exposition of the more obvious texts that were so often used against the mortalists: for example, the promise to the Good Thief, the story of Dives and Lazarus, and the verses that tell of the spirit returning to God who gave it, of St. Paul being caught up into Paradise, and of God being not the God of the dead but of the living (the texts are, respectively, Luke 23:43, 16:19-31, Eccles. 12:7, 2 Cor. 12:2-4, and Matt. 22:31-32).

Thnetopsychism did not make its appearance as a distinct variety of the English soul-sleeping heresy until 1549. In that

[28] *The Troubled Man's Medicine*, in *Writings of Edward the Sixth*, pp. 36–38.

year Bishop John Hooper wrote to Henry Bullinger, an authority on continental Anabaptism and a friend of the English Church, to complain of the Anabaptists who flocked to his public lectures to contend with him on doctrinal matters. The letter mentions some radicals who meet in conventicles, but it is chiefly valuable as the record of an important prelate's impressions of those nonseparatists who were attempting the reform of the Church of England along radical lines. Among the troublemakers were "some who deny that man is endued with a soul different from that of a beast, and subject to decay."[29]

In the next year England's struggle against the Anabaptist radicals resumed in earnest. A royal commission was established to combat Anabaptist errors (Hardwick, *History of the Articles*, p. 89), Bullinger's aid having already been indirectly enlisted in the fight. John Veron, prebendary of Worcester, had translated Bullinger's early dialogues against the Anabaptists and published them as *An Holsome Antidotus or Counterpoysen, agaynst the Pestylent Heresye and Secte of the Anabaptistes* (London, 1548).[30] Bullinger's dialogues touch on all the disputed doctrines, and in all instances Joiada, the mature, reasonable voice of moderate reform, wins out over Simon, the naïve, uncritical Anabaptist sympathizer. The tenth dialogue (sigs. N5v–P3v) is devoted to the Anabaptist opinion on the sleep of the soul, but Bullinger makes Simon such a weak representative of the Anabaptist view that the discussion is quite disappointing. Joiada, civil and conciliatory, easily gains Simon's assent to disputable points and carries the day with ridiculous ease. Simon, for example, expresses the familiar fear that the orthodox idea that the soul goes straight to heaven or hell at death makes the General Resurrection and the Judgment unnecessary, but he is satisfied with Joiada's evasion that the resurrection of the

---

[29] Hardwick, *History of the Articles*, pp. 88–89; Hooper also rejected psychopannychism (*Later Writings of Bishop Hooper*, ed. Charles Nevinson, Parker Society [Cambridge, 1852], p. 63).

[30] Veron worked from the Latin edition of Leo Inde; Bullinger's original German edition was *Von dem unverschämten Frevel* (Zürich, 1531).

body "perteyneth to the whole man" (sigs. N6v and O5v).

Simon presents Anabaptist mortalism as nothing more extraordinary than psychopannychism;[31] he makes no reference to the dissolution of the "whole man" in the grave, but speaks only of the sleep of the just in Abraham's bosom, a place he is unable to locate (sig. N7r). He is content to dispute only on the basis of Holy Scripture,[32] and Joiada often finds him too literal an interpreter: when Simon insists that Scripture often says a dead man has fallen asleep, Joiada complains that the Anabaptists do not understand synechdoche (sig. O4r). Joiada easily defeats Simon in a philosophical discussion of the nature of the soul, but Simon, well beyond his depth, properly gives the scornful Anabaptist rebuff to such human vanity: "Thou shuldest peraduenture haue persuaded somewhat, to Timeus, and Phedrus, Platos disciples, I had leauer heare Scriptures" (sigs. O6r–P1r). Simon's complaint ends Joiada's philosophical excursion none too soon, for Joiada had simply asserted that the soul is naturally active and thereby begged the question; Bullinger doubtless wanted to illustrate the Anabaptist's smug ignorance of reason and learning, but his own attempt to establish rationally the nature of the soul's intermediate state is unimpressive.

In 1549 Calvin's influence was thrown against the English Anabaptists when a translation of his *Briève Instruction Pour Armer Tous Bons Fidèles contre . . . la Secte Commune des Anabaptistes* (Geneva, 1544) was issued.[33] After the refutation of the more notorious Anabaptist errors, an abbreviated version of Calvin's *Psychopannychia* is appended in which he maintains that all those who believe the other Anabaptist doctrines are also soul sleepers (*A Short Instruction*, sig. G7v).

---

[31] Simon grants Joiada that "A sprite, is immortall, incorruptible, euerlasting or perpetuall" (sig. O6r), thereby taking a position that is comfortable for a psychopannychist but contradictory for a thnetopsychist.

[32] Some of his more formidable texts are: 1 Thess. 4:13–18; Phil. 3:11; John 5:28–29, 14:2–3; Acts 7:60; and 2 Tim. 4:7–8.

[33] Williams, *Radical Reformation*, p. 596. The translation is John Calvin, *A Short Instruction for to Arme All Good Christian People agaynst the Pestiferous Errours of the Common Secte of Anabaptistes* (London, 1549).

Since *Psychopannychia* has already been discussed sufficiently, it is only necessary to note in passing that the *Short
Instruction* restates the thnetopsychists' view of the soul:
"[some say] the soule is not a substāuce, or a creature hauīge
an essentiall beynge: but that it is only the vertue that mā
hath to breathe, to moue, and to do other actions of lyfe . . ."
(sigs. G7v–G8r).

The Anabaptists continued seriously to trouble the Established Church throughout the reign of Edward. John Veron
published two of Bullinger's dialogues against Anabaptism as
separate volumes in 1551.[34] In the same year, Archbishop
Cranmer drafted a statement of belief that was to form the
basis of the Forty-two Articles of 1553, sometimes called the
Edwardine Articles (Hardwick, *History of the Articles*, p. 72).
Many of these articles were directed against the Anabaptists,
and Archbishop Thomas Cranmer and his fellows apparently
thought soul sleeping had made gains enough to merit an
article condemning both psychopannychism and thnetopsychism.

> XL. *The soulles of them that departe this life doe
> neither die with the bodies, nor sleep idlie.*
> Thei whiche saie, that the soulles of suche as departe
> hens doe sleepe, being without al sence, fealing, or per-
> ceiuing, vntil the daie of iudgement, or affirme that the
> soulles die with the bodies, and at the laste daie shalbe
> raised vp with the same, doe vtterlie dissent from the
> right beliefe declared to vs in holie Scripture [Hardwick,
> *History of the Articles*, p. 348].

The Edwardine Articles defined the official doctrinal position of the Church of England for only a few months.[35] Ed-

---

[34] Henry Bullinger, *A Moste Sure and Strong Defence of the Baptisme
of Children, against ye Pestiferous Secte of the Anabaptystes,* tr. John
Veron (Worcester, 1551), and *A Most Necessary & Frutefull Dialogue,
between ye Seditious Libertin or Rebel Anabaptist, & the True Obedient
Christiā,* tr. John Veron (Worcester, 1551). The latter dialogue argues that
the civil power has authority in religious affairs.

[35] See Hardwick, *History of the Articles*, pp. 105–113, for a discussion of the circumstances of ratification; Hardwick concludes that the
Edwardine Articles may fairly be called "official" even though records of
their acceptance by concerned parties are incomplete.

ward VI died a few weeks after they were ordered printed, and Queen Mary quickly began her efforts to return England to the Roman fold, thereby setting back the Anabaptist cause temporarily and driving the movement underground.[36] Early in Elizabeth's reign, however, the Anabaptists were again in evidence. In 1560 Bishop John Jewel wrote: "We found at the beginning of the reign of Elizabeth a large and inauspicious crop of Arians, Anabaptists, and other pests, which I know not how, but as mushrooms spring up in the night and in darkness, so these sprang up in that darkness and unhappy night of the Marian times."[37] Cranmer's leniency and his reluctance to use force had encouraged the Anabaptists in Edward's reign to speak their minds; as we have seen, they even dared to challenge Bishop Hooper in public. After 1560, when Elizabeth ordered Anabaptists to conform or leave the country, it became clear that this Queen would not tolerate radical dissent in her kingdom any more readily than her predecessor had in hers. The Anabaptists appear to have grown cautious. The Queen's government was troubled by those who believed the individual soul was annihilated by death, but the evidence that soul-sleeping ideas remained current during Elizabeth's time is exceedingly slight and inconclusive until late in her reign.

In the 1571 edition of his *The Poore Mans Librarie*, William Alley, Bishop of Exeter, defended the orthodox view of the soul, but it is not clear that the mortalists he refutes are in England or even that they are his contemporaries. In this collection of his sermons on 1 Peter delivered in 1560 and first published in 1565, Alley includes extensive encyclopedic and discursive material. He cites the orthodox understanding of the nature of the soul: "The soule is a spirituall substaunce infused of God into the body of man, that being joyned thereto, may geue it life, direct and rule it, and beyng seperate from

---

[36] Horst thinks that perhaps 80 percent of the martyrs during Mary's reign were professing Anabaptists or their sympathizers and that the Marian persecutions thus cut short the separatist development of Anabaptism in England ("England," *Mennonite Encyclopedia*).

[37] Cited in Williams, *Radical Reformation*, pp. 781–782.

the body, doth not perish, but liue immortally and eternally."³⁸ Alley then states an objection that is made to this
definition: "The soule is no substaunce but a certaine vitall
power and quality in man"; although he does not indicate
the source of the objection, it is clearly the thnetopsychist
view. The Bishop's rebuttal is of little interest, consisting as
it does of the usual references to the Dives and Lazarus story,
Christ's promise to the Good Thief, and the souls of the martyrs crying out from under the altar (Rev. 6:9–10). Alley's examination of psychopannychism similarly fails to locate the
anonymous heretics in place or time and adds nothing new
to the scriptural arguments commonly used to refute them
(II, 58r–59r). Although Alley may have been concerned with
a contemporary English heresy, it is equally possible that he
was commenting on the soul sleeping he had read about in
Calvin and Bullinger.

The rest of the evidence that bears upon the currency of
soul-sleeping ideas throughout Elizabeth's reign is similarly
inconclusive. When the Edwardine Articles were revised in
1563, the article condemning the soul sleepers and other articles directed solely against the Anabaptists were excised. Although this change may mean that the offensive doctrines
no longer existed in England, it is safer to conclude that the
authorities were simply no longer seriously troubled by them
and welcomed the opportunity to make the Thirty-nine Articles less topical.³⁹ When in 1576 John Woolton, Bishop of
Exeter, published a defense of the orthodox view of the soul
that argues against soul-sleeping and traducian beliefs, he may
have been responding to Anabaptist attempts to subvert established doctrine, but he may simply have intended to write
a creditable pious work that was not too much trouble, for
his book is little else but a translation of Bullinger's sermon

---

³⁸ William Alley, *The Poore Mans Librarie*, 2 vols. (London, 1571),
I, 49v.

³⁹ The other possibility, that in less than a decade the Church had decided that soul sleeping was among the adiaphora, has its supporters, but
their position is difficult to defend (see Appendix, n. 9).

on the immortality of the reasonable soul.[40] The soul sleepers may have been prominent enough in the England of 1581 to encourage John Day to publish a translation of Calvin's *Psychopannychia,* but it is also possible that he wanted to publish an important work by a leading reformer to combat the Family of Love, whose mortalist tendencies had recently been brought to the public's attention.[41] Finally, in 1587 Arthur Golding may have completed and published Sidney's translation of Philip de Mornay's defense of the reasonableness of Christianity to convert English Anabaptists as well as atheists, Jews, Moslems, and pagans to orthodox views, but he may have thought that the atheism then current in England was sufficient to justify the effort.[42] Chapters 14 and 15 are devoted to arguments for the immortality of the soul drawn from reason and ancient authority; Mornay argues that the soul is the substantial form of the body and not just a quality of a living creature (p. 203).

Such slight evidence permits us to conclude only that the condition of the soul after death was not considered a wholly settled matter during most of Elizabeth's reign; it is not clear that soul sleepers were publicly professing their heresy. By 1597, however, soul sleepers were again spreading their opinions in England. John Payne, writing from Haarlem, exhorts his friends who frequent the Royal Exchange to beware of a variety of sins and heresies. In particular, he warns "of the dangerouse opinions of suche Englyshe Anabaptists bred here/ as whose parsons [persons] in part wth more store of there letters dothe crepe and spreade amongest you in cittie

---

[40] John Woolton, *A Treatise of the Immortalitie of the Soule* (London, 1576). Bullinger's sermons were not available in English until the next year: Bullinger, *Fiftie Godlie Sermons.* Bullinger's sermon against the soul sleepers is available in a nineteenth-century edition: *The Decades of Henry Bullinger: The Fourth Decade,* pp. 365–408.

[41] Calvin, *Treatise of the Immortalytie of the Soule.*

[42] Mornay, *The Trewnesse of Christian Religion.* In 1578 Lyly had in *Euphues* accused Oxford of harboring atheists: "Be there not many in Athens [Oxford] which think there is no God, no redemption, no resurrection?" (John Lyly, *Euphues: The Anatomy of Wit; Euphues & His England,* ed. Morris W. Croll and Harry Clemons [1916; reprint, New York: Russell & Russell, 1964], p. 128).

and contrey." Payne connects the heretics with a group of
English separatists who stayed for a time in Campen, then
Naarden, and finally Amsterdam; at some time after their
arrival in Holland their church, ridden with dissension, split
into at least two communities, the one still fundamentally in
doctrinal agreement with the Church of England, the other
full of horrible Anabaptist errors.[43] Burrage identifies the
parent church as Francis Johnson's Barrowist community,
which emigrated to Campen in 1593, thence to Naarden
about 1595, and to Amsterdam about 1597, where Johnson
joined them after his release from the Clink. Probably at
Campen in 1594 the congregation had expelled a group that
had adopted Anabaptist opinions.[44] Payne's account of these
radicals reveals them to be perhaps the first community of
English General (or Arminian) Baptists.[45] "Fyrst our Englishe
and Dutche here howld that Christ toke not his pure fleshe of
the Virgin Mary; and do denie her to be His naturall mother.
Secondly that the Godheade was subject to passions and to
deathe wch ys Impassible. Thyrdly that the infants of the
faythfull ought not to be baptysed. Fourthly that the soules
do slepe in grave wth the bodies vntill the resurrectiō. Fyfthly
that Matcstrates ought not to put malefactors to deathe. Sixtly
they condemne all warrs and Subiects in armure in the feyld.
Seventhly they denye the article of predestinatiō: they denye
the L.day. And finally they savour moch of the opinions of
fre wyll/ and the merit of works" (*Royall Exchange*, p. 22).
Thus belief in man's free will and in the sleep of the soul,
heresies long identified with the general radical movement,
can finally be located in a particular English sect. As we shall
see, soul-sleeping ideas were entertained among the English
General Baptists until after the Restoration. It is likely that
Richard Overton was simply a notable expositor of ideas

[43] John Payne, *Royall Exchange* (Haarlem, 1597), pp. 21–22, 48.
[44] Champlin Burrage, *The Early English Dissenters*, 2 vols. (Cambridge: Cambridge University Press, 1912), I, 155–156, 221–223.
[45] Burrage thinks that one of this company may have baptized himself
and then others in the congregation sometime before 1600, thus antici-
pating John Smyth as the first English se-baptist (*ibid.*, 223). In Mary's
reign Henry Hart's group, while Pelagian, did not practice adult baptism.

common among those who expressed the faith to which Overton had sworn allegiance in his youth.

Johann Mosheim lists chiliasm and the psychopannychist variety of soul sleeping among the doctrines of the English General Baptists.[46] There is, however, no reason to believe the General Baptists considered these doctrines necessary to salvation. W. T. Whitley has observed that the General Baptists were always willing to state their common beliefs when the need arose, but they were generally opposed to using such confessions as tests required for all those in their communion.[47] Their only comprehensive confession of enduring importance, *A Brief Confession or Declaration of Faith* (London, 1660), written to explain their church to the returning King, was indeed adopted officially by the church's General Assembly in 1663, but attempts to use even a document of such latitude as a test were not popular among Baptists.[48] The traditional General Baptist concern for church unity above doctrinal uniformity is perhaps best expressed by the General Assembly itself; attempting to reunite with some churches that had broken communion over doctrinal issues, the assembly in 1728 wrote their brethren a letter that said, in part:

> We find by long Experiance that in points Sublime & Difficult it cannot be Expected that we should be all Exactly of a Mind. The Christian World Contend in vain

[46] Johann Mosheim, *Institutes of Ecclesiastical History*, tr. James Murdock, 12th ed. (London, 1880?), p. 697.

[47] W. T. Whitley, *A History of the British Baptists* (London: C. Griffin, 1923), pp. 30–31, 93–95. In the middle of the eighteenth century a member of a General Baptist church in Kent refused to attend as long as the church erred. He wanted three doctrines established: "the mortality of the soul," the personal millennial reign of Christ, and the restoration of man and nature to the prelapsarian state. The church refused to accept these doctrines as conditions for membership; only when the member refused to accept this decision was he expelled (*Minutes of the General Assembly of the General Baptist Churches in England*, ed. W. T. Whitley, 2 vols. [London: Kingsgate Press, 1909–1910], I, xxiii–xxiv). Whitley supposes that "mortality" is a slip for "immortality." All three doctrines were formerly common enough among the General Baptists.

[48] *Minutes*, ed. Whitley, I, xviii; the 1660 Confession is reprinted here (I, 10–22). The General Baptists respected the decisions of the assembly, but reserved the right to test those decisions against Scripture (Whiting, *Studies in English Puritanism*, p. 95).

about Creeds & Humane Explications all the while the
Avouch the Holy Scriptures to the whole & Only Rule of
their ffaith & practise And Now as it is not Necessary for
Christians to be Determined by any Unscripturall fforms
Especially in points of abstruce Speculation which are
above the Capacities of Men in Comon So we propose it
as our Judgements that we lay all such forms asside and
Unite upon the Six principles of the Doctrine of Christians as Contained in Hebr. 6.1.2. Adding Only for Distinctions Sake that we believe the Doctrine of Universall
Redemption [*Minutes,* ed. Whitley, I, 149–50].

Late in the reign of Charles II the General Assembly also
adopted, for those members who could not agree on the content of the longer Confession of 1660, a formula of "Six Principles" based on Heb. 6:1–2: "the foundation of repentance
from dead works, and of faith toward God, Of the doctrine
of baptisms, and of laying on of hands, and of resurrection of
the dead, and of eternal judgment" (*Minutes,* ed. Whitley, I,
xviii–xix). The Confession of 1660 had been nakedly scriptural, a conflation of biblical texts, but if even it became a
barrier to fellowship, the General Baptists characteristically
were ready to move still farther down the latitudinarian path.

From the Confession of the Helwys-Murton church in
1611[49] through the adoption of the Confession of 1660 and
the Six Principles, General Baptist confessions say nothing
that would bar soul sleepers from the General Baptist fellowship: they make no mention of the souls of the dead and affirm only the resurrection of the body and eternal judgment.
In our period the individual General Baptist churches had not
yet joined in a synodical organization or agreed on a doctrinal
confession; judging from their later latitudinarian attitudes
about doctrine and from contemporary evidence, one may
reasonably conclude that the General Baptist churches before
the Restoration considered the intermediate state of the soul

[49] *A Declaration of Faith of English People Remaining at Amsterdam
in Holland* (Amsterdam? 1611), in *Confessions of Faith, and Other Public Documents, Illustrative of the History of the Baptist Churches of
England in the 17th Century,* ed. Edward Bean Underhill, The Hanserd
Knollys Society (London? 1854), pp. 1–10.

a question that is not clearly answered in Holy Scripture, a matter that might be clarified in debate based on the Word.

Although regular Baptist meetings are not known to have been held in England before 1612, when Thomas Helwys and John Murton led back to London those English people who had separated from John Smyth's congregation in Amsterdam, the English missionaries from Haarlem may have had an effect a generation earlier, as Payne feared. The anti-Trinitarian Edward Wightman, arrested in 1611, opposed infant baptism and maintained the same beliefs that Payne listed as the first four doctrines of the English Anabaptists in Holland. He was tried in Lichfield before great crowds and burned in 1612, the last man to be executed solely for heresy in England. Wightman appears to have been a fanatic convinced that he was a special emissary sent by God to comfort His people; his view of the soul's sleep after death, however, was not a private revelation but the thnetopsychist opinion common enough among the Anabaptists: "11. That the soul doth sleep in the sleep of the first death, as well as the body, and is mortal as touching the sleep of the first death, as the body is: And that the soul of our Saviour Jesus Christ did sleep in that sleep of death as well as his body. 12. That the souls of the elect saints departed, are not members possessed of the triumphant Church in Heaven."[50] Wightman's belief that the soul of Christ shared the death of his body is the same as that opinion which Payne attributed to the English Anabaptist community at Haarlem and to "T. M.," its missionary, who in 1597 was imprisoned at Norwich awaiting execution for denying that Christ was true God as well as true man (Payne, *Royall Exchange*, pp. 45–47). The Norwich mission of the Haarlem Anabaptists may have had some continuity, for in 1612 the antipaedobaptist William Sayer was imprisoned in Norfolk while George Abbot, Archbishop of

---

[50] The full list of the heresies Wightman revealed under examination is given in *A Complete Collection of State Trials*, ed. T. B. Howell, 21 vols. (London, 1811–1826), II, 734–736. Wightman was a native Englishman, a draper living in Burton upon Trent, Staffordshire, in the diocese of Coventry and Lichfield (Burrage, *Early English Dissenters*, I, 217); English Anabaptism was not limited to the eastern counties and London.

Canterbury, wrote the Bishop of Norwich suggesting that
Sayer be interrogated further on his denial of Christ's Godhead so that the civil authority could "frie him at a Stake" as
it had Wightman and Bartholemew Legate.[51]

By the Interregnum soul-sleeping ideas were most frequently associated with certain of those who, like Richard
Overton, were General Baptists. In his youth Overton had
joined the Trinitarian, Arminian church of the Waterland
Mennonites in Holland (Burrage, *Early English Dissenters*, I,
250). His Latin confession of faith, made about 1615, has for-
tunately been preserved (Burrage, *Early English Dissenters*, II,
216-218). In it Overton renounced his membership in the
Church of England and expressed his hope that, newly baptized in a true church, he would be able "after death to enter
into eternal life." There is no reason to believe that Overton
ever left the company of those "baptized believers" who were
convinced that Christ died so that all men who believe may
be saved. Thomas Edwards called him "a desperate Sectary"
and described Overton's activities at what was clearly a General Baptist meeting.[52] Whitley listed him as a General Baptist
leader.[53]

Overton was not reluctant to express General Baptist ideas
in *Mans Mortalitie*. When he enlarged his tract in 1655, Overton boldly observed that, among baptismal methods, only the
Baptist practice of total immersion properly symbolized the
thnetopsychist message of Scripture: "the death, burial, &
resurrection of Jesus Christ cannot in the external ordinance
of baptisme be represented . . . but by baptizing, that is, dipping or submerging the whole man into the water, the evidence that whole man shall die, and whole man be raised

[51] Part of the correspondence between Norwich and Canterbury is
printed in Burrage, *Early English Dissenters*, II, 169–171.

[52] Edwards, *Gangraena*, III, 148; II, 17–18.

[53] *Minutes*, ed. Whitley, I, xl. There Whitley calls him "Colonel," apparently confusing him with Robert Overton, although in the same place
he correctly identifies him as a prolific author (which Colonel Robert
Overton was not). Elsewhere Whitley rightly names him as the Baptist
author of *Articles of High Treason Exhibited against Cheap-side Crosse*
(1642) (*ibid.*, xv; Joseph Frank, *The Levellers* [Cambridge, Mass.: Harvard
University Press, 1955], p. 40) and calls him "an eccentric Baptist civilian"
(*British Baptists*, p. 76).

again, by the total death and total Resurrection of Jesus Christ."[54] In all editions Overton spoke with the Arminian understanding that Christ's sacrifice had freed man's will: ". . . Condemnation in Hell is not properly, but remotely the reward of *Adams Fall;* For properly Condemnation is the wages of *Infidelity,* or unbeleife in *Christ,* as Salvation is of *Beleife:* So that none can be condemned into Hell; but such as are actually guilty of refusing of *Christ,* because immortality or the *Resurrection* cannot be by Propagation or Succession, as mortality from *Adam* to his Issue, and so the Child though temporally, yet shall it not eternally be punished for his Fathers sin, but his Condemnation shall be of himself."[55] Overton is so committed to the General Baptist doctrine of universal grace that he extends it to all creatures in the expectation of *apokatastasis* (Acts 3:21): "the *Gospel* or *Glad Tydings* is unto all, all are under hope, and all things, *men, beasts, &c.* shall be made new, or restored at the Resurrection, and so *Death shall be swallowed up in victory . . ."* (*Mans Mortalitie,* p. 70). Although belief in "the restitution of all things" (including animals and plants) had been advocated by such moderate early reformers as Martin Bucer and John Bradford, later the Restitution was associated chiefly with those radicals who used it to support the doctrine of universal salvation or to argue that only the just will attain resurrection and immortality. In 1550 an Anabaptist synod met in Venice and decided that the soul sleeps until the Last Day, that the wicked are not resurrected, and that only the elect are raised to immortal life. Hobbes said that the wicked are ultimately condemned to extinction.[56]

Not all those committed to believer's baptism, however, were willing to take such unconventional doctrines under

---

[54] R[ichard] O[verton], *Man Wholly Mortal* (London, 1655), p. 55.

[55] *MM,* ed. Fisch, p. 11. Fisch's text is the 1644 edition, which corrected the printing errors in the first edition of 1643. All my references to *Mans Mortalitie* are taken from the Fisch edition except for a few references to material Overton added in his 1655 edition.

[56] For Reformation interest in the idea of the restoration of all things, see George H. Williams, *Wilderness and Paradise in Christian Thought* (New York: Harper, 1962), pp. 83–84, and *Radical Reformation,* pp. 843–844; D. P. Walker, *The Decline of Hell* (Chicago: University of Chicago Press, 1964), pp. 67, 73–74; C. A. Patrides, "The Salvation of Satan," *Jour-*

consideration. When Dr. Daniel Featley in 1645 identified
the Anabaptists with psychopannychism and blamed them
for the publication of *Mans Mortalitie*,[57] he was puzzled by
the fact that seven Baptist churches of London disavowed
responsibility for this and other heresies that had been
charged against them. Featley acknowledges that psychopannychism and some other errors "are not at this day generally owned by our Anabaptists" (*Dippers Dipt*, p. 153), but
suspects that those who signed the reasonably orthodox *Confession of Faith of Those Churches Which are Commonly
(Though Falsly) Called Anabaptists* (London, 1644) inadequately represent Anabaptism.[58] Featley came close to the
truth in his suspicions, for he is unaccountably ignorant of
the fact that the seven English churches represented by the
signatories of the confession (among whom were William
Kiffen and later Hanserd Knollys) were the relatively orthodox Particular (Calvinist) Baptist churches of London. These
predestinarians were so distant from the Arminian branch of
the "Dippers" that they would not accept as valid the baptism of the General Baptists (Whiting, *Studies in English
Puritanism*, p. 88). Featley would not have had to seek far
had he looked for soul sleepers among the General Baptists.

The General Baptists of the Interregnum were the true
heirs of Anabaptist radicalism. Their numbers were considerable, although the more recently founded, more conservative Particular Baptists were already showing the strength
that was to make them the dominant element in the English

---

nal of the History of Ideas, XXVIII (1967), 467–478. For Bradford's essay,
which is for the most part a translation from Bucer, see "The Restoration of All Things," in *The Writings of John Bradford*, ed. Aubrey Townsend, Parker Society (Cambridge, 1848), pp. 350–364. For the idea that the
wicked do not live eternally, see the account of the Venetian synod in Earl
M. Wilbur, *A History of Unitarianism* (Cambridge, Mass.: Harvard University Press, 1947), pp. 84–85; and Hobbes, *Leviathan*, pp. 342–344; Chap. 44.

[57] Daniel Featley, *The Dippers Dipt*, 6th ed. (London, 1651), sigs. A3v–
A4r. Featley does not seem to have grasped Overton's thnetopsychist view,
for he says the pamphlet casts the soul *"into an Endymion sleep"*; Featley
would surely have been even more indignant had he discerned that
Overton denied that the soul is a substance.

[58] *Ibid.*, pp. 177–179. The second edition (1646) of this confession is
reprinted in *Confessions of Faith*, ed. Underhill, pp. 11–48.

(and international) Baptist movement. Just after the Restoration, the General Baptists claimed that their Confession of 1660 was "owned and approved by more than 20,000" (Whiting, *Studies in English Puritanism*, p. 90). By one calculation, in 1660 the General Baptists had 115 congregations and the Particular Baptists 131.[59] A Particular Baptist of Ashford, Kent, complained that most of the Baptists in Kent and Sussex denied the doctrines of the Trinity and Christ's satisfaction and affirmed that after death the soul sleeps in the body (Whiting, *Studies in English Puritanism*, pp. 89–90); he was apparently referring to the General Baptists who, unlike the Particular Baptists, do not seem to have been interested in excluding devout people from their fellowship on doctrinal grounds.

Most of the soul sleepers mentioned in Thomas Edwards' *Gangraena* appear to have been Overton's spiritual brethren, members of the "Broad Church" wing of those who subscribed to believer's baptism. We hear briefly of "one Crab of Southwark side, a Dipper and a Preacher, who vents strange doctrines against the Immortality of the soul, &c."[60] When, in 1646, sectaries in Lancashire and Cheshire sent a petition to Commons requesting liberty of conscience, "a godly Christian in Lancashire" reported to Edwards that "it was framed and set on foot by the Members of the Church of *Duckingfeild*, but I am confident they admit to sign it Seekers, Soulsleepers, Anabaptists: Rigid Brownists, &c."[61] Perhaps Thomas Sidebotham of Lancashire was one of these sectaries, for he wrote Edwards two letters defending the sleep of the soul on the basis of Scripture (Edwards, *Gangraena*, III, 66–67).

[59] A. C. Underwood, *A History of the English Baptists* (London: Kingsgate Press, 1947), p. 85. The first Particular Baptist church was founded in London "not earlier than 1633, and not later than 1638" (*ibid.*, p. 58).

[60] Edwards, *Gangraena*, III, 110. This person does not seem to have been Roger Crabbe, the hermit and food faddist who, to judge from the *DNB* article (s.v.), had no Baptist connections. Edwards elsewhere refers to the Baptist Crab as a "feltmaker" (*Gangraena*, II, 9).

[61] Edwards, *Gangraena*, III, 166–167. The church referred to may have been at Dukinfield, Lancashire (now part of Manchester), but Samuel Eaton (not the Particular Baptist of the same name) led for many years an Independent congregation at Dukinfield Old Hall, Cheshire (McLachlan, *Socinianism*, p. 267).

The Presbyterian Edwards was, of course, utterly con-
founded both by the radicalism of the General Baptists and
by their lack of interest in formulating a comprehensive and
detailed doctrinal system. He has left a remarkable portrait of
the kind of man who was likely to find the General Baptist
fellowship attractive. Clement Wrighter (or Writer), a friend
of Richard Overton and William Walwyn,[62] might have
found among the General Baptists a church that would not
inhibit his spiritual development.

> There is one Clement Wrighter in London, but anciently
> belonging to Worcester, sometimes a Professor of Religion,
> and judged to have been godly, who is now an arch-Heret-
> ique and fearfull Apostate, an old Wolf, and a subtile
> man, who goes about corrupting and venting his Errors
> . . . . This man about 7 or 8 years ago fell from the Com-
> union of our Churches, to Independency and Brownisme,
> and was much taken with Mr. Robinsons Books, as that
> of the Justification of Separation; from that he fell to Ana-
> baptisme and Arminianisme, and to Mortalisme, holding
> the Soul Mortall; (he is judged to be the Author, or at least
> to have had a great hand in the Book of the mortality of
> the Soul). After that he fell to be a Seeker, and is now an
> Anti-Scripturist, a Questionist and Skeptick, and I fear an
> Atheist. This Wrighter is one of the chief heads of those
> who deny the Scriptures to be the Word of God . . . . This
> Clement Wrighter about Spring last did affirm to Mr.
> Farthing, (from whom I have it in writing, written in his
> own hand) That man hath no immortal Soul, but when
> he dieth, all of man sleepeth till the Resurrection . . . .[63]

Edwards' charge of atheism against Wrighter itself sufficiently justifies Milton's reference to "shallow *Edwards*" in
his poem "On the New Forcers of Conscience." In his eagerness to show the steps in a sectary's inevitable descent into
hell, Edwards multiplies distinctions to suggest Wrighter's
intellectual and spiritual giddiness, but there is nothing in
the portrait to indicate that Wrighter ever threw off the easy

---

[62] Edwards calls "Mr. Wallin" a "great friend" of Wrighter (*Gangraena*,
I, 116). Walwyn was notorious among the Presbyterians as a republican
political theorist and an advocate of unrestricted religious liberty.

[63] *Ibid.*, 113–114. I have found no evidence to suggest that the attribution of *Mans Mortalitie* to Wrighter need be taken seriously.

doctrinal yoke of the General Baptists. Even Edwards' claim that Wrighter denied that Scripture is the Word of God may merely have been a distortion of Wrighter's attempt to undermine the Presbyterian position: from the sectarian point of view, Presbyterian arguments from Scripture tended to be philological, bookish, and excessively logical—in a word, "dead." Sectaries often said that the Bible was but "ink and paper" in order to emphasize that "holiness," which they demanded of their members, was required to understand the Word rightly. This view of scriptural interpretation underlay the argument for "gathered" churches that could select their own members and leaders because, so the argument went, no state-supported parish church could select its members and ministry for their sanctity, and, therefore, no such church could perceive the Word of God behind the ink and paper. Even Ralph Cudworth, in his remarkable sermon to Commons, makes the point that sanctity is required for understanding by dealing harshly with those who revere Scripture in the wrong way:

> Inke and Paper can never make us Christians, can never beget a new nature, a living principle in us; can never form Christ, or any true notions of spirituall things in our hearts. The Gospel, that new Law which Christ delivered to the world, it is not merely a *Letter* without us, but a *quickning Spirit* within us. Cold Theorems and Maximes, dry and jejune Disputes, lean syllogisticall reasonings, could never yet of themselves beget the least glympse of true heavenly light, the least sap of saving knowledge in any heart. All this is but the groping of the poore dark spirit of man after truth, to find it out with his own endeavours . . . . Words and syllables which are but dead things, cannot possibly convey the living notions of heavenly truths to us . . . . The knowledge of Christ, and the keeping of his Commandments, must alwayes go together, and be mutuall causes of one another.[64]

This attitude toward Holy Scripture could, of course, unbridle the inclinations of the sects toward enthusiasm. We have already seen (Chapter Two, above) the result of an exaggerated contempt for the "dead letter" of Scripture in

[64] Cudworth, *A Sermon*, pp. 5, 7.

what Edwards called the Independent Churches in Somersetshire. Since these churches allowed a wide latitude in doctrine and, unlike the Congregationalists, denied the validity
of infant baptism, Edwards might more precisely have described them as General Baptist congregations. A minority
of these Somersetshire Baptists denied personal immortality
altogether, but the annihilationist opinion does not appear
to have been common among the General Baptists. Edwards
reports a meeting of some forty sectaries in a house on *"Red-
crosse* street or thereabouts." Although the meeting may not
have been General Baptist, the preacher's doctrines recall
the Socinianism of the Somersetshire Baptists and the views
of Clement Wrighter: "1. That Jesus Christ was not God,
not the Son of God. 2. That the Scriptures were not the word
of God . . . . 3. That the souls of men dye with their bodies"
(*Gangraena*, III, 93). Edwards does not give enough information to make clear whether the speaker is an annihilationist
or a thnetopscychist like Wrighter and Richard Overton.

Early in 1646 Richard Overton was involved in a General
Baptist meeting for which a debate on the immortality of
the soul had been arranged. It is curious that the author of
Mans Mortalitie was not the principal speaker for the mortalist side.[65] One "Battee" had that role, and Overton served
as moderator on his side.[66] Edwards' gossip is insufficient to
identify positively this Battee who was presumably thought
to be a more formidable opponent for the immortalists than
Richard Overton, but it is likely that he was the Arminian

[65] The debate is described by Edwards (*Gangraena*, II, 17–18) from the
report of "an eare and eye witnesse." Since Edwards does not give Overton's first name, the identification of this man as Richard Overton must
remain somewhat speculative. Either Robert Overton, thought by some
to have written *Mans Mortalitie*, or Henry Overton the bookseller might
have been the Overton at this meeting. Since no Overton can be positively linked with mortalism on grounds other than his being the author
of *Mans Mortalitie*, it is most reasonable to believe that the author of
that book was the Overton present at the debate. Most scholars think
that the evidence points to Richard Overton as the author of the tract;
the attribution will be discussed in the next chapter.

[66] Overton's office is further evidence of the General Baptist character
of the meeting. Whitley points out (*Minutes*, I, xxxi) that in their de-
bates the General Baptists liked to appoint a moderator for each side
and later created positions for two moderators in their General Assembly.

Battee who wrote *A True Vindication of the Generall Redemption of the Second Adam* (London? 1645), a book from which the Calvinist Edwards drew the doctrines relating to universal grace listed as errors 169 through 171 in his catalogue (*Gangraena*, I, 35). This same Battee was probably the "John Batty" listed as a member of Thomas Lamb's General Baptist congregation in London.[67]

By Edwards' account the debate was indecisive, both sides quoting proofs from Scripture and rambling. Although the narrative is disappointingly general, *Gangraena* indirectly clarifies the status of the doctrine of the soul among the General Baptists. John Batty's opponent was his minister, Thomas Lamb, who led the lively General Baptist congregation in Bell Alley, Coleman Street, and there preached universal grace and Arminianism.[68] The debate may, in fact, have been held in Lamb's house, which had in the past been used for Baptist meetings.[69] As far as we can learn from Edwards, the debate was not in the least acrimonious; the disputants kept to Scripture and avoided personal invective. We may well believe that the discussion would have been bitter had either party considered the right understanding of the nature of the soul an essential part of saving faith.

[67] *Ibid.*, xxxvi. It is less probable that Battee was the William Batty who, because he opposed paedobaptism, left Henry Jessey's Independent congregation in 1638 and joined the congregation of John Spilsbury (Burrage, *Early English Dissenters*, I, 327; II, 299–300). Spilsbury's was a Particular Baptist church, and Spilsbury signed the 1644 Confession of the Particular Baptists. Since a Calvinistic Baptist would be unlikely to take the mortalist side in such a debate, William Batty cannot be thought to be the mortalist Battee unless we are willing to believe, without evidence, that by 1646 William Batty had turned his theology quite around.

[68] Called "Lam" by Edwards. Alexander Gordon's identification of "Lam" with Thomas Lamb (*DNB*, s.v. "Lambe or Lamb, Thomas") is undoubtedly correct, for Edwards earlier described "*Lams* Church," which met in Bell Alley, Coleman Street, where "Lam" also boiled soap (*Gangraena*, I, 124–127). Gordon in the same article identifies the Overton at the debate as Robert Overton, but offers no evidence. Edwards' account of the ideas and activities of Lamb's church is a valuable portrait of an exciting, youthful group of radical sectaries in the Interregnum. Lamb's General Baptist work is described in Underwood, *English Baptists*, pp. 71, 86–87, and Whitley, *British Baptists*, p. 68.

[69] The debate was held at the "Spitle" (Edwards, *Gangraena*, II, 17). Lamb's home at the Spital in Norton Folgate had been one of the houses used for church meetings before the Bell Alley quarters became available about this time (*Minutes*, ed. Whitley, I, 1).

Lamb was so tolerant of dissent that he encouraged the preaching of Mistress Attaway,[70] a volatile lacewoman who believed in the mortality of the soul and in the imminent establishment of Christ's millennial Kingdom. Edwards uses the enthusiastic Mrs. Attaway to advantage throughout *Gangraena* as an example of the personal depravity and doctrinal madness toward which the sects must tend,[71] but she does not seem to have alienated Lamb by her strange doctrinal pronouncements. Edwards tells us that she deserted her husband and children to run away with her fellow sectary Will Jenney, a preacher who left children and a pregnant wife. She spoke favorably of "Master *Miltons* Doctrine of Divorce" and applied it to her own case, for she had "an unsanctified husband, that did not walk in the way of *Sion,* nor speak the language of *Canaan*" (*Gangraena*, II, 9). She and Jenney echoed the blasphemous perfectionism and some other doctrines often attributed to the Familists (they thought they were as free from sin as Christ had been), but their eschatology was far more carnal than that of the annihilationists among the experimental Christians. They believed that they would never die, but would live immortal in a restored Jerusalem with Abraham, Isaac, Jacob, and Christ. Their mortalism was of the soul-sleeping type, as millennial views required. "This *Jenney*, Mistress *Attaway* and some of their Tribe held no hell but what was in the conscience; the soules mortall; . . . and that there was *Esaus* world and *Jacobs* world; this was *Esaus* world, but *Jacobs* world was coming shortly, wherein all creatures shall be saved, yet there should be degrees of glory between those that have been Saints . . . and those who were the wicked, though now restored . . ." (*Gangraena*, III, 26–27). Instructed by an "imprisoned prophet"[72] to go to Jerusalem to prepare

[70] *DNB*, s.v. "Lambe or Lamb, Thomas."

[71] Edwards discusses her activities in all three parts of *Gangraena*: I, 116–121, 220–223 (falsely numbered 120–123); II, 9; and III, 26–27.

[72] John Robins and Thomas Tany (*DNB*, s.v.) were probably not this particular prophet, but their fanaticism and urge to greet Christ in Jerusalem give some idea of the influence that overcame Mrs. Attaway and Jenney.

it for the coming of the Kingdom, Mrs. Attaway and Jenney apparently left London to await the universal salvation in Jerusalem. It is not known that they ever reached the Holy Land, but they seem to have disappeared from English history after 1646.

Mortalism, as Tyndale saw, could serve to emphasize the importance of the events on the Last Day. When chiliasts like Mrs. Attaway shifted the emphasis to the time preceding the Last Day, to the apocalyptic events that were to establish Christ's thousand-year reign with his Saints in an earthly Kingdom, they found mortalism no less useful to their purpose. They, like Tyndale, wanted no part of any doctrine that detracted from the importance of the great eschatological drama, and in this period some chiliasts decided that if the imagination was to give the drama of the Kingdom its due attention the idea that souls are presently in bliss must be eliminated. These chiliasts "searched the Scriptures," of course, but they found there what others, more interested in the immediacy of the Christian's reward, could not find: the doctrine of the sleep of the soul. The chiliasts also found that Christians would not have to wait long for glory, for most chiliasts who risked making timetables from the scriptural clues calculated that the beginning of the apocalyptic events was imminent (the year 1666 having a special attraction since the last three digits were "the number of the beast" in Rev. 13:18). Then the Saints would be raised to rule the Kingdom as Christ's lieutenants, and the drama would be the better if they awakened to their glory and vindication instead of being recalled to duty in the war against evil after they had experienced for a time heavenly joy and reward.

The troubled social situation of the middle years of the seventeenth century brought on, then, not only an increase in chiliasm, but a smaller, parallel increase in Christian mortalism. In the years before Hobbes linked soul sleeping with the Millennium, a number of English Christians anticipated him. One of these was William Bowling of Cranbrock, Kent, a dissenter whose church affiliation is unclear. His opinions were reported to Edwards as those of a sectary, but a sectary protested that the sects "hold fundamentals in Religion" and called Bowling an atheist member of the Church of England (*Gangraena*, III, 39–40). His opinions do not necessarily identify him as a General Baptist, but that sect was strong in Kent. From the evidence given by Edwards we can be sure only that, amid overtones of Familism, Bowling took a Socinian view of the Atonement, thought Christ died for all living creatures, believed in the death of the soul pending the resurrection, and awaited the coming of Christ's earthly Kingdom. According to Edwards' correspondent, Bowling believed:

4. That Christs bloud did not purchase Heaven for any man. And being asked how came the Saints to be in Heaven: He answered, Heaven is a gift given to the Saints as a reward of Christs righteousnesse without relation to his Death and Suffrings which were endured for to be our example, not to purchase Heaven for us.

5. That Christ shed his bloud for kine and horses and all creatures, as well as for men . . . .

6. . . . that there is no other fire in Hell, then the Hell that is and shall be in mens consciences.

7. That the souls of Divels and all other men are mortall as well as their bodies, and that there was none immortall but God.

8. That if the soul which was the breath of God were not mortal, then the breath of God, which is part of God, should be eternally tormented in Hell.

9. That (those words) *to day*, or *this day shalt thou be with me in Paradise*, is so to be understood . . . [:] at the day of Resurrection when I come personally to reign upon earth a 1000 yeers, at that day shalt thou be with me in my Kingdom, for there is Gods Kingdom which Christ has now, and there is Christs Kingdom, which the Theif shall share in then.

10. He affirmed that place *Revel.* 20.6. to be meant of a personall reign of Christ in his body upon earth a 1000 yeers.

11. [Referring to Eccles. 12:7] . . . the soul may return to God that gave it, though it lay with the body in the grave,

for God is present every where, and the soul went no more
to God then the body did.
12. It is injustice in God to punish the souls of the wicked
in Hell while their bodies lay at rest in their graves, for
seeing both were sinners together, both must be sufferers
together, if God should punish the soul of Cain in Hell five
or six thousand yeers before he punish the body of Cain,
he would then shew himself partiall in his distribution of
justice [*Gangraena*, III, 36-37].

Even before Mrs. Attaway and Bowling preached their
chiliastic vision, chiliasm accompanied by soul sleeping had
established its appeal among the more sober Independent
churches. Like the General Baptists, some of the English
Independent or Congregational churches were reluctant to
make precise doctrinal definitions where they thought the
teaching of Scripture was unclear. Although they never ap-
proximated the doctrinal latitude of the General Baptists,
some of the Independents were more willing than the Presbyterians to leave gaps in their dogma. The Presbyterian
propagandists of the Interregnum were quick to seize upon
what they took to be the doctrinal looseness of the Independent churches. The Independents, foreseeing their inevitable defeat in the predominantly Presbyterian Assembly
of Divines, carried the appeal for toleration of their church
polity to Parliament: as a public defense of their fundamental
orthodoxy, Thomas Goodwin, Philip Nye, Sidrach Simpson,
Jeremiah Burroughs, and William Bridge published *An
Apologeticall Narration* (London, 1644). These leaders of
the Westminster Assembly's "Dissenting Brethren" told of
how their tender consciences had forced them into exile in
Holland during Laudian times though they were as orthodox
in doctrinal matters as the other members of the assembly.[73]
Now that the Independents were arguing their case outside
the assembly, the Presbyterians launched their massive assault in press and pulpit against the very idea of toleration,

[73] Thomas Goodwin *et al.*, *An Apologeticall Narration* (London, 1644),
p. 28, reprinted in *Tracts on Liberty*, ed. Haller, II, [306]–[339]. All references are to the pagination of the 1644 edition.

whether of church polity or doctrine. In their attempt to
prove that doctrinal error was a natural consequence of the
de facto toleration then existing because there was no established church, Presbyterians like Edwards, Prynne, Baillie,
and Alexander Ross energetically publicized the heresies that
abounded in England at the time.[74] They did not spare the
Dissenting Brethren themselves, but endeavored to show
that their Independent congregations in Holland had not
been doctrinally sound.

However skeptical one may be of the reliability of the
details in Presbyterian propaganda, it must be admitted that
Independent congregations were not likely to be as pure or
uniform in doctrine as the more disciplined Presbyterian
churches. Some Independents could subscribe wholeheartedly
to the main doctrines of Calvin's exposition of Christian
truth and yet not be bound by his opinion when the scriptural evidence was not clear. Goodwin and his associates
stated that it was one of their principles in Holland to sus-
pend judgment when Scripture did not clearly resolve a
question and that, although they were selective in accept-
ing members, they "took measure of no mans holinesse by
his opinion, whether concurring with us, or adverse unto
us . . ." (*Apologeticall Narration*, pp. 10, 12). There is, con-
sequently, reason to believe the Presbyterian assertions that
some Independents disbelieved Calvin's doctrine that the
elect soul at death flies directly to Christ in heaven and that
they also believed, again contrary to Calvin, that Christ
would come again to establish an earthly Kingdom.[75]

In his prompt answer to the *Apologeticall Narration*, Edwards challenged the claim Goodwin and his colleagues had
made to doctrinal orthodoxy. "Whether *in all matters of
Doctrine* all of you be *as Orthodox* in your Judgements as
your brethren themselves, I question it, (though in the most

[74] William Prynne's *Twelve Considerable Serious Questions touching
Chvrch Government* (London, 1644), p. 7, and Thomas Edwards' *Antapologia* (London, 1644), pp. 291–292, expressly blame mortalism on the
de facto toleration.

[75] Calvin insisted that Christ in his regal office would reign over a
spiritual kingdom only: Calvin, *Institutes*, I, 543–546; Bk. II, Chap. XV,
Sect. iii.

Doctrines and in the maine I grant it) I have been told of some odd things in matter of Doctrine preached by one of you five both in *England* and *Holland,* and of some points preached in the Church of Arnheim never questioned there, and since printed, not very Orthodox, as for instance (amongst others) that the soules of the Saints doe not goe to heaven to be with Christ, expresly contrary to the 2 *Cor.* 5.6, 8. and to *Philip* 1.23" (*Antapologia,* p. 261). Baillie makes it possible to clarify Edwards' apparent charge of mortalism: "Mr. *Archer,* and his Colleague, *T. G.* at *Arnheim,* were bold to set up the whole Fabricke of *Chiliasme,* which Mr. *Burrowes* in his *London* lectures upon *Hosea* doth presse as a necessary and most comfortabe [*sic*] ground of Christian Religion."[76] Earlier, Baillie had associated Goodwin and Nye with the Arnhem church (*Dissvasive,* p. 75). Edwards was obviously referring to the unorthodox views to be found in John Archer's *The Personall Reigne of Christ vpon Earth* (London, 1643), a popular millenarian work that also departs from Calvin's teaching on the intermediate state of the soul.

Archer is aware that Calvin's view that the elect soul is in heaven cannot easily be reconciled with the millenarian conviction that the dead Saints shall be raised up to rule the Kingdom for a thousand years.

> If you object, how can soules of *Saints* dead be fetched from heaven to live on earth againe, with men in their bodies, since it is a damage to be fetcht from heaven to earth, and from the bodily presence of Christ and face of God, and innumerable company of Angels, to converse againe on earth with men. I answer, this objection supposes the soules of the dead *Saints,* to be in the highest heavens, which is not so; . . . it is likely the soules of the dead *Saints* are not in the highest heavens, but in a middle place, better then this world, but inferior to the highest heavens, which is meant in the new Testament by *Paradise,* in which they have full joy and perfect happinesse, *Heb.* 12.23. and a speciall presence of Christ, *Phil.* 1.23. & 2 *Cor.* 5.6, 8. that is, a presence to their minds, which may

[76] Robert Baillie, *A Dissvasive from the Errours of the Time* (London, 1645), p. 224.

be, though they be not where Christs body is; and in this
place they are kept till this Kingdome of Christ come, and
then they shall assume their bodies, till the worlds end,
when with soule and body they with all other *Saints* shall
goe up into the highest heavens for ever.[77]

Archer defends his opinion out of Scripture and insists that
this state is the Paradise to which Christ's soul went (with
that of the Good Thief) until Christ's Resurrection (*Personall
Reigne*, p. 24). Archer's teaching not only controverts Calvin,
but comes perilously close to the Roman doctrine of purgatory (or, at least, the *limbus patrum*).[78] The *Personall Reigne*
is certainly not a mortalist work, but Archer avoids mortalism only at the risk of reviving the unscriptural "inven-
tions" of the Roman church. Those Independent millenarians
who would not countenance anything resembling the doctrines of Antichrist may well have substituted psychopannychist or thnetopsychist ideas for Archer's speculation about
the soul's conscious existence outside heaven.

Although the objectivity of the testimony of Edwards
and Ross may be doubted, they do not confuse Archer's
views with mortalism; nevertheless, they accuse the Independents of advocating or at least tolerating mortalism
in their congregations:

let me tell you, granting you five to be so Orthodox, . . .
yet there are many members of those Churches to which
you belong, besides many other members of Churches of
your way and communion, whom I suppose must be tolerated as well as your selves, that doe hold very odd and
strange things. Some of Arnheim hold strange conceits,
and some members of Mr. *Sympsons* Church hold some
of the points of the Anabaptists, and daily the Independ-

[77] Archer, *Personall Reigne*, p. 23; Archer's book was first published
in 1641. The disagreement so common among literal interpreters of Scripture is well exemplified here and in the citation from Edwards' *Antapologia* I have just given in the preceding paragraph: Archer and Edwards
both cite 2 Cor. 5:6–8 and Phil. 1:23 to prove distinct points.
[78] Archer (*Personall Reigne*, p. 25) argues that his Paradise is nothing
like purgatory because it is a place of joy, not punishment; many Protestants would argue, nevertheless, that it has no more scriptural warrant
than purgatory.

ent Churches like Africa doe breed and bring forth the Monsters of Anabaptisme, Antinomianisme, Familisme, nay that huge Monster and old flying serpent of the Mortality of the soul of man, and indeed there is no end of errours that the Independent principles and practices lead unto [Edwards, *Antapologia*, p. 262].

In his list of the errors of Goodwin's Arnhem church, Ross mentions both mortalism and Archer's view of the soul; since these views, as Ross presents them, cannot be reconciled, we must conclude that, if Ross is correct, the Arnhem Independents did not have a uniform doctrine of the soul's intermediate state. "[1.] They hold that Independency is a beginning of Christs temporal Kingdom here on earth, that within five years, (but these are already expired) Christ was to come in the flesh, and with an Iron Sword to kill most of his enemies, and then that he should raign here on earth with his Saints a thousand years, in all carnal delights.... 6. They teach that the soul is mortal. 7. That just mens souls go not into Heaven till the last day, but remain in the upper element of fire...."[79]

Neither Ross nor Edwards seems to be referring to *Mans Mortalitie*. Edwards may well have had in mind the Independent John Goodwin, who a few months later was to complain that his enemies had unjustly called him a mortalist. Perhaps Edwards himself was one of those who had maligned him. The Arminian Goodwin, that bugbear of the Presbyterians, had shown his Independent colors long before May, 1645, when the Presbyterians finally managed to have him ejected from his living at St. Stephen's, Coleman Street, for refusing the sacraments to some members of the parish

[79] Alexander Ross, *Pansebeia or, A View of All Religions in the World,* 5th ed. (London, 1675), p. 369; Ross's book was first published in 1653. Ross may not have based his statement about chiliasm at Arnhem on Archer's book; it is certainly a poor summary of Archer's views. Archer has nothing to say of "carnal delights," and he thought that Christ would institute his Kingdom about A.D. 1700 (*Personall Reigne*, p. 50). Since Thomas Goodwin left England in 1639 and returned at the beginning of the Long Parliament in November, 1640 (*DNB*, s.v. "Goodwin, Thomas"), the Presbyterians were presumably discussing the opinions held by the Arnhem church between those dates.

(*DNB*, s.v. "Goodwin, John"). Since he was not allowed to gather a church on Independent principles within the state-controlled ecclesiastical system, Goodwin defiantly founded his own Independent church on the same street, a church that was to remain prominent throughout the Interregnum. This notable propagandist for toleration was a natural target for the gossip-mongering author of *Gangraena*.

In July, 1646, Edwards contented himself with taunting John Goodwin: "What say you to the 84. and 85. errours laid down in the Catalogue? Is it not true that such things were preached in London?" (*Gangraena*, II, 128). The eighty-fourth error is "That the souls of the faithfull after death, do sleep till the day of judgement, and are not in a capacity of acting any thing for God, but 'tis with them as 'tis with a man that is in some pleasing dream." The eighty-fifth error concerns the technical point, often disputed in England, of whether the resurrection body shall be the same body that died, or some newly created body ("changed" from the natural and mortal, as is suggested by 1 Cor. 15) in which the immortal soul chiefly preserves the identity of the individual man (*Gangraena*, I, 26–27). In December, 1646, Edwards directly charged Goodwin with those heresies: "Many other passages I have from good hands of *Cretensis* [Goodwin] preaching, of his preferring Reason before Faith in points of Religion; of holding the sleeping of the soule till the Resurrection, of bodies that die not rising the same again, with divers such . . . ."[80]

But had not Goodwin clearly denied charges of mortalism in October, 1644? "I have oft been cast into the fire of mens zealous indignations, by an unclean spirit of calumny and slander; Some have reported, that I deny justification by Christ, i. that the Sun is up at noon-day; Others, that I deny the immortalitie of the soule, i. that I murthered my father

---

[80] Edwards, *Gangraena*, III, 117. John Goodwin, in his *Cretensis*, 2d ed. (London, 1646), had called Edwards a liar because the First Part of *Gangraena* had charged Goodwin with loose living. See *Tracts on Liberty*, ed. Haller, I, 83–84, for a brief account of how Goodwin preferred Reason before Faith in his *The Divine Authority of Scriptures* (London, 1647).

and my mother...."[81] Goodwin may have felt that he would no more deny immortality to the soul than he would murder his parents, but this passage from a book almost certainly read by Edwards does not mean that Edwards was so unfair as to charge a man with a heresy that he had freely denied. For Edwards charged Goodwin not with annihilationism or thnetopsychism (the only varieties of mortalism that, strictly speaking, deny the immortality of the soul), but with the psychopannychism described in the catalogue's eighty-fourth error. Nor must we think that, if Edwards' charge is true, Goodwin either equivocated in 1644 or changed his opinion by 1646: John Frith's defense of Tracy against the charge of thnetopsychism shows how indignant a psychopannychist could be when his views were misunderstood as thnetopsychism. Indeed, Edwards himself must have granted that Goodwin believed in the soul's immortality because, as Edwards states the matter in the eighty-fifth error of the catalogue, those who believed that the resurrection body is created anew had to depend on the soul's immortal substance to establish the body's identity. Goodwin does not seem to have denied Edwards' charge of psychopannychism.

Edwards probably thought that Goodwin's imputed Socinianism and psychopannychism were of a piece. To a strict Presbyterian, Goodwin's commitment to toleration and to a place for reason in religion was sufficient to place him in the shadow of Socinus, and evangelical rationalism had long been associated with soul sleeping in the Reformation.[82] When Joachim Stegmann, once Rector of the College

[81] John Goodwin, *Theomachia* (London, 1644), sig. A2r, reprinted in *Tracts on Liberty*, ed. Haller, III, [3]–[58].

[82] Williams (*Radical Reformation*, p. 24) stresses the importance of the mortalist ideas of the radical rationalists. A few passages from Williams that connect continental rationalists with psychopannychism and thnetopsychism may be noted here: Camillo Renato (pp. 548, 555), Michael Servetus (p. 609), Laelius Socinus (pp. 569, 631), and Faustus Socinus (pp. 750, 752). Williams also discusses in considerable detail the thnetopsychism of the proto-Socinian Renato and the significance of the idea among the reformers in northern Italy: "Camillo Renato (c. 1500?–1575)," *Italian Reformation Studies in Honor of Laelius Socinus* (1562–1962), ed. John A. Tedeschi, *The Proceedings of the Unitarian Historical Society*, XIV (1962–1963), 103–183.

in Socinian Rakow, published a tract that argued that right reason and tolerance could unify Protestantism and defeat Rome,[83] he followed the Socinian tradition and tried to dismiss with scriptural proofs the idea that the soul is conscious between death and resurrection. Stegmann's Latin tract was known in England soon after its publication in 1633, and in 1641 a committee appointed by the House of Lords denounced it as a dangerous book that was "vulgarly to be had" (McLachlan, *Socinianism*, p. 94). The Socinian John Bidle translated the tract under the title *Brevis Disquisitio: or, A Brief Enquiry touching a Better Way . . . To Refute Papists, and Reduce Protestants to Certainty and Unity in Religion* (London, 1653). The argument that the sleep of the soul destroys the basis of Roman superstition recalls the chief attraction the doctrine had for the psychopannychists who lived a century earlier: Luther, Tyndale, and Frith. ". . . [the "papists"] beleeve in effect that the dead live. . . . Now this is the foundation not only of Purgatory, but also of that horrible Idolatry practised amongst the Papists, whilest they invocate the Saints that are dead. Take this away and there will be no place left for the others. To what purpose is the fire of Purgatory, if souls separated from the bodies feel nothing? To what purpose are prayers to the Virgin *Mary*, to *Peter*, and *Paul*, and other dead men, if they can neither hear prayers nor intercede for you? On the contrary, if you admit this, you cannot easily overthrow the invocation of Saints."[84] In England, however, Socinianism played a minor role in the development of Christian mortalism until the Unitarian Joseph Priestley advocated thnetopsychism in the second half of the eighteenth century.

Against the disorderly growth of opinions and sects the Presbyterians wrote and legislated in vain. It is doubtful that

[83] [Joachim Stegmann,] *Brevis Disquisitio* (Eleutheropolis [Amsterdam], 1633). The tract is discussed in McLachlan, *Socinianism*, particularly on pp. 92–95.

[84] [Joachim Stegmann,] *Brevis Disquisitio: or, A Brief Enquiry . . .* [tr. John Bidle] (London, 1653), p. 27; McLachlan (*Socinianism*, p. 92) attributes the work to Stegmann and Bidle. The tract goes on (pp. 27–29) to cite proof-texts from Scripture, only the last of which is unusual in mortalist arguments: Matt. 22:31–32, 1 Cor. 15:30–32, 1 Pet. 1:5, 2 Tim. 4:8, Heb. 11:40.

they could have reversed the thrust of the Reformation toward sectarianism, but their ascendancy was far too brief seriously to hamper the development of a great variety of religious opinions. By the time the Assembly of Divines had defined a new doctrine and polity for a national church, the Presbyterian Parliament no longer had the power to make the country accept a new state church; it had become clear to all parties that the Independents in the Army, having shown themselves to be the main protectors of Parliament, were fully capable of destroying a Parliament that threatened their religious liberty. Against Christian mortalism the Presbyterians could do little more than preach. In its revision of the Thirty-nine Articles, the Westminster Assembly chose to insert a strong passage against both psychopannychism and thnetopsychism and to declare Calvin's view of the intermediate state the only true doctrine: "The bodies of men, after death, return to dust, and see corruption; but their souls (which neither die nor sleep), having an immortal subsistence, immediately return to God who gave them. The souls of the righteous, being then made perfect in holiness, are received into the highest heavens, where they behold the face of God in light and glory, waiting for the full redemption of their bodies: and the souls of the wicked are cast into hell, where they remain in torments and utter darkness, reserved to the judgment of the great day. Besides these two places for souls separated from their bodies, the Scripture acknowledgeth none."[85] But by 1646 it was too late to suppress soul sleeping or many other opinions: the political power of the sectaries was such that the Westminster Confession could not be imposed by law on the dissenters.

This chapter may fittingly close with an account of John Reeve and Lodowick Muggleton, for those mortalist tailors and their sect epitomize that eccentricity of the sectarian spirit which the Presbyterians so futilely opposed. The filiation of the Muggletonians is thoroughly obscure. Reeve and Muggleton repudiated their former admiration for the Ranters and scorned all those who thought the human spirit

[85] Chap. XXXII of the Westminster Confession, in *Creeds of the Churches*, ed. Leith, p. 228.

was part of the Divine Essence,[86] who were guided by a
spurious "Inner Light," and who lacked the authority given
only by the actual voice of God; yet the prophets also
scorned literalists like the Baptists who interpreted Scripture by the false light of their Satanic Reason[87] and also
lacked a clear commission from God. In short, "the two
last Commissionated Witnesses" thought no one capable of
interpreting Scripture but themselves. On three consecutive
days in February, 1652, Jesus Christ spoke to Reeve "by voice
of words" and commissioned him and his cousin Muggleton
as his last messengers, giving them understanding and authority and empowering them to curse or to bless particular persons for eternity.[88] Moses and Aaron had been the first so
commissioned, Christ and his Apostles the second, and these
London tradesmen were the third and final messengers, the
"two witnesses" spoken of in Rev. 11:2–13.[89]

It would be pointless to summarize here the peculiar doctrines of these prophets, for they had no need to construct a
coherent system out of their rag-ends of doctrine.[90] To those

[86] John Reeve and Lodowick Muggleton, *A Divine Looking-glass; or,
the Third and Last Testament of Our Lord Jesus Christ*, 4th ed. (London?
1760), pp. 11–12, reprinted in *The Works of John Reeve and Lodowicke
Muggleton*, 3 vols. (London, 1832), I. In the 1832 edition of the *Works*, the
individual tracts have separate title pages and only separate pagination.
A Divine Looking-glass was first published in 1656.

[87] John Reeve and Lodowick Muggleton, *Joyful News from Heaven*
(n.p., n.d.), pp. 33 ff., reprinted in *Works*, I. *Joyful News*, most of it written by the dying Reeve, was first published in 1658.

[88] John Reeve and Lodowick Muggleton, *A Transcendent Spiritual
Treatise* (London, 1822), pp. 1–4, reprinted in *Works*, I. This was the first
publication of the prophets, issued in 1652.

[89] Lodowick Muggleton, *A True Interpretation of the Eleventh Chapter of the Revelation of St. John* (London, 1753), pp. 196–197, reprinted
in *Works*, I. Muggleton first published the book in 1662, four years after
Reeve's death.

[90] Reeve and Muggleton have been little studied, but their doctrines
and lives have been usefully summarized: Alexander Gordon, "The Origins of the Muggletonians," *Proceedings of the Literary and Philosophical
Society of Liverpool*, XXIII (1868–1869), 247–279; Alexander Gordon,
"Ancient and Modern Muggletonians," *ibid.*, XXIV (1869–1870), 186–244;
Whiting, *Studies in English Puritanism*, pp. 242–258. Augustus Jessopp's
chapter on Muggleton ("The Prophet of Walnut-tree Yard") in his *The
Coming of the Friars* (London, 1889), pp. 302–344, is a shallow essay of
no value.

people who had adopted the "Seeker" attitude of denying the validity of all worship and ordinances until God sent new apostles to reestablish the Truth, Reeve and Muggleton offered themselves as the uniquely authoritative bearers of the Third Commission. They enunciated dogmas in abundance, but primarily "the Witnesses of the Spirit" were concerned with advancing their claim to be God's mouthpieces and silencing their competitors with the curse of eternal damnation; they are never so clear as when they are damning the Ranters, Baptists, and Quakers, all of whom were also attractive to the lost "Seekers." Belief in all the Witnesses' doctrines was required of all those who would be saved, and Reeve and Muggleton repeatedly insisted that the thnetopsychist view of the soul is a central teaching of Holy Scripture.

Although they expressly rejected chiliasm and cursed into obscurity the Ranters John Robins and Thomas Tany (both of whom had plans to lead their followers to Jerusalem to await the Millennium),[91] Reeve and Muggleton nevertheless taught an apocalyptic eschatology that stressed Christ's sudden Coming as the Lord of the Last Judgment. Thus soul sleeping again served to emphasize the eschatological drama that was central to the Adventist vision: "both the Soul and Body of *Adam* are in the Dust of the Earth dead asleep, void of all Life, Light, Motion, Heat, or any Thing appearing unto Life, until that second Man *Adam,* the Lord from Heaven, by the might Power of his Word doth, or shall raise him again, and all Mankind that are asleep with him in the Dust, at the last Day."[92] Thnetopsychism was, as late as 1870, one of the Six Cardinal Principles of Muggletonianism, subscription to which was required by all members.[93]

It is curious that the immiscible currents of pantheistic

[91] Reeve and Muggleton, *Divine Looking-glass,* pp. 205–209; *DNB,* s.v. "Robins, John," "Tany, Thomas."

[92] Reeve and Muggleton, *Divine Looking-glass,* pp. 164–165. Thnetopsychism runs through the prophets' work. It appears in their first work, *A Transcendent Spiritual Treatise,* and is featured in *Joyful News from Heaven.*

[93] Gordon, "Ancient and Modern Muggletonians," pp. 186–187, 226.

annihilationism and materialistic thnetopsychism succes-
sively flowed into the spiritual life of just one man, as far
as we know, and that man died a Muggletonian. The life
of Laurence Clarkson[94] would have made fine material for a
sermon by an orthodox divine who wanted to illustrate the
excesses to which a sectary must succumb if he denies all
external authority and throws himself entirely upon his own
spiritual resources. Clarkson was a Seeker to the last degree.
Born into the Church of England, he turned early to Presbyterianism, was briefly an Independent, then an Antinomian; he was rebaptized by immersion in November, 1644,
imprisoned for "dipping," and released in July, 1645, after
he had formally renounced Anabaptism. In 1648 the Presbyterians refused his petition for readmission to their church,
and by 1649 he was a prominent Ranter, remarkable even
in that group for his outrageous and licentious conduct. We
have already noted at the end of the preceding chapter the
extravagant lengths to which he carried the latent pantheism
of the experimental Christians.[95] He was prosecuted and
jailed briefly for his amoral tract *A Single Eye All Light, No
Darkness* (London, 1650). Clarkson did not find his spiritual
home until he met Reeve and Muggleton in 1658. After
Reeve's death in that year Clarkson made an abortive attempt to take over the leadership of the sect, but Muggleton
crushed the attempt and later generously readmitted Clarkson
to his flock. Spiritually the lost sheep was found, although
Clarkson died in Ludgate jail in 1667, imprisoned for the
debts he had incurred in an unsound venture into finance.

This Seeker found his rest in a characteristic way, for when
Clarkson accepted authority at last it was the authority of

[94] The following details of Clarkson's life are taken from *DNB,* s.v.
"Claxton or Clarkson, Laurence," which notes that Sir Walter Scott used
Clarkson's spiritual autobiography, *The Lost Sheep Found* (1660), as a
source for the character of the Independent Joseph Tomkins in *Wood-
stock;* for his slighting reference to the Muggletonians in that novel, a
member of the sect in 1826 informed Scott by letter that he was eternally
and irrevocably damned (Gordon, "Ancient and Modern Muggletonians,"
pp. 243–244).
[95] Cohn, *Pursuit,* pp. 349–359, contains a sketch of Clarkson's life and
invaluable selections from his writings that illuminate his Ranter phase.

two fanatic "Witnesses" whose concept of a transcendent and corporeal God required that Clarkson utterly reverse his previous "spiritual" views. Abandoning the extreme pantheism and amoralism of his Ranter years, Clarkson adopted the Muggletonian belief in a God who was sharply distinct from his corrupt Creation, a God who resided nowhere but in his own material body, which was in form like Adam's (*Divine Looking-glass*, pp. 98–105). Once content with the idea of an impersonal immortality as part of the Divine Essence, Clarkson now joined Reeve and Muggleton in the confident expectation that a personal immortality would begin when God graciously raised the bodies of his elect.[96] It appears that the inconstant Clarkson was in his later years constant only in the belief that the human personality does not have the "immortal subsistence" that the Westminster divines never doubted.

As we examine in the final chapter the thnetopsychism of intellectuals like Hobbes, Milton, and young Browne, and of that aspirant to the intellectual life Richard Overton, the Muggletonians may remind us that Christian mortalism was primarily the treasure of the ignorant and the outcast. The religious culture of the London slums produced Reeve, Muggleton, and Clarkson, all of whom repudiated human reason as a deception of the Devil. The established authorities, in their struggle to keep the immortality of the soul an unquestioned doctrine of English Protestantism, scolded Browne and Hobbes, made Milton cautious, and sought in vain for the author of *Mans Mortalitie*, but the battle had already been lost to enemies who were harder to discern because they rarely stated their mortalism in print. Before the Restoration, Christian mortalism in all its forms owed most of its success to the spoken word, preached by evangelists among the Familists, millenarians, Socinians, Anabaptists, Ranters, Adventists, Muggletonians, and General Baptists.

---

[96] The fact that Reeve and Muggleton were confirmed Calvinists on matters of predestination and believed in absolute election (*Divine Looking-glass*, p. 97) further indicates how far they stood from the thnetopsychists among the General Baptists.

Four / The Major Spokesmen for Soul Sleeping: Overton, Milton, and Hobbes

It is noteworthy that in the foregoing survey of Christian mortalist opinions—psychopannychism, thnetopsychism, and annihilationism—the disputants have both presented and attacked the mortalist positions virtually without recourse to rational argument and without appeal to philosophers. Bullinger touched on the philosophical arguments for immortality and William Hugh tried to associate the soul sleepers with Galen, but in general all parties seemed to recognize that Christian mortalism was based primarily on the Bible, not on philosophical speculation. Certainly no philosophical argument could have had the least effect on the "scriptural mortalism" of a Mrs. Attaway, a Muggleton, or a Winstanley.

After 1640, however, the most prominent Christian mortalists supplemented their scriptural exegesis with philosophical arguments and provoked their opponents to answer them in both modes of discourse. Milton, it is true, adhered almost entirely to Scripture, but his soul-sleeping ideas, clearly stated only in his unpublished *Christian Doctrine*, lay hidden for almost two centuries. His fellow thnetopsychists, Browne, Overton, and Hobbes, stated publicly that philosophy supported mortalist views, and they thereby elicited philosophical refutations. In this chapter I shall nevertheless slight the rational arguments that were advanced for and against mortalism, partly because they have been adequately discussed elsewhere,[1] but mostly because they are not central to this particular heretical tradition. Despite the title of his chapter on the Interregnum mortalist controversy, "Milton and the Mortalist Heresy," George Williamson has virtually nothing to say about Milton's mortalism; the chapter focuses on the Epicurean revival and the work of Walter Charleton and Pierre Gassendi, leaving no natural place for Milton's mortalism, supported as it is almost wholly by scriptural proofs. Williamson supposes that the

---

[1] Allen, *Doubt's Boundless Sea*, pp. 150–185; George Williamson, *Seventeenth Century Contexts* (Chicago: University of Chicago Press, 1961), pp. 148–177.

Interregnum controversy was a response to Browne's remark in *Religio Medici* that philosophy had not yet refuted mortalism, but, as we have seen, the mortalist controversy antedated Browne's book and most Christian mortalists cared little about philosophy.

It is a mistake to conclude that Browne, Overton, and Hobbes, because they referred to philosophical proofs, turned their backs on the still vital mortalist tradition of the Christian radicals and thought that rational argument took precedence over revelation. Like most philosophers in the Christian tradition, they thought that reason could be an aid to faith, but they did not presume to test the truths of revelation by rational processes; even Hobbes, whose credentials as a philosopher are unquestioned, believed that Scripture revealed truths beyond the reach of reason, and Browne, when he wrote *Religio Medici,* rejected mortalism on grounds of faith even though he did not believe philosophy could refute the doctrine. Although the Interregnum mortalists, particularly Overton, have often been confused with Deists, presumably because they used rational argument to support a doctrine contrary to the major Christian tradition, their conclusions about the soul are actually contrary to those of the Deists. Whereas the Deists believed that the doctrine of the immortality of the soul did not need the support of divine revelation because it was a truth evident to natural reason, these soul sleepers believed that reason and revelation both taught that immortality was not a natural property of the soul, but a consequence of the divine intervention (about which only revelation, not reason, teaches us) by which the bodies and souls of the dead will be raised on the Last Day. At bottom the Christian mortalists were immortalists, but their expectation of immortal life was based on faith, not reason, on Holy Scripture, not natural religion. Reason and Scripture taught them that the soul must die, but only Scripture taught them that it must live again. The eschatology of young Browne, Milton, Hobbes, Overton, and all the Anabaptist soul sleepers hinged upon faith in the General Resurrection, and not even Hobbes felt any compulsion to demonstrate the reasonableness of this resurrection. Thus the fact that the Interregnum soul sleepers sometimes buttressed their mortalist exposition of Scripture with rational arguments must not be allowed to obscure their close relationship with those Protestant radicals who were satisfied that their mortalist opinions were based only on the literal interpretation of Scripture.

Browne willingly grants that the resurrection of the body cannot be discovered by reason, his faith being sufficient not only to persuade him of the certainty of the event, but also to convince him that the bodies that will rise again will be the same that died: "How shall the dead arise, is no question of my faith; to beleeve onely possibilities, is not faith, but meere Philosophy; many things are true in Divinity, which are neither inducible by reason, nor confirmable by sense . . . . I beleeve that our estranged and divided ashes shall unite againe, that our separated dust after so many pilgrimages and transformations into the parts of mineralls, Plants, Animals, Elements, shall at the voyce of God returne into their primitive shapes; and joyne againe to make up their primary and predestinate formes."[2] The rational objections to this resurrection of the "numerical" body (with the same particles as the body that died) were so potent that Henry More refused to decide to whose body a particle from a cannibal's victim belongs and argued only that a transformed body not identical with the natural body will rise again.[3] Neither Hobbes nor Overton deals with the problem, but Milton also asserts that the body that rises will be the identical body that died.[4] Browne and Milton were evidently

[2] Sir Thomas Browne, *Religio Medici and Other Works*, ed. L. C. Martin (Oxford, 1964), I, 48 (all citations are from this edition, and all references are to the part and section numbers of *Religio Medici*).

[3] More, *The Grand Mystery of Godliness*, in *Theological Works*, pp. 152–153. In his *Observations vpon Religio Medici* (1643), Sir Kenelm Digby chided Browne for thinking that every atom of an individual body will "be raked together againe" when it is evident that the soul, the immortal, substantial form of the body, will sufficiently particularize the resurrected body (reprinted with separate pagination in Sir Thomas Browne, *Religio Medici* [Oxford: Clarendon Press, 1909], pp. 27–31).

[4] "The Christian Doctrine," in *CM*, XVI, 353; Bk. I, Chap. 33.

not disturbed by the rational considerations that troubled More; neither, surely, would most of the sectarian soul sleepers have struggled to reconcile Scripture and reason.

Browne was not, of course, a mortalist in any sense when, about 1635, he wrote *Religio Medici*. His mature view of the nature of the soul differs from Calvin's only in that Browne believed the soul immortal by nature rather than by grace. "... I beleeve that the whole frame of a beast doth perish, and is left in the same state after death, as before it was materialled unto life; that the soules of men know neither contrary nor corruption, that they subsist beyond the body, and outlive death by the priviledge of their proper natures, and without a miracle; that the soules of the faithfull, as they leave earth, take possession of Heaven ... " (*Religio Medici*, I, 37). Despite his present orthodoxy in the matter, Browne drew the censure of Sir Kenelm Digby and Alexander Ross when he confessed that in his "greener studies" he had believed the soul mortal and that he still believed that only faith, not philosophy, could refute that doctrine. Speaking of his youthful errors, Browne says:

> Now the first of mine was that of the Arabians, that the soules of men perished with their bodies, but should yet bee raised againe at the last day; not that I did absolutely conceive a mortality of the soule, but if that were, which faith, not Philosophy hath yet thoroughly disproved, and that both entred the grave together, yet I held the same conceit thereof that wee all doe of the body, that it should rise againe. Surely it is but the merits of our unworthy natures, if wee sleepe in darknesse, untill the last alarum: A serious reflex upon my owne unworthinesse did make me backward from challenging this prerogative of my soule; so I might enjoy my Saviour at the last, I could with patience be nothing almost unto eternity [*Religio Medici*, I, 7].

With readers as confident of their prowess in metaphysics as Digby and Ross, Browne was soon put back to school. Condescending as to a half-educated craftsman, Digby assured the doctor that if he had but known his metaphysics he would never have entertained the idea of a mortal soul. Digby then went on to suggest that Browne could learn the appropriate metaphysics from Digby's own forthcoming *Treatise . . . of Man's Soul, Out of Which the Immortality of Reasonable Souls Is Evinced* (1644), in the drafting of which he had recently filled nearly two hundred sheets (*Observations*, pp. 3–5). Ross, who was no kinder to what he considered the incompetent metaphysics of Digby's *Treatise* than to the ignorance of a physician, undertook properly to correct Browne's presumed ignorance of Plato and Aristotle and included a series of philosophical arguments for the immortality of the soul.[5] But Ross was so anxious to use all his scraps of learning that he inconsistently asserted that Browne's "*Arabian* opinion is not grounded upon *Philosophy*, but rather upon *Pope John* the 20. [sic] his heresie, for which hee was condemned by the *Divines of Paris*," a wild guess utterly without foundation.[6]

The concern of Digby and Ross for Browne's inadequate grounding in metaphysics is far from the mark. By his own account, Browne in his youth, like the other Christian soul sleepers, believed that the death of the soul was temporary, pending the resurrection of the body; such a thnetopsychist view could not have been developed on rational grounds alone, and Browne nowhere suggests that he was led into thnetopsychism by his reason. The truth is that Browne does not give a clear account of the genesis of his mortalist ideas. It is likely that his thnetopsychism began and ended during his Pembroke years. Mortalist ideas suggest an independence of

---

[5] Alexander Ross, *Medicus Medicatus: or the Physicians Religion Cured* (London, 1645), pp. 11–13. Ross treated Digby's metaphysics with contempt in *The Philosophicall Touch-stone* (London, 1645).

[6] Ross, *Medicus Medicatus*, p. 13. Ross meant Pope John XXII (1249–1334), who thought that the blessed departed did not see God until the Last Judgment; under pressure from theologians at Paris, Pope John joined in their opinion that the separated souls of the just enjoyed the Beatific Vision (*The Catholic Encyclopaedia*, ed. Charles G. Herbermann *et al.*, 15 vols. [New York: Appleton, 1907–1912], s. v. "John XXII"). John XXII is often mentioned in discussions of mortalism although his opinion does not approach even psychopannychism. Calvin was probably instrumental in spreading the idea that John XXII was a mortalist: Calvin, *Psychopannychia*, in *Tracts*, tr. Beveridge, III, 415.

mind and a self-confidence too great to attribute even to young Thomas Browne when he was a schoolboy at Winchester, and at the beginning of his sojourn on the Continent he argued for the immortalist position: "I remember a Doctor in Physick of Italy, who could not perfectly believe the immortality of the soule, because *Galen* seemed to make a doubt thereof. With another I was familiarly acquainted in France, a Divine and man of singular parts, that on the same point was so plunged and gravelled with three lines of *Seneca*, that all our Antidotes, drawne from both Scripture and Philosophy, could not expell the poyson of his errour" (*Religio Medici*, I, 21). Browne's later medical studies in Padua and Leiden were too advanced and, at the time *Religio Medici* was written, too recent properly to be called "greener studies."

Browne's youthful errors included, besides thnetopsychism, an inclination to pray for the dead and Origen's belief that the damned will not suffer forever. It is curious that he describes his errors as "not any begotten in the latter Centuries, but old and obsolete, such as could never have been revived, but by such extravagant and irregular heads as mine . . . " (*Religio Medici*, I, 6), yet prayer for the dead was obviously a flourishing Roman practice, and his own church along with the Swiss and Scottish churches had opposed soul sleeping and the idea of universal salvation for almost a century. The mortality of the soul was certainly far from being an "old and obsolete" idea. In the year *Religio Medici* was probably written, Alexander Gill in his *Sacred Philosophie of Holy Scripture* (1635) distinguished the English Christian mortalist positions of the time, and in 1642, when *Religio Medici* was first printed, Henry More published his *Psychodia Platonica*, which included "Antipsychopannychia, or the Confutation of the Sleep of the Soul," a long, verse attack on those who believe that the soul is unconscious after it separates from the body at death. Although More's poem is completely based on Neoplatonic arguments and does not use scriptural proofs, it is clear from the fourth stanza of Canto I that he is disputing against Christian mortalists who think the sleeping soul will awake to join the body at the promised General Resurrection:

What profiteth this bare existency,
If I perceive not that I do exist?
Nought longs to such, nor mirth nor misery.
Such stupid beings write into one list
With stocks and stones. But they do not persist,
You'll say, in this dull dead condition.
But must revive, shake off this drowsie mist
At that last shrill loud-sounding clarion
Which cleaves the trembling earth, rives monuments of stone.

Unfortunately, More gives no hint of the identity of his psychopannychist opponents (he is clearly not responding to Browne's thnetopsychism), but he must have thought them formidable enough to merit over a hundred Spenserian stanzas of refutation. The soul sleepers were unlikely to be persuaded by More's talk of the soul's innate ideas, "self-essentiall omniformity," and "centrall self-vitality"; like Bullinger's Anabaptist Simon, they "had leuer heare Scriptures."

Although Browne's celebrated book lacked philosophical and scriptural support for the soul-sleeping idea, Richard Overton soon supplied both sorts of argument in abundance. *Mans Mortalitie* was the first English defense of soul sleeping to be published since the time of Tyndale, and in the religious ferment of the first civil war the tract received considerable attention. Probably printed on a secret press in London by Overton himself, the first edition, bearing the date 1643 on the title page, was acquired by George Thomason on January 19, 1644. Apparently the sales exceeded Overton's expectations, for in 1644 the pamphlet was entirely reset and corrected; like the first edition, it carried the bogus imprint of John Canne and named Amsterdam as its place of publication. R[ichard] O[verton], *Man Wholly Mortal* (London, 1655) was called on its title page "The second Edition, by the Author corrected and enlarged." Overton deleted some passages, added more, and rearranged the chapters. This edition did not sell out, however, and the sheets were reissued in 1675 with a cancel title. All four versions identified the author only as "R.O."[7] The full title of the first edition boldly trumpeted the pamphlet's heterodox contents and truculent manner: *Mans Mortallitie, or a Treatise Wherein 'Tis Proved, Both Theologically and Phylosophically, That Whole Man (as a Rationall Creature) Is a Compound Wholly Mortall, Contrary to That Common Distinction of Soule and Body: and That the Present Going of the Soule into Heaven or Hell Is a Meer Fiction: and That at the Resurrection Is the Beginning of Our Immortallity, and Then Actuall Condemnation, and Salvation, and Not Before. With All Doubtes and Objections Answered, and Resolved, Both by Scripture and Reason; Discovering the Multitude of Blasphemies, and Absurdities That Arise From the Fancie of the Soule. Also Divers Other Mysteries, as, of Heaven, Hell, Christs Humane Residence, the Extent of the Resurrection, the New Creation &c. Opened, and Presented to the Tryall of Better Judgments.*

The pamphlet does not retreat from this confident beginning. Overton was never a man to lead his opponents into the truth; in him the English soul sleepers had a gifted and articulate propagandist who intended to win the argument, a polemicist who would hammer the "soularies" into submission. His self-assurance is complete. Hesitances and vagueness such as we have seen in Tyndale's discussion of the matter have no place in *Mans Mortalitie*. Overton, as always, is spoiling for a fight. In 1645 he chided his Presbyterian adversaries for not publishing refutations he could counter. "Here the Authour of that Booke, intituled, *Mans Mortality*, desires Mr. *Edwards* with those that are so invective against it in their Pulpits that they would cease their railing at it there, and come forth in Print against it; for the thing being so rare, so little questioned, and the contrary so generally concluded as a principle of faith, any *bumbast stuffe* will passe there for authentike with the people without tryall, but if it be put

---

[7] The case for attributing *Mans Mortalitie* to Richard Overton need not be repeated here since it is convincingly argued in P[erez] Zagorin, "The Authorship of *Mans Mortallitie*," *The Library*, 5th Ser., V (1950–1951), 179–182; in Frank, *Levellers*, pp. 263–265; and in Don M. Wolfe, "Unsigned Pamphlets of Richard Overton: 1641–1649," *Huntington Library Quarterly*, XXI (1957–1958), 167–201.

forth to publike vew, it must expect an encounter by one or other, and therein the Authour of that Booke observeth the policie of his Presbyterian Adversaries to maintain their repute with the people, in being so hasty in the Pulpit and so slow to the Presse."[8]

Overton's wish was granted in the same year, though one response, at least, did not come from the Presbyterians. The Jesuit Guy Holland, from the Royalist camp in Oxford, wrote *The Prerogative of Man* (1645) to frustrate those who, having destroyed the Church's hierarchy, in their frenzy now sought to destroy "the sacred rights of Princes" and to divest their own nature of its "cheifest ornaments."[9] Holland is perhaps the ablest of the Interregnum critics of mortalism and is aware that the mortalists believe in an eternal afterlife for body and soul resurrected together, but he nevertheless accuses them of being Epicureans who want to believe in the soul's mortality so that they may indulge their lusts.[10] Overton, like Browne, thought thnetopsychism could increase a man's sense of dependence on God, but Holland, like the other immortalists, cherishes man's "prerogative": "of late a sorry Animal, . . . having stept into the crowde of Scriblers in the defense of an old rotten heresy condemned and suffocated by consent of the wise, almost at the houre of the birth, hath met with some soules so unhappy as to be perswaded by him, and to thinke as meanely of themselves as the wisest of all ages did of beasts; . . . not elevating Beasts to the degree of reason, . . .

[8] [Richard Overton,] *The Araignment of Mr. Persecvtion* (London? 1645), p. 20, reprinted in *Tracts on Liberty*, ed. Haller, III, [205]–[256]. Overton's pamphleteering and other activities in the Leveller cause increased in 1645 and after, and he never replied to the printed attacks on *Mans Mortalitie*.

[9] [Guy Holland,] *The Prerogative of Man: or, His Soules Immortality, and High Perfection Defended, and Explained against the Rash and Rude Conceptions of a Late Authour Who Hath Inconsiderately Adventured to Impugne It* (Oxford? 1645), pp. 2–3. In his later version of the pamphlet, *The Grand Prerogative of Humane Nature* (London, 1653), Holland expanded his attack on Epicurism and complained that his first edition had been cut by the censor at Oxford (Williamson, *Seventeenth Century Contexts*, p. 157 n.).

[10] Holland, *Prerogative of Man*, pp. 31–32, sig. A2r, and p. 45 (misnumbered "43").

but contrariwise reproachfully depressing man even as low as bruite beasts, and ascribing to them both a mortality alike" (*Prerogative of Man*, pp. 1-2). Neither did Alexander Ross see anything Christian in the Christian mortalist position: in characteristically shrill passages he associates the mortalists with the Cynics and Epicureans and says that if the mortalist opinion is generally accepted "wee must bid farewell to *lawes* and *civility*, nay, to *Religion* and *Christianity*. We must bid adieu to *vertuous actions*, and to all *spirituall comforts* . . . . Admit but such *Lucretian* doctrine, you may shake hands with heaven and hell." Ross concludes that the souls of mortalists are "fitter to dwell with *Nebuchadnezzars* in a beasts body, then in their owne . . . ."[11]

In ordinary circumstances it would not be necessary to defend Overton and the soul sleepers from such abuse. This reaction of orthodox Christians to Overton's mortalism shows how deeply committed they were to the doctrine of the immortal soul, but it tells us nothing about Overton's real views or those of the Christian soul sleepers. Overton's orthodox contemporaries could not conceive of a Christian faith that did not include belief in the immortal, incorporeal substance called soul; thus they naturally thought of the soul sleepers as pagan rationalists. The error of seventeenth-century orthodoxy could be dismissed with a passing note were it not for the fact that many modern scholars, ignorant of the tradition of mortalism among radical Christian groups in the Reformation, also consider soul sleeping an unchristian idea and link Overton with the beginnings of Deism or even with a totally irreligious naturalism (see Appendix).

Although modern scholars are not so shrill as Ross, they emphasize Overton's rationalism at the expense of his scripturalism and conclude that he is not so much a Christian as an early proponent of natural religion. Certainly Overton's

[11] Alexander Ross, *The Philosophicall Touch-stone: or Observations upon Sir Kenelm Digbie's Discourses of the Nature of Bodies, and of the Reasonable Soule . . . . And the Weak Fortifications of a Late Amsterdam Ingeneer, Patronizing the Soules Mortality, Briefly Slighted* (London, 1645), pp. 123, 126–127.

style has done much to foster this misconception. *Mans Mortalitie* brought to the discussion of Christian doctrine the manners and taste of an Anabaptist debate: traditional opinions are not shown due respect, and those who hold them are assumed to be deceivers, fools, and blasphemers. Overton's favorite device is the *reductio ad absurdum,* and in his margins he calls attention to no less than seventy-six absurdities in the immortalist position.[12] His book is full of the irreverent ridicule of the "soularies" that caused David Masson to think Overton did not expect an immortal afterlife at all. He is not above coarse comedy; when, for example, he ridicules the idea that the soul has faculties whose existence does not depend on the body, he lists the multiplicity of souls that the idea supposes: "a *Phantasticke Soul,* a *Rationall Soul,* a *Memorative Soul,* a *Seeing Soul,* a *Hearing Soul,* a *Smelling Soul,* a *Tasting Soul,* a *Touching Soul,* with divers other *Souls* of all sorts, and sizes: as, *saving your presence,* an *Evacuating Soul,* &c."[13] (That last "&c." indicates that Overton had some respect for decorum.) Such ridicule is doubtless offensive to believers in the soul's immortality and dignity, but Overton's impudent manner must not be allowed to obscure the fact that he vigorously states his belief in the truth of revelation and in salvation through Christ alone. Like soul sleepers since Tyndale, Overton sees no contradiction between Christian faith and belief in a soul whose vitality depends on the body.

Among those who take Overton's Christian faith to be superficial or even insincere, A. S. P. Woodhouse is preeminent; his comments on Overton's views are representative of the almost unanimous judgment of current scholarship.[14] "In seventeenth-century England (as in the Europe of the Reformation) currents which in spirit belong to no religious

[12] Because of errors in enumeration, Overton's count came to only sixty-nine.

[13] *MM,* p. 26.

[14] Overton's professed Christianity is taken seriously only in H. N. Brailsford, *The Levellers and the English Revolution,* ed. Christopher Hill (Stanford: Stanford University Press, 1961), pp. 52–53, and in Wilhelm Schenk, *The Concern for Social Justice in the Puritan Revolution* (London: Longmans, Green, 1948), pp. 168–171.

tradition but rather to libertinism, seek a temporary alliance with radical Protestant thought. In Overton there is a militant naturalism and a thinly veiled hostility to dogmatic religion. He champions the mortalist heresy in the name of scripture and reason and advances a materialistic view of man and the world. He claims to have attempted a proof of the main truths of revelation from nature and reason; it is difficult to judge of his motives, but the method seems to link him with the beginnings of Deism."[15] The alliance between mortalism and "radical Protestant thought," reaching as it does from the earliest days of the Reformation to the present, cannot properly be called "temporary," but Woodhouse, unaware of that religious tradition, naturally thinks Overton is somehow more fundamentally related to the rationalism of the libertines and the Deists. I have already touched on the essentially nonrational character of soul sleeping even when Hobbes and Overton found rational grounds to support the conclusions of their scriptural exegeses. The libertinism that attracted most attention in seventeenth-century England was the antinomianism that was so common among the Family of Love and the Ranters, but Overton has nothing in common with those experimental Christians. Like Milton, Overton prefers the traducian doctrine of the origin of the soul because he thinks the creationist doctrine of the soul's divine origin makes God the author of sin (*MM*, pp. 62-63); he insists on the literal interpretation of the Bible and makes no claim of immediate revelations from God; and he asserts a personal afterlife of rewards and punishments that will follow the literal resurrection of body and soul together from the grave. Like any Protestant radical, Overton shows "hostility to dogmatic religion" whenever he thinks dogmatic religion departs from Holy Scripture; his is the hostility of the radical sectary toward unscriptural dogmatism, but it is far from being hostility toward the Christian religion. His mortalism has its roots in Reformation Christianity, as does his "materialistic

---

[15] *Puritanism and Liberty*, ed. A. S. P. Woodhouse, 2d ed. (Chicago: University of Chicago Press, 1951), Introduction, p. 55.

view of man and the world" (if, indeed, that phrase represents Overton's opinions).[16] The truth is that the conclusions drawn in *Mans Mortalitie* differ in no important way from Milton's thnetopsychism in the *Christian Doctrine*; nor, although we have no detailed knowledge of it, does Browne's thinking when he entertained the thnetopsychist opinion appear to have differed from the conclusions of Milton and Overton. Since scholars do not habitually relate the mortalist opinions of Milton or of Browne in his "greener studies" to the beginnings of Deism, perhaps it is only Overton's "method" that suggests he is a proto-Deist.

Woodhouse's suspicion that Overton's method is Deistic is based on Overton's own description of a manuscript taken from him by one of Cromwell's officers during Overton's arrest in 1649 on political charges:

> he took away certain papers which were my former Meditations upon the works of the Creation, intituled, *Gods Word confirmed by his Works*; wherein I endeavoured the probation of a God, a Creation, a State of Innocencie, a Fall, a Resurrection, a Restorer, a Day of Judgment, &c. barely from the consideration of things visible and created: and these papers I reserved to perfect and publish as soon as I could have any rest from the turmoils of this troubled Common-wealth: and for the loss of those papers I am only troubled: all that I desire of my enemies hands, is but the restitution of those papers, that what-ever becomes of me, they may not be buried in oblivion, for they may prove usefull to many.[17]

Overton's meditations were, unfortunately, "buried in oblivion," but from his description there seems to have been

[16] Overton certainly argued that man's soul was not an "incorporeal substance," but, unlike Hobbes and Milton, he does not discuss the "corporeality" of angels or of God. Overton takes a monistic view of man, but we cannot be sure that he extended that monistic view to the whole universe.

[17] Richard Overton, John Lilburne, and Thomas Prince, *The Picture of the Councel of State* (London? 1649), p. 28, reprinted in *The Leveller Tracts: 1647–1653*, ed. William Haller and Godfrey Davies (New York: Columbia University Press, 1944), pp. 191–246.

nothing remarkable about them. What orthodox Christian did not think God's word was confirmed by his works? In his *Institutes* (Bk. I, Chap. 5) Calvin said that the created world manifested God and his attributes. There is in Overton's extant work no sign of the Deists' tendency to prune revealed religion of those doctrines that could not be demonstrated by reason and "natural religion." If the attempt to show that the truths of revealed religion can be demonstrated rationally in itself indicates a movement toward Deism, then Overton's opponents (to say nothing of Thomas Aquinas and the Scholastics) tend toward Deism no less than he.

Overton's method in *Mans Mortalitie* is by no means foreign to Christian apologetics, though his appeal to reason to support doctrines derived from Scripture must have seemed irrelevant to most sectarian mortalists. When he published *Mans Mortalitie* Overton took Christian mortalism outside the conventicles in an effort to convert the "Gentiles," and like St. Paul he used terms the Gentiles would understand. Overton's opponents did not criticize him for reasoning against the immortality of the soul, but for reasoning badly. In addition to countering the mortalists' scriptural exegesis, Ross and Holland advance rational proofs of immortality, and the anonymous author of *The Immortality of Mans Soule* devotes almost all his effort to rational rather than scriptural argument.[18] John Bachiler, the book licenser, contributed his mite to the dispute by reissuing the arguments for the immortality of the soul that had been set forth in Philip de Mornay's popular apology for Christianity and translated into English in 1587 by Sir Philip Sidney and Arthur Golding as *A Worke concerning the Trewnesse of Christian Religion.*[19] Bachiler's selection, like the whole of

[18] *The Immortality of Mans Soule, Proved Both by Scriptvre and Reason. Contrary to the Fancie of R. O. in His Book Intituled Mans Mortality* (London, 1645).

[19] Philip de Mornay, *The Soul's Own Evidence for Its Own Immortality*, ed. John Bachiler, tr. Sir Philip Sidney and Arthur Golding (London, 1646).

Mornay's original work, avoids scriptural proofs and argues for the soul's immortality on rational grounds alone.

Whereas the Deists liked to appeal for support to the *consensus gentium,* Overton is aware that mortalism is a minority opinion and speaks contemptuously of the pagan philosophers who developed their immortalist views by the light of their unaided natural reason. After listing the incongruous opinions about the soul that form our heritage, Overton scorns the confused results of natural reasoning, which has misled even Christians: "Divers other conceptions and fancies there be, to uphold this ridiculous invention of the Soule traducted from the *Heathens,* who by the Book of Nature understood an immortality after Death; but through their ignorance how, or which way; this invention (reported to be *Platoes*) was occasioned, and begat a generall beliefe: and so they, and after them the Christians have thus strained their wits to such miserable shifts, to define *what it is,* but neither conclude any certainty, or give satisfaction therein" (*MM,* p. 19).

Overton's ethics is, similarly, not based on a "militant naturalism" and would have been as unacceptable as his attitude toward natural religion in any company of Deists. As a dedicated social revolutionary, Overton sought to destroy the aristocratic structure of English society; as a General Baptist who believed with his fellows that Christ's sacrifice offered saving grace to all men, he could see no privilege established by divine ordinance. Overton had no respect for the Calvinist conception of an order of grace that established a spiritual aristocracy of the elect.[20] When he suffered in the cause of social melioration, Overton was sustained in his

[20] Woodhouse cites a passage in which Overton speaks of the natural equality of all men (*Puritanism and Liberty,* Introduction, p. 69) and considers it evidence of Overton's secularism. Although it is true that the idea repudiates Calvin's doctrine of election, it is misleading to call it secular. The "levelling" implications of the General Baptist doctrine of universal grace were realized in Overton's political writing, but he does not suggest that all men are created innocent, as Rousseau did. For Overton all men needed redemption from sin, an attitude far from secularism.

trials by a Christian, not a social, ideal. Like Milton and Browne, Overton could see no suitable reward for virtue in this life and looked forward with no less eagerness than they to Resurrection and Judgment.[21] When Overton with some other Leveller leaders was dragged before the Council of State because he had provoked Cromwell to anger, the Baptist printer and propagandist was able to defy this awesome assemblage because of his Christian (and apparently mortalist) faith in the resurrection of the body to immortal life: "for I know my Redeemer liveth, and that after this life I shall be restored to life and Immortality, and receive according to the innocency and uprightnesse of my heart: Otherwise, I tell you plainly, I would not thus put my life and wel-being in jeopardie, and expose my self to those extremities and necessities that I do; I would creaturize, be this or that or any thing else, as were the times, eat, drink, and take my pleasure; turn Judas or any thing to flatter great men for promotion . . . ."[22] There is a rugged eloquence in Overton's statement of the faith that sustained him, but the ethical position would not have been admired by a Deist like Shaftesbury. Of a man whose behavior is governed by his expectation of future rewards and punishments, Shaftesbury in his *An Inquiry concerning Virtue or Merit* (1699) says: "There is no more of rectitude, piety, or sanctity in a creature thus reformed, than there is meekness or gentleness in a tiger strongly chained, or innocence and sobriety in a monkey under the discipline of the whip."[23]

[21] Browne considered the Stoic idea "That vertue is her owne reward" to be "but a cold principle" (*Religio Medici*, I, 47), and Milton in his *Christian Doctrine* argued that the General Resurrection is necessary because God's justice would not be vindicated if the righteous were left miserable and the wicked happy, as they are on earth (*CM*, XVI, 351–353; Bk. I, Chap. 33).

[22] Overton, Lilburne, and Prince, *Picture of the Councel of State*, p. 41. In *Mans Mortalitie* also Overton saw the Christian idea of an afterlife of rewards and punishments as the only barrier to the "Epicurean Blasphemy" (*MM*, pp. 65–66).

[23] Anthony Ashley Cooper, *Characteristics of Men, Manners, Opinions, Times, etc.*, ed. John M. Robertson, 2 vols. (London: G. Richards, 1900), I, 267.

Overton's rational arguments for soul sleeping are, for the most part, not anticipations of rationalism, but tedious adjuncts to the main, scriptural arguments. Although some of his arguments seem quite "modern" (for example, his insistence, based on the observations of the French physiologist Ambrose Paré, that man differs from the beast only in degree, and his argument that the rational faculty is a function of the body's health and maturity [*MM*, pp. 26–29]), Overton's reasoning is Scholastic both in method and terminology. He is undistinguished in such disputing, although our opinion of his abilities in philosophical argument will not suffer if we compare his arguments with the philosophical refutations of mortalism published by Holland, Ross, and the author of *The Immortality of Mans Soule*.

Overton's mortalist exegesis of Scripture deserves more attention than it has yet received, not only because the soul-sleeping idea was traditionally based on Scripture, but also because his scriptural arguments closely correspond to Milton's mortalist arguments, which are almost wholly scriptural. No discussion of the parallels in the scriptural arguments of Milton and Overton can be conducted without the question of influence naturally arising. Was Denis Saurat right in suggesting that Milton learned his mortalism from Overton's pamphlet, became friendly with Overton and his circle, and helped revise the pamphlet for the new edition of 1655?[24] Robert Adams has taught us to be cautious in our attempts to identify influences on Milton's mind,[25] but if our caution is too great we shall fall into the error of making Milton impossibly independent, a figure who stood aloof from the intellectual and social ideas of his time and unassisted developed his own views of man and God. It is particularly easy to exaggerate Milton's independence in religious matters, for while he was deeply religious he was no churchman: in his desire to be free of ecclesiastical discipline, he repudiated episcopacy and Presbyterianism, stayed

[24] Saurat, *Milton*, p. 279.

[25] Robert Martin Adams, *Ikon: John Milton and the Modern Critics* (Ithaca: Cornell University Press, 1955), pp. 128–176.

clear of the Independent congregations, and even avoided the easier yoke of the General Baptists.[26] In his *Christian Doctrine* Milton approves of a congregational sort of church whose voluntary members exercise discipline as a group over individual members in matters concerning Christian living and the regulation of meetings, but he denies the church as well as the state any authority over doctrine (*CM*, XVI, 267; Bk. I, Chap. 30). For all that, it is probable that Milton was influenced by some of the doctrines of the Christian churches of England.

But did not Milton himself assert his independence from the doctrinal positions of his day in his preface to the *Christian Doctrine*?

> For my own part, I adhere to the Holy Scripture alone —I follow no other heresy or sect. I had not even read any of the works of heretics, so called, when the mistakes of those who are reckoned for orthodox, and their incautious handling of Scripture first taught me to agree with their opponents whenever those opponents agreed with Scripture. If this be heresy, I confess with St. Paul, Acts xxiv. 14. "that after the way which they call heresy, so worship I the God of my fathers, believing all things which are written in the law and the prophets"—to which I add, whatever is written in the New Testament. Any other judges or paramount interpreters of the Christian belief, together with all implicit faith, as it is called, I, in common with the whole Protestant Church, refuse to recognize [*CM*, XIV, 15].

There is nothing in this statement that would not gain the assent of most of the radical sectarian congregations of seventeenth-century England. Milton is speaking of authority and, in common with the practice of the sectaries and the theory of the more orthodox Protestants, he maintains that only the Holy Scripture (interpreted under the guidance of the Holy Spirit) has authority in matters of faith. Milton,

---

[26] John Toland said Milton was a member of no church in his later years: *The Early Lives of Milton*, ed. Helen Darbishire (London: Constable, 1932), p. 195.

who refused to bow to the authority of Calvin or the Fathers, was not likely to adopt a doctrine on the authority of a Richard Overton, but he would certainly be glad to adopt a doctrine that, in his opinion, passed the test of Scripture literally interpreted.

Although Milton acknowledged no authority but Holy Scripture in matters of faith, it is surely unreasonable to suggest that he closed his eyes and ears to all influences in matters of faith. But that is the position George N. Conklin takes when he says: "By the very terms of his hermeneutics and the philological capability of his exegesis, Milton through his Biblical criticism developed alone, with Puritan independence and Renaissance talent, his system of Christian doctrine."[27] It may be that Conklin's statement is more sweeping than he intended, for surely he did not mean that Milton discovered the doctrines of original sin and justification by faith through his independent study of the Bible and owed no debt to Augustine and Luther. Perhaps he meant to say only that Milton's mortalist and materialist heresies (which are the main subject of Conklin's study) are "independently adduced and beholden to none" (*Biblical Criticism,* p. 6). Although I think it is improbable that Milton's thinking about mortalism originated during his study of the Bible when it is clear that the heresy was much discussed in London long before Milton completed the basic draft of the *Christian Doctrine* (about 1658–about 1660),[28] it is possible that he heard nothing of it before he derived the heresy from his scriptural study. Conklin's admiration for Milton's exegetical powers is so great, however, that he goes well beyond claiming that Milton's mortalism was independently derived from Scripture and asserts that Milton's mortalism was an extraordinary conception, that there are no close, contemporary parallels to the *Christian Doctrine*'s

> ... two theses that, for sheer heterodoxy, go far beyond even the rampant *Fratres Poloni*. These two beliefs are, in

---

[27] George N. Conklin, *Biblical Criticism and Heresy in Milton* (New York: King's Crown Press, 1949), p. 5.

[28] Maurice Kelley, *This Great Argument* (Princeton: Princeton University Press, 1941), p. 68.

fact, so individual (one of them appears to be uniquely
Milton's) and so singular in textual genesis, namely, his
mortalism and his pantheistic materialism, that parallels
to the ideas in one case are rare and approximate, and in
the other simply nonexistent. It is to Milton's "rule of
Scripture" and to his conception of interpretation that we
must turn for explicit exposition of these extreme conclusions. With Milton's hermeneutics definitely propounded
and his exegetical equipment and technique so manifest,
there may be no great need to search for the sources of
his theological irregularities. It is quite probable that the
ideas, the reasoning, and the proofs are wholly Milton's;
the parallels, wherever they occur, merely coincidental
[*Biblical Criticism*, pp. 4–5].

That Milton's mortalism is "singular in textual genesis"
and that parallels to it are "rare and approximate" are assertions of historical fact that may be evaluated without reference to the more difficult question of whether Milton was
influenced by previous expressions of mortalism. Conklin's
failure to make a serious study of the history of mortalist
ideas led him to his erroneous conclusion. He rightly per-
ceives that Milton believes in the death of the soul, not just
in its sleep,[29] but Conklin supposes that Milton originated
thnetopsychism: " . . . Milton's basic argument, unlike all
others, is based upon, and begins with, the mortality of the
soul (the whole man) rather than the sleep of the soul and
the problem of the intermediate state."[30] Conklin thinks
Calvin attacked only psychopannychism (p. 75), and he is
unaware of the thnetopsychist views of young Browne,

[29] Conklin, *Biblical Criticism*, p. 89. Harry F. Robins is not quite clear
on this point and seems to think that Milton also expressed psychopannychism in the *Christian Doctrine*; Robins, however, does not imagine
that Milton originated thnetopsychism (*If This Be Heresy* [Urbana: University of Illinois Press, 1963], p. 145).

[30] Conklin, *Biblical Criticism*, p. 83. Conklin (pp. 117–118) thinks that
other mortalists, like the Socinian Joachim Stegmann (author of *Brevis
Disquisitio*), espoused mortalism more because it was useful in com-
bating purgatory than because it was a truth of Scripture. Like good
Protestants before and since, Milton based his mortalism on Scripture,
but like them also he did not fail to recommend the doctrine for its
utility against Rome: "if it be true . . . that the soul as well as the body
sleeps till the day of resurrection, no stronger argument can be urged
against the existence of a purgatory" ("The Christian Doctrine," *CM*,
XV, 341; Bk. I, Chap. 16).

Hobbes, and Overton. Had Conklin studied *Mans Mortalitie* instead of dismissing it because Saurat thought it connected with Robert Fludd and the Cabala,[31] he would have found a mortalist exegesis of Scripture comparable to Milton's own.

The more one knows of the currency of mortalist ideas in Interregnum England, the more hesitant one becomes to suggest that Milton was stimulated by any particular person or book to examine the Scriptures for proofs of soul sleeping. Detailed knowledge of the English tradition of Christian mortalism does not support Saurat's contention that the idea, shared by Milton and Overton, that the Bible does not teach the doctrine of a separate soul was "sufficiently rare in the seventeenth century to be in itself a proof of connection" (*Milton*, p. 277); knowledge of the mortalist tradition does indicate that Richard Overton was not the originator of thnetopsychism in England, not the sole cause of the idea's increased popularity after 1643, and perhaps (if we remember his secondary role in the Anabaptist debate on the idea) not even its chief prophet. It is probable, however, that Milton read *Mans Mortalitie* when it was first published, unless we can believe that Milton, just before he wrote *Areopagitica*, was not curious about a book that the Company of Stationers in a formal complaint to Commons paired with his own *Doctrine and Discipline of Divorce* as a book worthy of suppression.[32]

Milton's poetry offers no certain clues about when the poet adopted mortalism. Many of the poems written before *Paradise Lost* implicitly state the orthodox Protestant opinion of the soul's immortality; *On the Death of a Fair Infant, At a Solemn Musick, An Epitaph on the Marchioness of Winchester, Lycidas, Comus,* and Sonnet XIV all express belief in "those just Spirits that wear victorious Palms." The trans-

[31] Conklin, *Biblical Criticism*, p. 118; Saurat, *Milton*, pp. 270–272. Certainly Saurat's association of Overton with cabalism is farfetched, but it seems to have discouraged Conklin from reading *Mans Mortalitie*.

[32] On August 26, 1644, Commons ordered its Committee on Printing " 'diligently to inquire out the authors, printers, and publishers of the Pamphlets against the Immortality of the Soul and *Concerning Divorce*' " (Masson, *Life of Milton*, III, 164–165).

lations of Psalms 7, 86, and 88 indeed use "soul" in the Hebrew sense (for "life" or "whole man"), but not more noticeably than the translations of the Authorized Version. In *Paradise Lost*, X, 782–792, the fallen Adam, whom Michael has not yet told of the General Resurrection and the Judgment, reasons out that God's sentence of death must also apply to the soul, which has life and responsibility; much the same argument is used in Bk. I, Chap. 13 of the *Christian Doctrine* (*CM*, XV, 217–219). Milton may not, of course, have thought it appropriate to propound such a disputable doctrine as mortalism in his poetry; thus the immortalism of his verse is no certain evidence of his beliefs. However that may be, mortalism plays an insignificant role in Milton's poetry and is not even hinted at before the publication of *Paradise Lost*. Nevertheless, there are numerous parallels (some of which I shall point out shortly) between Overton's scriptural arguments and those of Milton in the *Christian Doctrine*.

Those parallels are not so striking in either exegetical content or expression as to demonstrate that Milton owed any debt to Overton directly. At most we may conclude that such a debt is possible. It is, I think, more likely that Milton and Overton both drew ideas from the lively discussion of mortalism that was conducted first among the sects and then, as the orthodox preachers tried to combat the idea from their pulpits, more generally among Christian Londoners as they tested against Scripture what was told them from tub and pulpit.

The oral tradition of soul sleeping in Interregnum England did not depend on *Mans Mortalitie*, though Overton's book doubtless intensified the discussion. Although the mortalist opinion was not defended in print from Tyndale to Overton, we have seen how the orthodox turned to Scripture to refute the heretics and referred to the obvious texts: Christ's words to the Good Thief, the Dives and Lazarus story, St. Paul wanting to be with Christ, Christ's answer to the Sadducees that God is the God of the living, not of the dead, and John's vision of the souls under the altar. The mortalists had been

active for some time in advancing their interpretation of
Scripture. When Digby encountered thnetopsychism in *Religio Medici*, well before Overton's book appeared, he had
already drafted his philosophical defense of the soul's immortality. Ross thought Digby did so badly in refuting the
soul's detractors that in his *Philosophicall Touch-stone*
(1645) he tried to improve on Digby's arguments. Ross gave
scriptural[33] as well as rational proofs for immortality and
listed nine arguments of the thnetopsychists, two of them
based on Eccles. 3:19 and Job 14 (*The Philosophicall Touch-
stone*, pp. 117–122). Then, only as an afterthought, Ross
briefly cuffed aside the author of *Mans Mortalitie* as a completely unworthy opponent who had just been brought to
his attention (almost a year and a half after the publication
of Overton's book).[34] Interregnum London did not lack exegetes to expound the mortalist meaning of Holy Scripture;
nor did it lack teachers who confidently refuted soul sleeping by explaining Scripture in pulpit and press. In such a
milieu, it would be bold to credit either Overton or Milton
with much originality. It is likely that, in company with
many other Londoners, they were familiar with the arguments advanced by each side in the dispute; since Overton
and Milton both took the same side, it is not surprising that
their arguments from Scripture should closely correspond.

The *Christian Doctrine* shows that Milton shared a number of other doctrines with Overton's General Baptist associates. Milton was not, of course, a General Baptist insofar
as the name suggests a person who attends the sect's meetings and feels a social bond with other members of the sect;

[33] Ross, *The Philosophicall Touch-stone*, pp. 100, 109–110. Most of
Ross's proof-texts are the familiar ones about the spirit returning to God
(Eccles. 12:7), Christ commending his spirit into the hands of his Father
(Luke 23:46), God not being the God of the dead, but of the living (Matt.
22:32), Lazarus' soul being carried to Abraham's bosom (Luke 16:22),
Christ promising Paradise to the Good Thief (Luke 23:43), and Christ
advising his disciples not to fear those who can kill the body, but not
the soul (Matt. 10:28).

[34] Ross, *The Philosophicall Touch-stone*, pp. 123–127. Thomason dated
his copy of *The Philosophicall Touch-stone* "June 27" (1645) and his
copy of Overton's first edition "Jan. 19" (1644).

a man of Milton's learning would have found no congenial company in Bell Alley. Nevertheless, Milton was willing to subject all ideas to the test of Scripture, and, in addition to soul sleeping, many of the central General Baptist ideas passed that test to Milton's satisfaction. Milton's Arminianism is well known; he considered baptism a meaningful ceremony only when it was administered to adult believers by total immersion in running waters; he denied the civil magistrate any authority in matters of religion; he insisted on the freedom (indeed, the obligation) of every believer to interpret Scripture for himself; and he thought that all church members (except women) had the right to "prophesy" according to their gifts, being voluntary members under the guidance of a particular congregation only and subject to the congregation's rebuke or excommunication only in matters of conduct.[35] Without being a member of any church, Milton in the *Christian Doctrine* adopted an attitude toward freedom of belief and toward the role of the church in a Christian's life that was, among the Interregnum churches, most closely realized in the General Baptist congregations.

Milton seems to have known that mortalism was much discussed in his day. He refers to a "controversy," which suggests that he was aware of the scope of the dispute. Like many General Baptists, he considers the question of the soul's immortality adiaphorous. "Is it the whole man, or the body alone, that is deprived of vitality? And as this is a subject which may be discussed without endangering our faith or devotion, whichever side of the controversy we espouse, I shall declare freely what seems to me the true doctrine, as collected from numberless passages of Scripture; without regarding the opinion of those, who think that truth is to be sought in the schools of philosophy, rather than in the sacred writings" (*CM*, XV, 219; Bk. I, Chap. 13). Milton may have meant to censure Overton's philosophical mode of argument

---

[35] Milton, "The Christian Doctrine," *CM*, XVI, 169–171, 265–267, 321–337; Bk. I, Chaps. 28, 30, 32. In *Paradise Lost*, XII, 441–445, Michael describes the baptizing of believers in running waters as the apostolic practice.

as well as that of such immortalists as Henry More, Digby, Ross, and Holland, but he would not have found much to quarrel with in Overton's scriptural argument; in their conclusions, in their selection of proof-texts, and in their interpretation of those texts, Milton and Overton are in substantial agreement.

About the origin of the soul Milton and Overton have the same opinion—the traducian view that the soul is, by the process of natural generation, transmitted from the parents to the child;[36] they therefore oppose the creationists, who believe that God performs a separate act of creation for each particular soul (at least for each rational soul, with the faculties of reason and will) and infuses it into the embryo in an early stage of development. The question of the soul's origin is closely related to the question of the soul's fate, as the disputants well knew. Ross says: "As the *dissolution* or *corruption* of the body dissolveth not the soule, neither doth the *constitution* or *generation* of the body give being to the soul; for if she hath her being from the body, she must decay with the body."[37] Overton sees that traducianism is an excellent support for mortalism: "that which is immortall cannot generatively proceed from that which is mortall, as Christ saith, *that which is borne of the flesh is* (as it selfe is, corruptible, mutable) *flesh, John 3.6* . . ." (*MM*, p. 59). Milton argues that if souls are not generated "in a natural order" God did not finish his creation in six days, but left himself rather with "a vast, not to say a servile task . . ., without even allowing time for rest on each successive sabbath," creating souls daily "at the bidding of what is not seldom the flagitious wantonness of man" (*CM*, XV, 43; Bk. I, Chap. 7); the same points (save the delicate thrust that the creationists would have God labor every Sabbath) are made by Overton

[36] *MM*, pp. 58–72; *CM*, XV, 43–53; Bk. I, Chap. 7. Although Browne inclined toward creationism, he thought both the creationist and traducian theories "consist well enough with religion" (*Religio Medici*, I, 36). Hobbes listed creationism among the absurdities of Scholasticism (*Leviathan*, p. 371; Chap. 46).

[37] Ross, *The Philosophicall Touch-stone*, p. 99; cf. Holland, *Prerogative of Man*, p. 26.

(*MM*, pp. 61, 66), who characteristically seizes the opportunity to be offensive: "so Whoremongers and Adulterers sets God a work to create *Souls* for their *Bastards,* which is to make God a slave to their lusts."

Milton connects the problem of the origin of the soul with the origin of sin and, like the mortalists opposed by Ross (*The Philosophicall Touch-stone,* p. 119), he makes capital of Augustine's uncertainty in the matter: ". . . Augustine was led to confess that he could neither discover by study, nor prayer, nor any process of reasoning, how the doctrine of original sin could be defended on the supposition of the creation of souls." Since, as the creationists say, the soul comes from God, it must be pure; if it be pure, but "destitute of original righteousness" (as they say), then it is unjust of God to put this defenseless soul into a corrupt body (*CM,* XV, 45–49; Bk. I, Chap. 7). Overton similarly tries to put the creationists in the position of believing that God is either the author of sin or an unjust tyrant:

> And so Gods immediate hand is the cause of all sin, that man had better been without this soul; for it must needs be some damnable wicked spirit, or some Devil that God puts in him . . .: No marvell then if Reprobates must needs sin and be damned, since God *infuses* such a *malignant Soul,* that councels them with *Jobs* wife to *curse God and dye,* yea such a one as wholly works out their condemnation: This is as if a man should break his horses legs and then knocke out his brains for halting. If it be said the soul comes pure from God, and it is the body that corrupteth it. I Answer, that this to excuse God one way, makes him like the tyrant *Mezentius,* that bound living men to dead bodyes, till the putrefaction and corruption of the stinking corps had killed them [*MM,* p. 63].

Although their arguments for traducianism are similar, Milton's discussion contains no ideas or expressions that must necessarily be thought to have originated with Overton. Milton differs from Overton in two matters. Whereas Overton argues that the creationist hypothesis denies that Christ has a human soul (*MM,* p. 61), Milton says that, since

Christ's soul was generated supernaturally, the origin of his soul has no bearing on the traducian argument (*CM*, XV, 53; Bk. I, Chap. 7); and Milton uses the Scholastic idea that the whole soul is in every part of the body to argue that the soul is in the father's seed (*CM*, XV, 47–49; Bk. I, Chap. 7) without regard to Overton's reiterated scorn for this particular Scholastic idea. If, Overton says, we ask the "Soularies" where the soul is, "they *flap us i'th mouth* with a *Ridle, tota in toto, & tota in qualibet parte,* the whole in the whole, and the whole in every part . . . . So that it must either be held to be *ubiquitory,* which is an *Attribute* peculiar to God; or else multiplicable by corpulent division: and so, were a man minced into *Atomes,* cut into innumerable bits, there would be so many innumerable whole Souls, else could it not be wholly in every part" (*MM*, p. 72). In the arguments for mortalism proper, we shall find a comparable situation: the central ideas of Milton and Overton are identical and their arguments are often similar, but each man employs material not used by the other, and they sometimes disagree on subordinate issues.

Milton and Overton both believe in the thnetopsychist variety of mortalism. They have nothing to do with the psychopannychist opinion of an immortal substance that sleeps somewhere out of the body until it is awakened to rejoin the body on the Last Day. They do not share the mystical views of the experimental Christians, who thought the human soul was part of the Divine Essence.[38] Their scriptural argument turns on the meaning of Gen. 2:7, on the question of precisely what it was that God created when he made Adam from the dust of the earth. According to Milton, God breathed into the body of Adam a "measure of the divine virtue or influence," just as "every living thing receives animation from one and the same source of life and breath."

---

[38] Milton explicitly denied that the soul was part of God, or participated in the divine nature (*CM*, XV, 39; Bk. I, Chap. 7); Overton thought God in Gen. 2:7 merely gave man the "property of life" (*MM*, p. 7).

Nor has the word "spirit" any other meaning in the sacred writings, but that breath of life which we inspire, or the vital, or sensitive, or rational faculty, or some action or affection belonging to those faculties.

Man having been created after this manner, it is said, as a consequence, that "man became a living soul"; whence it may be inferred (unless we had rather take the heathen writers for our teachers respecting the nature of the soul) that man is a living being, intrinsically and properly one and individual, not compound or separable, not, according to the common opinion, made up and framed of two distinct and different natures, as of soul and body, but that the whole man is soul, and the soul man, that is to say, a body, or substance individual, animated, sensitive, and rational; and that the breath of life was neither a part of the divine essence, nor the soul itself, but as it were an inspiration of some divine virtue fitted for the exercise of life and reason, and infused into the organic body; for man himself, the whole man, when finally created, is called in express terms "a living soul [*anima vivens*]" . . . .

Where however we speak of the body as of a mere senseless stock, there the soul must be understood as signifying either the spirit, or its secondary faculties, the vital or sensitive faculty for instance . . . . But that the spirit of man should be separate from the body, so as to have a perfect and intelligent existence independently of it, is nowhere said in Scripture, and the doctrine is evidently at variance both with nature and reason, as will be shown more fully hereafter. For the word "soul" is also applied to every kind of living being; Gen. i. 30. "to every beast of the earth," &c. "wherein there is life [*anima vivens*]." vii.22. "all in whose nostrils was the breath of life [*spiritus vitae*], of all that was in the dry land, died"; yet it is never inferred from these expressions that the soul exists separate from the body in any of the brute creation [*CM*, XV, 39–43; Bk. I, Chap. 7].

Conklin, supposing the "whole man" concept to have originated when Milton came to understand a subtle point in philology, presents the results of his own study of the Hebrew word "nephesh" (*anima*, soul) in the lexicons of the period, "for these would be the first tool of reference in Milton's private perusal of Scripture" (*Biblical Criticism*,

p. 77). Milton may indeed have consulted lexicons, but he probably was provoked to do so by an interpretation of Genesis that he had already heard discussed. Both Overton and (as we shall see) Hobbes had earlier expressed the idea that in Scripture "soul" means "the whole man" or a "living creature." Indeed, it is difficult to imagine how the thnetopsychists in the first days of the Reformation could have argued from Scripture in any very different way; Calvin, it may be remembered, tells us in his *Psychopannychia* they "will sooner admit anything than its [the soul's] real existence, maintaining that it is merely a vital power which is derived from arterial spirit on the action of the lungs, and being unable to exist without body, perishes along with the body, and vanishes away and becomes evanescent till the period when the whole man shall be raised again" (*Tracts,* tr. Beveridge, III, 419). The idea that "soul" in Scripture refers to any living being and that "spirit" simply means "life" or "thought" permeates *Mans Mortalitie* and is behind most of the exegesis. Unlike Milton, Overton does not introduce the concept in general terms, and so it is difficult to find passages by Overton in which the idea is not expressed too narrowly in the exposition of particular texts. For the purpose of comparison with Milton, the following comments of Overton on scriptural texts are of sufficient generality to indicate at least that he anticipated the essential elements in Milton's analysis of the scriptural meaning of "soul" and "spirit."

To the idea that Gen. 2:7 proves the soul of man is immortal, Overton answers:

> Then so is the soul of a Beast; for *Solomon* saith, *their breath is all one, Eccl.* 3.19. and *David* reckoning up the creatures and man amongst them, saith indifferently of them all, God *hideth* his *face, and they are troubled,* he *taketh away their breath, they dye, and returne to their dust, Psal.* 104.29. and this is further amplified in *Gen.* 1.30. *to every thing in the Earth wherein there is a living soul &c.* and *cap.* 7.21.22. *all flesh dyed, in whose nostrils was the breath of life:* and *Num.* 31.28. all which make no

difference betwixt them, *but as the one dyeth, so dyeth the other, and man hath no preheminence above a beast: For what man is he that liveth, and shall not see death, or deliver his soul from the hand of the grave? Selah. Psal. 89.48 [MM, p. 55].*

Commenting on 1 Cor. 6:20 ("therefore glorify God in your body, and in your spirit"), Overton refuses to believe the Apostle implied a metaphysical distinction:" by *body* and *spirit,* is meant whole man, aiming at a thorough and perfect *sanctification,* as well in that which respecteth thought, [*the spirit*] as in that which respecteth action, [*the body:*] inwardly to glorifie God, as well as outwardly *to flee fornication, &c* (MM, p. 57; the brackets are in Overton's text). Finally, in the terms of the "schools," Overton states the thnetopsychist opinion on the inseparability of body and soul:

> ... Man is but a creature whose severall parts and members are endowed with proper natures or Faculties, each subservient to other, to make him a living Rationall Creature; whose degrees or excellencies of naturall Faculties make him in his kind more excellent then the Beasts: ... it doth not follow, that those Faculties together are a Being of themselves immortall: For as the members cannot be perfect members without them, so they cannot be faculties without their members; and separation cannot be without destruction of both: ... The *Forme* is so in the *Matter,* and the *Matter* so in the *Forme;* as thereby, and not else, is an *Existence,* or *Humane Entity* [MM, p. 22].

Like all the soul sleepers, Milton and Overton passionately believed in an afterlife of rewards and punishments, for it was in that life that God's justice would be vindicated. Unorthodox as Milton and Overton were, their understanding of Christian doctrine was far more traditional, far more "literal," than that of those experimental Christians who rejected the doctrines of the General Resurrection and of a personal, immortal life after death. In taking the Hebrew view that "spirit" was "breath" and "soul" was "living creature," Milton and Overton rejected the Christian heritage that led away from the Hebrew monistic view of man to the Greek dualism of body and soul, matter and spirit, but they, like the soul sleepers before them, reconciled their doctrine of total death with traditional Christian eschatology. In addition to the traditional "last things"—Death, Judgment, Heaven, and Hell—the soul sleepers stressed a fifth event, Resurrection, not because they believed the immortalists actually denied the General Resurrection (though Overton, like Tyndale, in the heat of controversy accused them of denying it in effect), but because the unscriptural doctrine of the soul's immortality pushed the scriptural doctrine of the resurrection of the whole man into a minor, if not irrelevant, position in the Christian eschatological drama. Once the scriptural doctrine of Death is properly understood, they argued, Resurrection will again assume the essential role it once had in the teaching of St. Paul.

Overton and Milton found the key texts for Pauline mortalism in 1 Cor. 15, particularly in the seventeenth to nineteenth verses. It is curious that the sincerity of Overton's professed belief in the General Resurrection has been frequently doubted and Milton's has not. It will therefore be necessary to show here how passionately (far less temperately than Milton) Overton expressed his faith in the General Resurrection. Overton says of St. Paul:

all his hope of future life was grounded upon the Resurrection, and that his hope was altogether grounded thereon, he confirmes, 1 *Cor.* 15. arguing, *If Christ be not risen, the dead should not rise:* and (ver. 18.) *They which are fallen asleep in Christ are perished,* and (ver. 14.) *Then is our faith also in vaine; whose end* (1 Pet. 1.9.) *is the salvation of our soules.* How should then all be in vaine, if our *soules,* as soone as breath is out of the body enter into glory and salvation? For by *that,* though there were no *Resurrection* of the flesh, we should receive the end of our *Faith,* the *Salvation of our Soules:* Nay further, he maketh *all our hope to be in this life, if there be no Resurrection;* for *ver.* 19. having shown the evils that follow the denyall of the Resurrection, saith; *If in this life onely we have hope in Christ, we are of all men most miserable:* whence plainly appeares, that the deniall of the Resurrection con-

fines all our hopes within this life, and so all our suffer-
ings, persecutions, prayers, faith, &c. were to no purpose:
which could not be by this *Soulary* fancy of present reward
of beatitude after this life [*MM*, pp. 13–14].

The last few lines anticipate the emphasis the Baptist political agitator was to put on the resurrection of the dead and
heavenly rewards when, five years later, he defied the Council of State. The conclusion of *Mans Mortalitie* shows how
the mortalist doctrine actually serves to direct a Christian's
attention to the essentials of a scriptural faith: "Thus having
found Mans Foundation to be wholy in the *Dust,* from
thence taken, and thither to returne: Let this then be the
use of all: That man hath not wherewith at all to boast no
more then of dirt under his feet, but is provoked wholy out
of himself, to cast himself wholy on *Jesus Christ* with whom
in God *our lives are hid,* that when he *who is our life* shall
appear, he might also with him appear in glory, to whom
be the honour of our immortality for ever, and for ever.
Amen" (*MM*, p. 76). One may, I suppose, dismiss this statement as the pretense of a sly rationalist who is actually
trying to undermine the essentials of the Christian religion,
but it is not so clear that belief in the immortality of the
soul is an essential doctrine of Christianity. If it is, then
Milton no less than Overton must be denied the title of
"Christian."

It would be tedious to discuss all the numerous places in
which Milton and Overton argue mortalism from the same
texts, for the parallels that may be observed are not so
striking as to suggest that Milton was directly indebted to
Overton. It will be useful, nevertheless, to note a few of the
more unusual ideas that are common to both authors lest
anyone conclude rashly that Milton broke ground when he
was in fact working tilled soil.

In his attempt to account for St. Paul's apparent belief that
his death would bring him immediately into the presence
of Christ (Phil. 1:23), Milton points out, alluding to Aristotle,
that the dead have no sense of time (*CM*, XV, 241–243; Bk. I,
Chap. 13); Overton explains Paul's "desire to depart" in the

same way (though without reference to Aristotle), and Baxter later complains that one "Lushington" resorted to the same "evasion."[39] Countering another strong text for the "Soularies"—"the spirit shall return unto God that gave it" (Eccles. 12:7)—Milton and Overton both observe that "spirit" means "life" because if it meant the orthodox "soul" then we would have to believe that even the souls of the wicked go to God (*MM*, p. 55; *CM*, XV, 237; Bk. I, Chap. 13). Both mortalists agree that the story of Dives and Lazarus, so often cited as a proof by the orthodox disputants, is a parable, and, as such, it cannot be cited as a record of historical fact.[40]

Milton's opinion that "the soul even of Christ was for a short time subject unto death on account of our sins"[41] may seem shocking, but the idea would not have been surprising in radical circles: Overton asserts the total death of Christ plainly and vigorously (*MM*, pp. 17, 41–42), and, as we have seen, earlier the Anabaptist Edward Wightman and the English General Baptist community at Haarlem had the same opinion. To oppose such blasphemy, the orthodox had a text ready at hand: "[Christ] being put to death in the flesh, but quickened by the Spirit: By which also he went and preached unto the spirits in prison" (1 Pet. 3:18–19). These dark verses had often been used as a proof-text for belief in the existence of purgatory and in the harrowing of hell by Christ's soul before the Resurrection, meanings clearly unacceptable to Milton. Milton therefore had to reach into his philological knowledge to show that in the Syriac version "in prison" is given as "in the grave" (*CM*, XV, 243; Bk. I, Chap. 13). Milton's exegesis, however, does not satisfy, since he leaves

[39] *MM*, pp. 32–33; Richard Baxter, *Saints Everlasting Rest* (London, 1650), p. 258. It may be that Baxter refers to Thomas Lushington, an Anglican divine who was once Browne's tutor at Pembroke.

[40] *MM*, pp. 55–56; *CM*, XV, 243; Bk. I, Chap. 13. Hobbes makes the same point in Chap. 44 of *Leviathan* (p. 342).

[41] *CM*, XV, 231; Bk. I, Chap. 13. In *Paradise Lost*, III, 245–249, the Son acknowledges that as Christ he will die totally, his "Soule" dwelling in the "loathsom grave" until he is raised by the power of the Father (the passage echoes Acts 2:31). The Son's reservation—"All that of me can die"—in this context is difficult to understand, especially since in the *Christian Doctrine* Milton insists that Christ died in his divine as well as in his human nature (*CM*, XV, 307–309; Bk. I, Chap. 16).

us with the idea that Christ preached to "dead spirits," which seems a futile activity. Overton, without evident knowledge of the Syriac version, also interprets "prison" as "the grave" and provides a fuller explanation; although his exegesis is not lucid, he does argue that Christ in his (preincarnate?) Godhead preached (inwardly?) to the wicked in the days of Noah, who are *now* dead (*MM*, pp. 56–57). Some such reading as this might quite possibly be what Milton meant to say. This is not the only place where Overton's handling of a troublesome verse of Scripture is superior to Milton's.[42]

It is surprising that Milton, since he believed that Christ was in the grave soul and body until the Resurrection, so lacks confidence when he discusses the chief proof-text of the immortalists—Christ's promise to the Good Thief (Luke 23:43), "Verily I say unto thee, Today shalt thou be with me in Paradise" (*CM*, XV, 243–245; Bk. I, Chap. 13). Indeed, when Milton's exegesis is compared with Overton's, particularly the greatly expanded exegesis of the 1655 edition (*Man Wholly Mortal*, pp. 75–85; *MM*, pp. 41, 46—47), Milton's efforts must be judged feeble. To be sure the verse was, as Milton observes, troublesome to the mortalists, but it is difficult to see why, having asserted the total death of Christ, Milton did not argue, like Overton (*Man Wholly Mortal*, pp. 75–77), that Christ was not in Paradise himself on the day of his execution; he might even have disturbed his opponents by pointing out the difficulty of reconciling the belief that Christ harrowed hell after his death with the belief that Christ was then with the Thief in Paradise. Instead Milton hesitantly says, without urging that the emendation

---

[42] Milton, however, in Bk. I, Chap. 13, of the *Christian Doctrine* noted the mortalist implications of some texts that Overton largely overlooked. Milton fully exploits the potential of 1 Thess. 4:13–17, a text that Tyndale had recognized as a powerful weapon for the soul sleepers, whereas Overton in all versions of *Mans Mortalitie* fails to give the passage his attention. Similarly, Milton makes good use of John 11:1–44 on the raising of Lazarus, a story Overton neglected until his revision of 1655 (*Man Wholly Mortal*, pp. 52–53, 63–64), where he does not make Milton's point that Christ addressed the soul of Lazarus in the grave, not in heaven. The location of Lazarus' soul before he was raised was part of Browne's "catalogue of doubts, never yet imagined nor questioned, as I know, which are not resolved at the first hearing . . ." (*Religio Medici*, I, 21).

is justified, that some people claim the passage has been erroneously punctuated and that the comma should follow "today" and not "thee." Conklin finds the emendation was recommended by the Socinian Valentin Smalcius and Josua Stegmann (*Biblical Criticism*, pp. 81–82), but Milton would more likely have garnered it from Overton's 1655 edition or from the popular *Gangraena*, where Edwards reported that a "Captain B.," arguing for mortalism with a member of Commons, had parried the Good Thief text in this way; Edwards added that this sectary was not the first to propose the change in punctuation.[43]

Although Overton did not argue for the transposition of the comma until the 1655 edition of his book (*Man Wholly Mortal*, pp. 84–85), he may have had the emendation in mind when he wrote his first exposition of the text late in 1643. Then Overton offered two readings, both consistent with mortalism: the first requires no repunctuation of the verse, but the second, which Overton favors, ignores the immediacy of reward that the unaltered text suggests and may well have assumed the transposed comma.

> If it [Paradise] be taken of any condition to be in that present day, it must be the same he was in himselfe; for he was to be *with* him, and that was *at rest, where the wicked cease from troubling, Job* 3.17. *where the prisoners rest together, and hear not the voice of the oppressour, Ver.* 18. If not to respect the present day, or any condition therein, (as is most probable) then it must be meant, (as the *Malefactour* desired) when he was in his *Kingdome*, which could not be before his Resurrection: therefore, the *Malefactour* could enjoy no such *soulary* beatitude, as from hence is supposed, and that before he had received this *Kingdome* himselfe; but must receive the *Paradise* as Christ did, by a totall Resurrection: wherefore it may well be he was one of the Saints that rose again soone after Christs Resurrection, *Mat.* 27.53 [MM, pp. 46–47].

[43] Edwards, *Gangraena*, III, 100–101. Baxter also rejects the transposition of the comma (*Saints Everlasting Rest*, p. 256).

In this exposition there is more uncertainty than is usual in Overton; evidently the Good Thief verse troubled him until he was able to handle it with the utmost confidence in his revised edition of 1655. Even in his earliest effort to explain the verse, however, Overton did not flounder about as Milton did, and he did not abandon the field to the enemy as Milton did when he concluded: "Nor is it necessary to take the word 'to-day' in its strict acceptation, but rather for a short time, as in 2 Sam. xvi. 3. Heb. iii. 7. However this may be, so much clear evidence should not be rejected on account of a single passage, of which it is not easy to give a satisfactory interpretation." Since Milton failed to show any difficulties in the orthodox interpretation of the verse (the immortalist reading has, after all, a fair claim to being "literal" and plain), he left himself vulnerable to the charge that only a mortalist could find it "not easy to give a satisfactory interpretation" of the passage.

It may seem strange, at first, to find the "atheist" Hobbes in the company of those who wrestled with Holy Scripture to discover truth, but there is nothing in Hobbes's mortalist exposition of Scripture that distinguishes his view of the soul from that of such devout thnetopsychists as young Browne, Milton, and Overton. As a philosopher Hobbes, of course, also grounds his mortalism on reason and on his contemptuous analysis of "Schoole Divinity," but when he argues that thnetopsychism is the doctrine of Scripture he does so without recourse to philosophical analysis. Like any other man, Hobbes cannot interpret Scripture without using his rational faculty or his knowledge of earlier Christian thought, but he does not suggest that Scripture must teach the mortality of the soul because it is the only doctrine conformable to reason. Like Milton and like Overton in his chapters on the scriptural doctrine, Hobbes interprets Holy Scripture primarily by evidence drawn from Scripture itself: he assembles the texts that support mortalism and seeks the meanings of such words as "soul" and "spirit" only in the context of scriptural usage.

Hobbes is best known today as the builder of a formidable materialistic philosophy; that philosophy, of course, denied the existence of incorporeal substances and insisted that all real substances are subject to the physical laws that govern matter. Such a system seems, on the face of it, to be incompatible with Christianity, but Hobbes devotes fully one-half of *Leviathan* to the demonstration that all his central ideas are clearly taught in Holy Scripture. One may view Hobbes's biblicism as an elaborate sham, or as a concession to the prejudices of his age, or as the aberration of a man so conditioned by the dominant Christian culture that he could not himself see the absurdity of using Scripture to support his essentially irreligious philosophy, but the fact remains that when Hobbes argued from Scripture he argued like a Protestant, maintaining that Scripture itself and not reason was his supreme authority.

Those contemporaries who did not like Hobbes's conclusions could, and did, denounce him as an atheist who perverted Scripture to destroy Christianity, but at a distance of three centuries we are perhaps obliged to arrive at a calmer judgment. We may not like his absolutist politics, we may deplore his extreme Erastianism, we may judge his anticlericalism immoderate and the theology he derives from Scripture perverse, but we must nevertheless be slow to declare insincere Hobbes's professed Christian faith and his avowal that the word of God as revealed in Holy Scripture gives us truths that are beyond the reach of reason (*Leviathan*, p. 199; Chap. 32). As the foregoing chapters of this study suggest, if we limit our concept of Protestant doctrine to those ideas which were acceptable to any of the established churches of England, Switzerland, and Germany, we shall exclude from even this copious fold the beliefs of many devout Reformation people who were themselves sure that they were Christians. Our increasing knowledge of the vitality and fecundity of the Radical Reformation has made it extraordinarily difficult to take a synoptic view of Christian doctrine in the first century of reformation. We may, of course, at the risk of falling into dogmatism, decide what the "true line" of Christian belief was in the period, but if such a definition excludes on the grounds of mortalism the troublesome Hobbes from the company of Christians, there is danger that it will also, with more offense to our sensibilities, exclude the poet of *Paradise Lost*.

But this is not the place to decide whether Hobbes was a sincere Christian. It will be enough at this time to establish that his denial that the soul is an immortal, incorporeal substance is not in itself evidence that he was attempting, as Basil Willey suggests, to undermine the Christian religion.[44] It will not be necessary here to present Hobbes's thnetopsychist doctrine in detail, for even a cursory reading of Chapters 38 and 44 of *Leviathan* will reveal that his mortalism differs in no important respect from the thnetopsychist views of Milton, Overton, and (as far as we know them) those of young Thomas Browne and the earlier exponents of the heresy. By the analysis of the "signification" of the words of Scripture Hobbes arrives at the same conclusions as Milton and Overton: "The *Soule* in Scripture, signifieth alwaies, either the Life, or the Living Creature; and the Body and Soule jointly, the *Body alive*," and "That the Soul of man is in its own nature Eternall, and a living Creature independent on the body; or that any meer man is Immortall, otherwise than by the Resurrection in the last day, (except *Enos* and *Elias*,) is a doctrine not apparent in Scripture."[45] As might be expected, most of his proof-texts and some of his interpretations of them are the same as those of Milton and Overton; like them, Hobbes notes with obvious pleasure that his view of the soul destroys the foundation of many Roman abuses, in particular the belief in purgatory, indulgences, ghosts, and the invocation of saints.[46]

[44] Willey, *Seventeenth Century Background*, pp. 100–106.

[45] Hobbes, *Leviathan*, pp. 337, 243; Chaps. 44, 38. Hobbes also attacks the immortalist opinion on rational grounds in his general attack on the "vain philosophy" of the "schools" (*ibid.*, pp. 368–370; Chap. 46), but he keeps his rational analysis strictly separate from his scriptural exegesis.

[46] *Ibid.*, pp. 338–339; Chap. 44; "The Christian Doctrine," *CM*, XV, 341; Bk. I, Chap. 16. In his textual notes, Fisch gives from the 1643 edition the passage that was dropped in the 1644 edition and restored in abbreviated form in the 1655 edition: *MM*, p. 102.

Like the soul sleepers since the time of Calvin, then, Hobbes insisted that the immortal life promised in Scripture would not begin until the Second Coming and the General Resurrection. According to Basil Willey, who does not seem to know that this doctrine appealed to such Christians in good standing as Tyndale, Luther, and Browne,[47] Hobbes expressed his expectation of immortality for the just on the Last Day merely to save appearances: "That far-off divine event was sufficiently distant and hypothetical to be safely admissible into Hobbes's scheme. To say that dead men wake on the Day of Judgment is, for him, as good as to say that they wake up never, only it has the advantage of sounding much more orthodox" (*Seventeenth Century Background*, p. 105). Willey assumes what is to be proved, that Hobbes was no Christian and therefore could have no sincere belief in the General Resurrection. Indulging a hostility toward Hobbes akin to that of the seventeenth-century divines, Willey suspects that the rest of Hobbes's eschatology is a mockery of the Christian religion (*Seventeenth Century Background*, p. 106), but he does not make clear how Hobbes's views undermine Christian values. The eschatology in *Leviathan* is certainly unusual. For one thing, the Kingdom of God is to be established on earth, and not just for a thousand years, but for eternity. The revivified just will live immortally as Christ's subjects in that Kingdom, and the reprobate will suffer in an earthly hell outside the Kingdom until they die the Second Death, for only the race of the damned, not the individuals, will have immortall life (*Leviathan*, pp. 342–344; Chap. 44). These ideas of Hobbes are neither antichristian nor particularly extraordinary, for they preserve the concept of an afterlife of rewards and punishments and are merely variants of the common radical beliefs that Christ will establish an earthly political Kingdom

---

[47] Willey notes that Milton was also a mortalist (*Seventeenth Century Background*, p. 105), but he does not compare the mortalism of Milton and Hobbes. Knowledge of Milton's mortalism does not moderate Willey's view that Hobbes advocated the doctrine to subvert Christianity, nor does it lead him to think that Milton too was an enemy of Christianity.

and that God will, in his mercy, not allow the damned to be tormented forever.[48] Nevertheless, according to Willey Hobbes must be undermining something essential to Christianity: "Even to-day the reader has a queer sense of lost bearings as he beholds all the splendours and glooms of Christian eschatology being thus given, by this prosaic intellect, a local habitation and a name" (p. 106). The millenarians so common in Interregnum England would not have felt this "queer sense of lost bearings," nor would twentieth-century millenarians like the Jehovah's Witnesses, the Christadelphians, and the Seventh-day Adventists.

We need not suppose that Hobbes was a spiritual brother of the Anabaptists because his scriptural exegesis parallels theirs in numerous places. Indeed, it is difficult to imagine a man who would be less likely than Hobbes to support men who called for an absolute separation of church and state, who defied the Erastian churches of their time, and who opposed their consciences to the might of "Leviathan"; nor would those who were proud of their martyrs have had anything to do with a man who advised Christians to deny their beliefs when the magistrate threatens them with punishment if they do not (*Leviathan*, p. 270; Chap. 42). Hobbes has none of the zeal and enthusiasm of such millenarians as Mrs. Attaway and the Fifth Monarchy Men, and his doctrine of absolute obedience to the civil authority sharply dissociates him from such rebellious sectaries. It is doubtful, however, that Hobbes would have conceived of the Kingdom of God as an earthly political kingdom ruled by Christ if the same view had not been expressed by innumerable radical Protestants since the early days of reformation. Like Milton, Hobbes was no sectary, but he was not ashamed to incorporate into his own system whatever he thought sound in the revisionist theology of the sects.

The most notable mortalists of the Interregnum were not all "Anabaptists," but neither were they men naturally

---

[48] For a good account of the religious motives of those seventeenth-century Christians who wanted to limit the duration of damnation, see Walker, *The Decline of Hell.*

averse to new ideas, certainly not to those that could with
some cogency be presented as the original doctrines of the
apostolic church. Among them only Browne has any claim
to doctrinal orthodoxy, and his orthodoxy was clearly a
hard-won prize, representing the victory of his faith over
his "extravagant and irregular" head. Hobbes, Milton, and
Overton all had, in varying degrees, the radical temperament,
and all willingly indulged it; even Hobbes, though he taught
absolute obedience to the sovereign power, was the "bugbear of the nation." In an age in which social and religious
doctrines were thoroughly interdependent, they were ready
to subvert the religious as well as the social traditions of a
civilization that, in their opinion, needed drastic overhaul.
The defender of the absolute power of the state, the defender of the regicides and of minority rule, and the defender
of the Leveller ideal of a republic built on what was very
nearly universal manhood suffrage—all could agree in their
dislike for the social and religious institutions that arose in
the Christian world under the leadership of the Church of
Rome. All expressed their contempt for Scholasticism and
thought its sophistries could be purged by a serious examination of the literal meaning of the Bible. Although Milton
and Overton wanted a church whose separate congregations
were free of interference from both external ecclesiastical
authority and civil power while Hobbes wanted a national
church that was rigorously controlled by the civil power,
none of the three had any interest in preserving the doctrines
of the postapostolic church which, in their opinion, had
degenerated in the hands of a self-seeking hierarchy and
usurped the prerogatives both of individual Christians and
civil rulers. The radicalism of the Anabaptists consisted in
their uncompromising challenge to the doctrines and polity
of the medieval Church, and with that challenge even
Hobbes, who left no room in his commonwealth for the
expression of dissent or the exercise of Christian liberty,
had sympathy.

The impact of radical Protestant doctrine on the intellectual life of seventeenth-century England has been obscured

by the force of the commonplace observation that under the spirit of the "Elizabethan Compromise" England's continuing religious strife concerned not so much the doctrine of the Church of England as its polity.[49] Even in the Interregnum the Independents quarreled with the Presbyterians primarily over matters of church government. But from the earliest days of the English Reformation there were many dissenters who were anxious to restore the doctrines and polity of the apostolic church insofar as they could be recovered by the careful study of Scripture. These radicals were ready to scrutinize in the light of Scripture all the traditional doctrines and practices of the Christian Church and would not limit themselves to examining such questions as the proper vestments and ceremonies to be used in worship or the right of each congregation to choose its own ministers and conduct its own affairs. Looking from the vantage point of three or four centuries, we can see a more uniform doctrine among English Christians in the first century or so of reformation than George Joye, or Bishop Jewel, or Thomas Edwards and Samuel Rutherford could see, for we can be more certain than they could that the radical ideas of some Christians would not flourish in the English climate.

In the midst of the doctrinal radicalism of the sectaries, the orthodox could take no comfort in the thought that Christian doctrine was largely a settled matter in England. Contemporary discussion in the first century of the English Reformation shows that the orthodox had good reason for being alarmed by the radicals' challenge to the official doctrinal position of the Church of England. If the idea that the soul is so dependent on the body that it cannot live without it seems to us a very modern idea that reflects the boldness with which seventeenth-century science and philosophy were prepared to attack medieval ideas, we shall

---

[49] Doctrinal dissent in England has not, of course, been ignored, as is testified by my references to such intellectual historians as George Huntston Williams, Champlin Burrage, W. T. Whitley, and H. John McLachlan.

fail to see that mortalism had far more support among radical, even fanatic, Christians than among natural philosophers, and that this Reformation attack on a medieval concept called not for an advance into the scientific future, but for a return to the apostolic past revealed in Scripture. When Mrs. Attaway the lacemaker or Lodowick Muggleton the tailor preached about the death of the soul, they did not speak to their flock of the laws of motion but of the nearness of the Second Coming, when God would destroy this contemptible world. When the Ranter Jacob Bauthumley taught the death of the personal soul he brought a joyous message of the return of the divine spark in man to God, the Alpha and the Omega. When Overton and other General Baptist mortalists taught the death of the soul, they hastened to speak of the forthcoming conquest of death and the "rising up of the corpses." And when Milton and Hobbes taught the death of the soul, they too argued for its being the restored doctrine of Christ and the prophets. Hobbes tried to synthesize that doctrine and his own doctrine of a world wholly consisting of matter in motion, thereby giving to his mortalism a flavor more familiar to modern readers, but the fact remains that Milton and Hobbes agreed about the scriptural doctrine of the soul.

The efforts of the Reformation sectaries to restore primitive Christianity as they conceived it are, for the most part, obscure to literary historians because sectarian ideas apparently seldom touch the lives and minds of men of literary stature and because a satisfactory understanding of these ideas is inordinately difficult to achieve. For the most part their ideas are recorded in hostile accounts, and their spoken words, the chief means by which their ideas were communicated to their contemporaries, are quite lost to us. But sectarian preaching spread radical theological doctrines in England effectively enough at the time, and particularly during the Interregnum these radical ideas were so widely dispersed that they seemed to the orthodox to threaten religion, civil society, and even the sanity of considerable portions of the population. In such a setting, it is not surprising that Hobbes and Milton, uncommitted to many medieval doctrines, were provoked to reconsider the scriptural support for many traditional Christian doctrines and to set down in their thnetopsychist analysis of Holy Scripture what was essentially an Anabaptist doctrine of the soul.

Epilogue

Although the soul-sleeping view was reasonably common in sectarian circles during the first century of the English Reformation, it remained a decidedly minority view which most churchmen, whether of the Anglican, Presbyterian, or Independent persuasion, did not examine on its own merits. In the three centuries since then the situation has changed, and those interested in the growth of support for the soul-sleeping concept may consult the second volume of LeRoy Edwin Froom's *The Conditionalist Faith of Our Fathers,* where that story is told in detail. It may be of interest here, however, to suggest briefly how commonplace among the major contemporary Protestant theologians is a doctrine of the soul that is Hebraic rather than Platonic. I do not mean to suggest, of course, that the following review represents a consensus of Protestant theologians about the meaning of "eternal life," or that the theologians mentioned have identical views on the subject, or that it is a complete account of contemporary Christian mortalists. The reader who wants an exact understanding of the views of these theologians should turn to the works referred to; I mean only to suggest the continuing vitality of some of the fundamental ideas of the English Reformation's mortalist radicals. In so doing, I shall supply particular references to support the general observation of Elmer G. Homrighausen, Dean of Princeton Theological Seminary, that a reaction against Greek body-spirit dualism with a consequent emphasis upon the resurrection of the body rather than the immortality of the soul is a significant movement in contemporary Christian theology.[1]

Most biblical scholars would agree with Johannes Pedersen[2] that the Jews of Old Testament times thought soul *(nephesh)* and body so interdependent that they could not conceive of true personality apart from a living body. Yet when Oscar Cullmann, Professor of the Theological Faculty

---

[1] *The Nature of Man in Theological and Psychological Perspective,* ed. Simon Doniger (New York: Harper, 1962), pp. 214–215.

[2] Johannes Pedersen, *Israel: Its Life and Culture,* tr. Aslaug Møller, 4 vols. in 2 (1926; reprint, Copenhagen: Branner Og Korch, 1964), I–II, 170–181, 335.

of the University of Basel and of the Sorbonne, argued that the very same position was also the uniform view of the New Testament texts, his opinion generated much discussion. Delivering Harvard's Ingersoll Lecture for 1954-1955, Cullman declared that the New Testament teaches that death encompasses both soul and body and that the Christian hope of immortality rests on the promise of a New Creation, the resurrection of the dead on the Last Day.[3]

Cullmann doubtless drew attention to the soul-sleeping doctrine because he argued it at length from an eminent platform, but the opinion has been common enough among noted twentieth-century theologians. Indeed, Emil Brunner, Professor of Theology at Zürich (where Bullinger had thundered against the mortalists), writes: "this dying will be a dying of the whole man and not merely of the body. The whole man must pass through an experience of annihilation which affects the whole man since the whole man is a sinner . . . . But through Christ this death has lost its sting, for indeed the sting of death is sin, and this has been removed by Jesus Christ; it stands no longer between me and God."[4] Rudolf Bultmann's analysis shows St. Paul's understanding of "soul" to be the same as that of Old Testament tradition so that Paul's whole hope for immortality lay in the resurrection of the dead through Christ at the Parousia; Bishop John A. T. Robinson's study of Paul yields essentially the same conclusion.[5] Paul Tillich rejects the concept of the soul as a naturally immortal substance, calling it superstitious and unchristian, and he finds that "man's participation in eternal life beyond death is more adequately expressed by the highly

[3] Oscar Cullmann, *Immortality of the Soul or Resurrection of the Dead?* (New York: Macmillan, 1958). Despite the apparent thnetopsychism, Cullman elsewhere so interprets the dead "being with Christ" that his view is closer to the psychopannychism of Luther and Tyndale: *Christ and Time,* rev. ed., tr. Floyd V. Filson (Philadelphia: Westminster Press, 1964), pp. 138–141.

[4] Emil Brunner, *Man in Revolt: A Christian Anthropology,* tr. Olive Wyon (London: Lutterworth Press, 1939), pp. 475–476.

[5] Rudolf Bultmann, *Theology of the New Testament,* tr. Kendrick Grobel, 2 vols. (London: SCM Press, 1952), I, 203–210, 345–348; John A. T. Robinson, *The Body: A Study in Pauline Theology* (London: SCM Press, 1952), pp. 11–14, 81–83.

symbolic phrase 'resurrection of the body.' "[6] Reinhold
Niebuhr, too, finds that selfhood and the historical dimension
of experience are better preserved by the Hebraic idea of the
resurrection of the body than by the Greek idea of the immortality of the soul, which has "usurped" the Hebraic idea's
place in popular piety.[7]

Nor is the soul-sleeping idea limited to those theologians
whom some might consider "revisionist" or "modernist."
Apart from the fundamentalist sects discussed in the Introduction, mortalist attitudes may be found in more "orthodox"
places. The articles on "Resurrection" and "Soul Concept" in
The Encyclopedia of the Lutheran Church are distinctly committed to thnetopsychism, and Karl Barth, noting that St.
Paul in 1 Cor. 15 ignores the immortality of the soul in favor
of the persistence of the body, says "We are waiting for our
Body's redemption; if the body is not redeemed to obedience,
to health, to life, then there is no God . . . ."[8] Later, Barth expresses himself in a way that recalls Luther's contempt for
views of immortal life that he thought "heathen" rather than
distinctly Christian:

> And now the Christian man looks forward. What is the
> meaning of the Christian hope in this life? A life after
> death? An event apart from death? A tiny soul which, like
> a butterfly, flutters away above the grave and is still pre-
> served somewhere, in order to live on immortally? That
> was how the heathen looked on the life after death. But
> that is not the Christian hope. "I believe in the resurrection
> of the body." Body in the Bible is quite simply man, man,
> moreover, under the sign of sin, man laid low. And to this
> man it is said, Thou shalt rise again. Resurrection means
> not the continuation of this life, but life's completion.[9]

[6] Paul Tillich, *Systematic Theology,* 3 vols. (Chicago: University of
Chicago Press, 1951–1963), III, 409–414.

[7] Reinhold Niebuhr, *The Self and the Dramas of History* (New York:
Scribner's, 1955), pp. 77–78, 236–242.

[8] *The Encyclopedia of the Lutheran Church,* ed. Julius Bodensieck,
3 vols. (Minneapolis: Augsburg Publishing House, 1965); Karl Barth, *The
Resurrection of the Dead,* tr. H. J. Stenning (New York and London:
Fleming H. Revell Company, 1933), pp. 196–197 [the italics are Barth's].

[9] Karl Barth, *Dogmatics in Outline,* tr. G. T. Thomson (New York:
Philosophical Library, 1949), p. 154.

Thnetopsychism plays an important, perhaps an essential role in Bishop Anders Nygren's view that Divine Agape is an utterly unmotivated love and that to be unmotivated it must have for its object a being that is inherently worthless, destitute of any quality that may be thought to merit love. "Thus having found Mans Foundation to be wholy in the *Dust*, from thence taken, and thither to returne: Let this then be the use of all: That man hath not wherewith at all to boast no more then of dirt under his feet, but is provoked wholly out of himself, to cast himself wholly on *Jesus Christ* with whom in God *our lives are hid*, that when he *who is our life* shall appeare, he might also with him appeare in glory, to whom be the honour of our immortality for ever, and for ever," concludes Overton, and it may well be that his contentious spirit would have seen that the implications of his own theology were most fully developed in Bishop Nygren's synthesis of the doctrine of thnetopsychism and the doctrine of God's Agape:

> In the course of history these two—belief in the immortality of the soul and belief in the resurrection of the dead—have constantly been blended together; yet in fact they belong to two opposite religious and ethical worlds. Wherever the natural immortality of the soul becomes the fundamental religious dogma, we can be fairly certain that we are within the sphere of Eros. But where the Agape motif is dominant, it regularly expresses itself in belief in the resurrection of the dead. If participation in the eternal life of God is possible for man, the possibility is not based on any natural quality or endowment of man, but simply and solely on a mighty act of God. Just as it is God who makes the sinner righteous, so it is God who makes the dead to live. Resurrection is the sign-manual of the Divine Agape. It has nothing to do with the contrast between soul and body, as if one part of man's being were by nature divine and immortal while the other was impure and perishable. Death is the judgment of God upon human life in its entirety, and resurrection is the renewal of human life, likewise in its entirety, by God's love. It was a true sense of the issues involved in the contrast in question that led early Christian writers to insist on the belief in the "resurrection of the flesh" in op-

position to the "spiritualising" tendencies of Græco-Hel-
lenistic thought. It is therefore highly misleading when
modern scholars treat this belief as evidence of a "natural-
istic" outlook. So far from its being a piece of naturalism, it
shows a determination to resist the naturalism of Eros-reli-
gion, which treats eternal life as a natural product dependent on the inborn quality of the soul, instead of seeing in
it the personal operation of God's omnipotence and love.[10]

[10] Anders Nygren, *Agape and Eros*, tr. Philip S. Watson (Philadelphia:
Westminster Press, 1953), pp. 224–225.

Appendix

A Critical Survey of the Scholarship on
English Christian Mortalism

The study of English Christian mortalism has been hampered by the lack of a comprehensive history of the movement. Studies of individual mortalists (chiefly Milton) have therefore been unduly circumscribed and have often led to erroneous conclusions.

Despite its promising title, Archdeacon Francis Blackburne's history, first published in 1765, is disappointingly tendentious and incomplete: *An Historical View of the Controversy concerning an Intermediate State and the Separate Existence of the Soul between Death and the General Resurrection, Deduced from the Beginning of the Protestant Reformation to the Present Times*, 2d ed. (London, 1772). Blackburne, a Latitudinarian, defends the idea that the soul is unconscious until it is reunited with the body by presenting it as an opinion that had a status among the reformers comparable to that of the immortalist position. If we make due allowance for the exaggeration of the polemicist, we shall find that his book gives us a useful though limited outline of Reformation belief in soul sleeping. It is seriously deficient on the history of the idea among the sectaries, from the early Anabaptists to the sleepers of Overton's time. Blackburne is unaware of the relevant opinions of Browne, Hobbes, and Milton (the *Christian Doctrine* was still lost when he wrote) as well as those of the annihilationists discussed in Chapter II, above. Blackburne's faults are not rectified in the historical sections of Joseph Priestley's *Disquisitions* or his *A History of the Corruptions of Christianity*, 2 vols. (Birmingham, 1782).

Leonard N. Wright's "Christian Mortalism in England (1643–1713)" improves on Blackburne mostly in its survey of the soul-sleeping ideas of Overton's contemporaries, but the survey is nevertheless far from complete. Although he reports the opinions of the ancients and the Fathers on the soul, Wright is unable to identify any English Christian mortalists before Overton, not even Tyndale and Browne. Wright's later essay does not improve on the dissertation: "Christian Mortalism: a Prospectus for the History of an Idea," in *The Great Torch Race; Essays in Honor of Reginald Harvey Griffith*, ed. Mary Tom Osborne (Austin: University of Texas Press, 1961).

George H. Williams' *Radical Reformation* contains an informative discussion of mortalism that is, however, brief and scattered; the latter weakness is not entirely compensated by the excellent index, where the relevant references are grouped under the heading "psychopannychism." Ezra Abbot's bibliography, "The Literature of the Doctrine of a Future Life," published as an appendix to William R. Alger's *A Critical History of the Doctrine of a Future Life*, is a comprehensive and well-indexed survey of the literature. It contains information on most of the major books relating to the controversy about the sleep of the soul, but it neglects those works which argued the irrevocable annihilation of the personal soul.

By far the most comprehensive survey of the defenders of the temporary death or sleep of the soul is LeRoy Edwin Froom's *Conditionalist Faith*. Written to advocate the Seventh-day Adventist thnetopsychist position on the soul, Froom's study ignores the annihilationists, but it provides, often in microscopic detail, a history of the soul-sleeping concept from Old Testament times to the present. Despite the enormous length of his study, Froom does not treat our period adequately: because he is insufficiently aware of the popularity of soul-sleeping ideas among the English sects, his discussions of Tyndale, Milton, and Overton make them appear to be solitary figures standing against the tide of belief in the soul's innate immortality. Although his conclusions from his evidence are sometimes not warranted (he finds mortalism in *Paradise Lost* [Froom, *Conditionalist Faith*, II, 156] and assumes Overton was imprisoned for his mortalism [II, 162–163] rather than for his politics), Froom's history, with its numerous citations and large bibliography, is a useful starting place for the study of soul sleeping. It was, unfortunately, published too recently to affect most of the scholarship discussed here, and I became aware of it only at the conclusion of my own work.

Studies of individual mortalists have for the most part been limited to Milton and Overton, viewed in isolation from their mortalist contemporaries and the mortalist tradition. Denis Saurat, for example, like David Masson before him, is unaware of any English mortalists except Milton and Overton and his "sect"; therefore, assuming that the advocates of so unusual an idea must have been acquainted, Saurat argues on slender textual evidence that Milton helped Overton revise his pamphlet for the edition of 1655.[1] Had Saurat known that insistence on the resurrection of the body and soul to immortality had been an integral part of two varieties of the heresy for a century before the publication of *Mans Mortalitie*, he surely would not have cited the increased emphasis on the General Resurrection in the 1655 edition as evidence of Milton's

[1] Saurat, *Milton*, pp. 278–282. The same assumption lies behind Saurat's idea that a "sect" was organized around the mortalist doctrine (pp. 268–269). There were, of course, a good many soul sleepers in England in Overton's day, but the doctrine by itself would not have provided a very substantial basis for a religious group distinct from other sectarian associations. It is more likely that the sleepers maintained their membership in various Independent and General Baptist congregations, where their belief was tolerated and often encouraged. Masson's discussion of the "mortalist sect" is, in fact, limited to a paraphrase of *Mans Mortalitie: Life of Milton*, III, 156–157.

hand.[2] George N. Conklin also credits Milton with far too much originality in his mortalist argument: despite the fact that Milton clearly states that he is trying to settle an existing controversy, Conklin considers Milton's position "exceedingly esoteric."[3] Conklin's judgment (*Biblical Criticism*, pp. 117–118, n. 2) is based on the misapprehension that other mortalists derived their heresy not, like Milton, from Holy Scripture, but from a desire to eliminate all possibility of purgatory and thus frustrate Rome. Overton and Hobbes were both conscious of how soul sleeping hurt the Roman position, but they no less than Milton derived their belief from Scripture. In Bk. I, Chap. 16 of the *Christian Doctrine*, Milton himself remarks on the strength of the soul-sleeping position as an argument against purgatory (*CM*, XV, 341). Harry F. Robins rejects the likelier sources of Milton's mortalism among contemporary and nearly contemporary Protestant radicals[4] and seeks out the heresy in Origen. Not only do his citations from Origen fail to support his contention that "Origen and Milton hold identical mortalist theories" (*If This Be Heresy*, pp. 145–146), but Robins is also ignorant of Eusebius' report that Origen persuaded the third-century Arabian mortalists to give up their heresy.

Scholars have often not sufficiently recognized the scriptural and sectarian elements in English mortalism. Masson doubts Overton's professed belief that immortal life will follow the resurrection of the body, apparently because of Overton's "nauseous" arguments against the "Soulites" (*Life of Milton*, III, 157). Saurat agrees with Masson about Overton's secularism because he sees too little emphasis on the General Resurrection in the first edition of *Mans Mortalitie*; when, in the 1655 edition, Overton increases his emphasis on the General Resurrection, Saurat attributes that to Milton's influence (*Milton*, pp. 278–279). Masson's impressionism and Saurat's logic might both have been improved had they known something of the simple, pious, even fanatic Christians who had always constituted the great majority of English mortalists. W. K. Jordan,

---

[2] Saurat (*Milton*, pp. 277–278) also sees significance in the fact that Overton and Milton agree that soul and body are both generated naturally in procreation, but there was nothing new or even very unusual about traducianism in 1643. [Henry Woolnor,] *The Trve Originall of the Sovle* (London, 1641), a work that is essentially traducianist, was simply a recent expression of an old minority opinion. Luther was a traducianist (Williams, *Radical Reformation*, p. 582).

[3] "The Christian Doctrine," in *CM*, XV, 219; Bk. I, Chap. 13; Conklin, *Biblical Criticism*, p. 75. C. A. Patrides' brief article suggests the considerable alarm caused in orthodox circles by the popularity of mortalist opinions throughout the Reformation: "Psychopannychism in Renaissance Europe," *Studies in Philology*, LX (1963), 227–229.

[4] Robins, *If This Be Heresy*, pp. 7–8.

Joseph Frank, Perez Zagorin, A. S. P. Woodhouse, David Petegorsky,
and Eduard Bernstein all suggest that Overton belongs to a tradition
that was skeptical and secular rather than religious, but they do not
demonstrate much knowledge of the relevant religious tradition.[5]
It may seem impertinent to class Woodhouse, whose knowledge of
Puritanism is admirable, with men (Jordan excepted) whose interest
is primarily in political history, rather narrowly conceived. To be
sure, Woodhouse does interpret Overton against a Puritan setting,
but because he does not allow Anabaptism a sufficient role in the
background of sectarian Puritanism Woodhouse sees Overton as
tending toward secularism when he is actually well within the
century-old tradition of English Anabaptism. H. N. Brailsford and
Wilhelm Schenk, despite their less impressive knowledge of Puritanism in general, know just enough about the Anabaptist soul-
sleeping tradition to argue that Overton must be viewed as a Baptist,
not as a secularist or proto-Deist.[6] George Mosse joins Frank in
the opinion that Overton's God is similar to the "removed God"
of Deism although there is nothing in *Mans Mortalitie* that is incompatible with the idea of a God who exerts his providence in the
smallest matters.[7] In his effort to find forerunners of the Deists,
unaware that he is confusing two distinct and incongruous types
of Christian mortalism, Mosse links Overton with Thomas Webbe
and the Ranters ("Puritan Radicalism," p. 437) even though both of
the latter denied personal immortality altogether. George Williamson discusses Milton and Overton in the context of English interest
in Epicurean materialism (*Seventeenth Century Contexts*, pp. 148–
177) although Milton argued for mortalism from Scripture, not
reason, and Overton vigorously repudiated the *carpe diem* morality
associated with Epicurism. Since he overlooks the theological tradition of mortalism, Williamson leaves the impression that the
increase in the published defenses of the soul's immortality during

[5] Jordan, *The Development of Religious Toleration in England*, IV,
190–196; Frank, *Levellers*, pp. 40–44; Perez Zagorin, *A History of Political
Thought in the English Revolution* (London: Routledge & Kegan Paul,
1954), pp. 19–25; *Puritanism and Liberty*, ed. Woodhouse, Introduction,
pp. 55, 69; David W. Petegorsky, *Left-Wing Democracy in the English
Civil War* (London: Victor Gollancz, 1940), pp. 72–73; Eduard Bernstein,
Cromwell and Communism, tr. H. J. Stenning (1930; reprint, London:
Cass, 1963), pp. 90–93.

[6] Brailsford, *The Levellers and the English Revolution*, pp. 52–53;
Schenk, *The Concern for Social Justice in the Puritan Revolution*, pp.
168–171.

[7] Mosse, "Puritan Radicalism," 431–437; Frank, *Levellers*, pp. 43–44.
All the texts Mosse cites (pp. 434–435, nn. 54, 58, 60) to prove that Overton's God was the "removed God" of Deism are drawn from Overton's
argument for traducianism. There Overton insists that God has no direct
role in the creation of the soul, but nothing suggests that in any other
matter God does not intervene in the affairs of the natural order.

the Interregnum came in response to the challenge Browne issued when he said that philosophy had not yet disproved the mortality of the soul (*Seventeenth Century Contexts*, pp. 148–149). Although the philosophical implications of Christian mortalism need not be disregarded, Williamson, in failing to give an adequate account of even the Interregnum sectaries, seems to limit the mortalist controversy to a quarrel among philosophers and classicists.

Nathaniel Henry's neglected article stands as the first significant attempt to relate Interregnum mortalism to a native theological tradition.[8] Although he has no knowledge of the "antiresurrectionists," the annihilationists among the experimental Christians, Henry is well enough informed about the history of soul sleeping to conclude "that Milton's 'mortalism' is best explained in terms of dogmatic theology, even in the commonplaces of theology, rather than in terms of philosophy ... " ("Mortalism and the Intermediate State," p. 235). Suitably adapted to the more general study of all the English Christian mortalists, annihilationists as well as soul sleepers, Henry's conclusion was the working hypothesis of my own investigation.

Although they do not invalidate Henry's insight, the shortcomings of his article are numerous. His knowledge of the English mortalist tradition is sketchy at best; he can, for example, find no evidence of soul sleepers between 1560 and 1642 ("Mortalism and the Intermediate State," p. 239, n. 13). His grasp of historical fact is uncertain, and the bases for his historical judgments are sometimes obscure.[9] His interpretation of texts may fairly be called superficial,

---

[8] Nathaniel H. Henry, "Milton and Hobbes: Mortalism and the Intermediate State," *Studies in Philology*, XLVIII (1951), 234–249. Schenk (*Concern for Social Justice*, pp. 169–171) briefly pointed the way in 1948.

[9] Henry ("Mortalism and the Intermediate State") says that the Forty-two Articles of Edward were framed in 1533 (p. 238) and adopted in 1549 (p. 239, n. 13). Cranmer did not begin to draft the articles until 1551, and they were adopted in 1553: Hardwick, *History of the Articles*, pp. 111–113. Edward VI was not born, of course, until 1537. Henry also thinks that soul sleeping was not considered a heresy during the reigns of Elizabeth, James I, and Charles I (until 1642) because the Thirty-nine Articles did not include the condemnation of mortalism that the Edwardine Articles had enunciated ("Mortalism and the Intermediate State," p. 239, n. 13). Hardwick says (*History of the Articles*, pp. 134–135) that three of the Edwardine Articles that had been promulgated specifically to combat the Anabaptists were dropped because the Anabaptist threat had abated. If Henry's judgment on soul sleeping were correct, we would have to conclude that in the same reigns it was not heretical to believe that all men will eventually be saved or that resurrection from the dead means only a rising from sin in this life, for these opinions were also no longer condemned in the Thirty-nine Articles. Blackburne (*Historical View*, p. lxxi) says that the Church "has declined ... to interpose her judgment of this controversy for more than two hundred years ... ," but this is merely a polemical point, made in the hope of reopening the question of soul sleeping among Anglicans.

perhaps even perverse: in the face of their clear statements to the contrary, Henry speculates that Overton may have believed in the preexistence of souls (p. 245) and insists that Hobbes was not a soul sleeper (pp. 241–245). In the light of Overton's reiterated traducianism and the relevant passages in Hobbes, these views do not seem worth disputing.

Nevertheless, further study of the English mortalists corroborates Henry's primary conclusion that the Interregnum mortalists ought to be viewed as part of a minor scriptural tradition. Harold Fisch, apparently independently of Henry, arrives at substantially the same conclusion in his study of Hebraic influence in seventeenth-century English culture and in the introduction to his edition of Overton's tract.[10]

The annihilationists among the experimental Christians have been little studied, probably because they had no representative as important as Hobbes or Milton. One may get a view of the complexity and continental scope of this general approach to Christianity from Williams' *Radical Reformation*, where the references are indexed under "spiritualism." The best short account of the general tenets and mood of these popular mystics in England is George H. Sabine's lucid introduction to the works of Winstanley, though Rufus M. Jones's studies in Protestant mystics of the Reformation are also valuable.[11] Sabine is not informative about the continuity of the movement throughout the English Reformation, and neither Sabine nor Jones shows much interest in the enthusiasts' doctrine of the soul's destiny. Robert Barclay and Norman Cohn give valuable samples of Ranter writings; A. L. Morton stresses the political significance of the Ranters and includes generous citations from the works of Abiezer Coppe and Laurence Clarkson.[12]

[10] Fisch, *Jerusalem and Albion* (New York, 1964), and *MM*.

[11] Winstanley, *Works*, esp. pp. 21–51. The relevant works of Jones are *Studies in Mystical Religion, Spiritual Reformers,* and *Mysticism and Democracy.* An excellent aid to the understanding of the "enthusiastic" temper is Joe Lee Davis' "Mystical versus Enthusiastic Sensibility," *Journal of the History of Ideas,* IV (1943), 301–319.

[12] Barclay, *Inner Life,* Appendix to Chap. XVII; Cohn, *Pursuit,* pp. 287–330; Morton, *The World of the Ranters.*

Bibliography

Sixteenth- and Seventeenth-Century Sources

Acts and Ordinances of the Interregnum, 1642–1660. Ed. C. H. Firth and R. S. Rait. 3 vols. London: His Majesty's Stationery Office, 1911.

Alley, William. *The Poore Mans Librarie.* 2 vols. London, 1571.

Archer, John. *The Personall Reigne of Christ vpon Earth.* London, 1643.

Baillie, Robert. *Anabaptism, The Trve Fovntaine of Independency, Brownisme, Antinomy, [and] Familisme.* London, 1647.

———. *A Dissvasive from the Errours of the Time.* London, 1645.

Barlow, William. *A Dyaloge descrybing the Orygynal Group of These Lutheran Faccyons.* London, 1531.

Bauthumley, Jacob. *The Light and Dark Sides of God.* London, 1650. [Selections in Barclay, *Inner Life*, and Cohn, *Pursuit.*]

Baxter, Richard. *The Autobiography of Richard Baxter.* Ed. J. M. Lloyd Thomas. London: J. M. Dent, 1925.

———. *The Reasons of the Christian Religion.* London, 1667.

———. *Saints Everlasting Rest.* London, 1650.

Bradford, John. *The Writings of John Bradford.* Ed. Aubrey Townsend. Parker Society. Cambridge, 1848.

A Brief Confession or Declaration of Faith. London, 1660. [Reprinted in *Confessions of Faith.*]

Browne, Sir Thomas. *Religio Medici and Other Works.* Ed. L. C. Martin. Oxford: Clarendon Press, 1964.

Bullinger, Henry. *The Decades of Henry Bullinger: The Fourth Decade.* Tr. H. I. Ed. Thomas Harding. Parker Society. Cambridge, 1851.

———. *Fiftie Godlie Sermons.* Tr. H. I. 3 vols. London, 1577.

———. *An Holsome Antidotus or Counterpoysen, agaynst the Pestylent Heresye and Secte of the Anabaptistes.* Tr. John Veron. London, 1548.

———. *A Moste Sure and Strong Defence of the Baptisme of Children, against ye Pestiferous Secte of the Anabaptystes.* Tr. John Veron. Worcester, 1551.

———. *A Most Necessary & Frutefull Dialogue, between ye Seditious Libertin or Rebel Anabaptist, & the True Obedient Christiā.* Tr. John Veron. Worcester, 1551.

———. *Von dem unverschämten Frevel.* Zürich, 1531.

Calvin, John. *An Excellent Treatise of the Immortalytie of the Soule.* Tr. T. Stocker. London, 1581.

———. *Institutes of the Christian Religion.* Tr. John Allen. 7th American ed. 2 vols. Philadelphia: Presbyterian Board of Christian Education, 1936.

————. *Psychopannychia* (1542). In *Calvin's Tracts*. Tr. Henry Beveridge. 3 vols. Edinburgh, 1851, III, 413–490.

————. *A Short Instruction for to Arme All Good Christian People agaynst the Pestiferous Errours of the Common Secte of Anabaptistes*. London, 1549.

Clarkson, Laurence. *The Lost Sheep Found*. London, 1660. [Selections in Cohn, *Pursuit*.]

————. *A Single Eye All Light, No Darkness*. London, 1650. [Selections in Cohn, *Pursuit*.]

A Complete Collection of State Trials. Ed. T. B. Howell. 21 vols. London, 1811–1826.

Confession of Faith of Those Churches Which Are Commonly (Though Falsly) Called Anabaptists. 2d ed. London, 1646. [Reprinted in *Confessions of Faith*.]

Confessions of Faith, and Other Public Documents, Illustrative of the History of the Baptist Churches of England in the 17th Century. Ed. Edward Bean Underhill. The Hanserd Knollys Society. London, 1854.

The Creeds of Christendom. Ed. Philip Schaff. 4th ed. 3 vols. New York: Harper, 1919.

Creeds of the Churches. Ed. John H. Leith. Garden City, N.Y.: Doubleday Anchor, 1963.

Crisp, Stephen. *A Faithful Warning & Exhortation to Friends: To Beware of Seducing Spirits*. London, 1684.

Cudworth, Ralph. *A Sermon Preached before the Honourable House of Commons at Westminster, March 31, 1647*. Cambridge, 1647; reprint, New York: Facsimile Text Society, 1930. Ser. III, Vol. 2.

A Declaration of Faith of English People Remaining at Amsterdam in Holland. Amsterdam? 1611. [Reprinted in *Confessions of Faith*.]

Dexter, Franklin B. "A Report of the Trial of Mrs. Anne Hutchinson before the Church in Boston, March, 1638." *Proceedings of the Massachusetts Historical Society*, 2d Ser., IV (1887–1889), 159–191.

Digby, Sir Kenelm. *Observations vpon Religio Medici*. London, 1643; reprinted in Sir Thomas Browne, *Religio Medici*, Oxford: Clarendon Press, 1909.

A Discovery of the Abhominable Delusions of Those, Who Call Themselues the Family of Loue. London? 1622.

Donne, John. *The Sermons of John Donne*. Ed. George R. Potter and Evelyn M. Simpson. 10 vols. Berkeley and Los Angeles: University of California Press, 1953–1962.

The Early Lives of Milton. Ed. Helen Darbishire. London: Constable, 1932.

Edwards, Thomas. *Antapologia*. London, 1644.

———. *Gangraena*. 2d ed. London, 1646.

Everard, John. *Some Gospel Treasures*. Germantown, Pa., 1757.

Featley, Daniel. *The Dippers Dipt*. 6th ed. London, 1651.

Foxe, John. *The Acts and Monuments of John Foxe*. Ed. Josiah Pratt. 4th ed. 8 vols. London, 1877.

Frith, John. *A Disputacion of Purgatorye Made by Iohn Frith*. N.p., 1531?

Gardynare, Germen. *A Letter of a Yonge Gentylman . . . Wherein Men May Se the Demeanour & Heresy of John Fryth*. London, 1534.

Gill, Alexander. *The Sacred Philosophie of Holy Scripture*. London, 1635.

Goodwin, John. *Cretensis*. 2d ed. London, 1646.

———. *Theomachia*. London, 1644. [Reprinted in *Tracts on Liberty*.]

Goodwin, Thomas, Philip Nye, Sidrach Simpson, Jeremiah Burroughs, and William Bridge. *An Apologeticall Narration*. London, 1644. [Reprinted in *Tracts on Liberty*.]

Gorton, Samuel. "Samuel Gorton's Letter to Nathaniel Morton." In *Tracts and Other Papers*. Ed. Peter Force. Vol. IV, No. 7. Washington, D.C., 1846.

The Harleian Miscellany. Ed. William Oldys and Thomas Park. 10 vols. London, 1808–1813.

Hobbes, Thomas. *The English Works of Thomas Hobbes*. Ed. William Molesworth. 11 vols. London, 1839–1845.

———. *Leviathan*. Everyman's Library. London: J. M. Dent, 1965.

H[olland], G[uy]. *The Grand Prerogative of Humane Nature*. London, 1653.

———. *The Prerogative of Man: or, His Soules Immortality, and High Perfection Defended, and Explained against the Rash and Rude Conceptions of a Late Authour Who Hath Inconsiderately Adventured To Impugne It*. Oxford? 1645.

Hooper, John. *Later Writings of Bishop Hooper*. Ed. Charles Nevinson. Parker Society. Cambridge, 1852.

Hugh, William. *The Troubled Man's Medicine* (1546). In *Writings of Edward the Sixth*. British Reformers, Vol. 3. Philadelphia, 1842.

Hutchinson, Roger. *The Image of God, or Layman's Book* (1550). In *The Works of Roger Hutchinson*. Ed. John Bruce. Parker Society. Cambridge, 1842.

The Immortality of Mans Soule, Proved Both by Scriptvre and Reason. Contrary to the Fancie of R.O. in His Book Intituled Mans Mortality. London, 1645.

Jessop, Edmond. *A Discovery of the Errors of the English Anabaptists*. London, 1623.

Joye, George. *An Apology Made by George Joy, To Satisfy, If It May Be, W. Tindale.* Ed. Edward Arber. English Scholar's Library, No. 13. Birmingham, 1882.

Kennet, White. *A Register and Chronicle Ecclesiastical and Civil ... from the Restauration of King Charles II.* London, 1728.

Knewstub, John. *A Confutation of Monstrous and Horrible Heresies, Taught by H. N. and Embraced of a Number, Who Call Themselues the Familie of Loue.* London, 1579.

The Leveller Tracts: 1647–1653. Ed. William Haller and Godfrey Davies. New York: Columbia University Press, 1944.

Locke, John. *The Reasonableness of Christianity.* Ed. George W Ewing. Gateway Ed. Chicago: Henry Regnery, 1965.

Luther, Martin. *D. Martin Luthers Werke.* Kritische Gesamtausgabe. Weimar: Hermann Böhlau, 1883–

————. *An Exposition of Salomons Booke, Called Ecclesiastes or the Preacher.* London, 1573.

————. *Luther's Works.* Ed. Jaroslav Pelikan and Helmut T. Lehmann. 55 vols. American Ed. St. Louis: Concordia Publishing House; Philadelphia: Fortress Press, 1955–

————. *What Luther Says.* Ed. Ewald M. Plass. 3 vols. St. Louis: Concordia Publishing House, 1959.

Lyly, John. *Euphues: The Anatomy of Wit; Euphues & His England.* Ed. Morris W. Croll and Harry Clemons. 1916; reprint, New York: Russell & Russell, 1964.

Marston, John. *The Dutch Courtesan.* Ed. M. L. Wine. Regents Renaissance Drama Ser. Lincoln: University of Nebraska Press, 1965.

[Middleton, Thomas.] *The Famelie of Love.* London, 1608.

Milton, John. *The Works of John Milton.* Gen. ed. Frank A. Patterson. 18 vols. New York: Columbia University Press, 1931–1938.

Minutes of the General Assembly of the General Baptist Churches in England. Ed. W. T. Whitley. 2 vols. London: Kingsgate Press, 1909–1910.

More, Henry. *An Explanation of the Grand Mystery of Godliness* (1660). In *The Theological Works of ... Henry More.* London, 1708.

————. *Psychodia Platonica.* Cambridge, 1642.

More, Sir Thomas. *The Dialogue concerning Tyndale.* Ed. W. E. Campbell. London: Eyre and Spottiswoode, 1927.

————. *The Workes of Sir Thomas More Knyght ... Written by Him in the Englysh Tonge.* London, 1557.

Mornay, Philip de. *The Soul's Own Evidence for Its Own Immortality.* Tr. Sir Philip Sidney and Arthur Golding. Ed. John Bachiler. London, 1646.

————. *A Worke concerning the Trewnesse of Christian Religion.* Tr. Sir Philip Sidney and Arthur Golding. London, 1592.

Morton, Nathaniel. *New-Englands Memoriall.* Cambridge, Mass., 1669; reprint, Boston: Club of Odd Volumes, 1903.

Muggleton, Lodowick. *A True Interpretation of the Eleventh Chapter of the Revelation of St. John.* London, 1753. [Reprinted in Reeve and Muggleton, *Works.*]

[Nicholas, Henry.] *Evangelivm Regni: A Joyfull Message of the Kingdom.* Amsterdam? 1575?

[Overton, Richard.] *The Araignment of Mr. Persecvtion.* London? 1645. [Reprinted in *Tracts on Liberty.*]

————. *Mans Mortalitie.* Ed. Harold Fisch. English Reprints Ser., No. 21. Liverpool: Liverpool University Press, 1968.

————. *Mans Mortallitie.* Amsterdam (London), 1643.

————. *Mans Mortalitie.* Amsterdam (London), 1644.

————. *Man Wholly Mortal.* London, 1655.

————. *Man Wholly Mortal.* London, 1675.

————, John Lilburne, and Thomas Prince. *The Picture of the Councel of State.* London? 1649. [Reprinted in *Leveller Tracts.*]

Payne, John. *Royall Exchange.* Haarlem, 1597.

Pomponazzi, Pietro. *On the Immortality of the Soul* (1516). Tr. William H. Hay II. In *The Renaissance Philosophy of Man.* Ed. Ernst Cassirer *et al.* Chicago: University of Chicago Press, 1948, pp. 280–381.

A Proclamation against the Sectaries of the Family of Loue. London, 1580.

Prynne, William. *Twelve Considerable Serious Questions touching Chvrch Government.* London, 1644.

Reeve, John, and Lodowick Muggleton. *A Divine Looking-glass; or, the Third and Last Testament of Our Lord Jesus Christ.* 4th ed. London? 1760. [Reprinted in Reeve and Muggleton, *Works.*]

————, and Lodowick Muggleton. *Joyful News from Heaven.* N.p., n.d. [Reprinted in Reeve and Muggleton, *Works.*]

————, and Lodowick Muggleton. *A Transcendent Spiritual Treatise.* London, 1822. [Reprinted in Reeve and Muggleton, *Works.*]

————, and Lodowick Muggleton. *The Works of John Reeve and Lodowicke Muggleton.* 3 vols. London, 1832.

A Relation of Severall Heresies. London, 1646.

R[ogers], J[ohn]. *The Displaying of an Horrible Secte of Grosse and Wicked Heretiques, Naming Themselues the Familie of Loue.* London, 1578.

Rogers, Thomas. *The Catholic Doctrine of the Church of England.* Ed. J. J. S. Perowne. Parker Society. Cambridge, 1854.

Ross, Alexander. *Medicus Medicatus: or the Physicians Religion Cured.* London, 1645.

————. *Pansebia* or, *A View of All Religions in the World.* 5th ed. London, 1675.

————. *The Philosophicall Touch-stone: or Observations upon Sir Kenelm Digbie's Discourses of the Nature of Bodies, and of the Reasonable Soule . . . . And the Weak Fortifications of a Late Amsterdam Ingeneer, Patronizing the Soules Mortality, Briefly Slighted.* London, 1645.

Rutherford, Samuel. *A Survey of the Spirituall Antichrist.* 2 vols. in 1. London, 1648.

[Stegmann, Joachim.] *Brevis Disquisitio.* Eleutheropolis [Amsterdam], 1633.

————. *Brevis Disquisitio: or, A Brief Enquiry touching a Better Way . . . To Refute Papists, and Reduce Protestants to Certainty and Unity in Religion.* [Tr. John Bidle.] London, 1653.

A Svpplication of the Family of Loue. Cambridge, 1606.

Taylor, Jeremy. *The Great Exemplar of Sanctity and Holy Life.* London, 1653.

Tracts on Liberty in the Puritan Revolution: 1638–1647. Ed. William Haller. Columbia University Records of Civilization, No. 18. 3 vols. New York: Columbia University Press, 1933–1934.

Tyndale, William. *An Answer to Sir Thomas More's Dialogue.* Ed. Henry Walter. Parker Society. Cambridge, 1850.

————. *The Exposition of the Fyrst Epistle of Seynt Iohn.* Antwerp? 1531.

————, tr. *The New Testament.* Ed. N. Hardy Wallis. Cambridge: Cambridge University Press, 1938.

Wilkinson, William. *A Confutation of Certaine Articles Deliuered unto the Familye of Loue.* London, 1579.

Winstanley, Gerrard. *The Works of Gerrard Winstanley.* Ed. George H. Sabine. Ithaca: Cornell University Press, 1941.

[Winthrop, John.] *A Short Story of the Rise, Reign, and Ruin of the Antinomians, Familists & Libertines, That Infected the Churches of New England.* London, 1644.

[Woolnor, Henry.] *The Trve Originall of the Sovle.* London, 1641.

Woolton, John. *A Treatise of the Immortalitie of the Soule.* London, 1576.

[Wyclif, John.] *Wicklieffes Wicket.* N.p., 1548?

Other Sources and Secondary Works

Abbot, Ezra. "The Literature of the Doctrine of a Future Life." In William R. Alger. *A Critical History of the Doctrine of a Future Life.* 10th ed. New York, 1878.

Adams, Robert Martin. *Ikon: John Milton and the Modern Critics.* Ithaca: Cornell University Press, 1955.

Allen, Don Cameron. *Doubt's Boundless Sea*. Baltimore: Johns Hopkins Press, 1964.

Althaus, Paul. *The Theology of Martin Luther*. Tr. Robert C. Schultz. Philadelphia: Fortress Press, 1966.

Augustine, St. *The De Haeresibus of Saint Augustine*. Tr. Liguori G. Müller. Catholic University of America Patristic Studies, Vol. XC. Washington, D.C.: Catholic University of America Press, 1956.

Barclay, Robert. *The Inner Life of the Religious Societies of the Commonwealth*. London, 1876.

Barth, Karl. *Dogmatics in Outline*. Tr. G. T. Thomson. New York: Philosophical Library, 1949.

————. *The Resurrection of the Dead*. Tr. H. J. Stenning. New York and London: Fleming H. Revell Company, 1933.

Berens, Lewis H. *The Digger Movement in the Days of the Commonwealth*. London: Simpkin, Marshall, 1906.

Bernstein, Eduard. *Cromwell and Communism*. Tr. H. J. Stenning. 1930; reprint, London: Cass, 1963.

Bicknell, E. J. *A Theological Introduction to the Thirty-nine Articles*. 3d ed., rev. H. J. Carpenter. London: Longmans, 1955.

[Blackburne, Archdeacon Francis.] *An Historical View of the Controversy concerning an Intermediate State and the Separate Existence of the Soul between Death and the General Resurrection, Deduced from the Beginning of the Protestant Reformation to the Present Times*. 2d ed. London, 1772.

Brailsford, H. N. *The Levellers and the English Revolution*. Ed. Christopher Hill. Stanford: Stanford University Press, 1961.

Brunner, Emil. *Man in Revolt: A Christian Anthropology*. Tr. Olive Wyon. London: Lutterworth Press, 1939.

Bultmann, Rudolf. *Theology of the New Testament*. Tr. Kendrick Grobel. 2 vols. London: SCM Press, 1952–1955.

Burrage, Champlin. *The Early English Dissenters*. 2 vols. Cambridge: Cambridge University Press, 1912.

Butterworth, Charles C., and Allan G. Chester. *George Joye*. Philadelphia: University of Pennsylvania Press, 1962.

The Catholic Encyclopaedia. Ed. Charles G. Herbermann *et al.* 15 vols. New York: Appleton, 1907–1912.

Clebsch, William A. *England's Earliest Protestants: 1520–1535*. Yale Publications in Religion, No. 11. New Haven: Yale University Press, 1964.

Cohn, Norman. *The Pursuit of the Millennium*. Rev. ed. New York: Oxford University Press, 1970.

Cole, Marley. *Jehovah's Witnesses: The New World Society*. New York: Vantage Press, 1955.

Conklin, George N. *Biblical Criticism and Heresy in Milton.* New York: King's Crown Press, 1949.

Cooper, Anthony Ashley. *Characteristics of Men, Manners, Opinions, Times, etc.* Ed. John M. Robertson. 2 vols. London: G. Richards, 1900.

Cullmann, Oscar. *Christ and Time.* Rev. ed. Tr. Floyd V. Filson. Philadelphia: Westminster Press, 1964.

——. *Immortality of the Soul or Resurrection of the Dead?* New York: Macmillan, 1958.

Davis, Joe Lee. "Mystical versus Enthusiastic Sensibility." *Journal of the History of Ideas,* IV (1943), 301–319.

The Dictionary of National Biography. Ed. Sir Leslie Stephen and Sir Sidney Lee. 27 vols. London: Oxford University Press, 1937–

Eironnach. "Notes on Certain Theosophists and Mystics." *Notes and Queries,* 4th Ser., I (1868), 597–600.

The Encyclopedia of the Lutheran Church. Ed. Julius Bodensieck. 3 vols. Minneapolis: Augsburg Publishing House, 1965.

Eusebius. *Church History.* Tr. Arthur C. McGiffert. In *A Select Library of Nicene and Post-Nicene Fathers.* Ed. Philip Schaff and Henry Wace. 2d Ser., 14 vols. New York, 1890–1900. Vol. I.

Fisch, Harold. *Jerusalem and Albion.* New York: Schocken, 1964.

Frank, Joseph. *The Levellers.* Cambridge, Mass.: Harvard University Press, 1955.

Froom, LeRoy Edwin. *The Conditionalist Faith of Our Fathers.* 2 vols. Washington, D.C.: Review and Herald Publishing Association, 1965–1966.

Gordon, Alexander. "Ancient and Modern Muggletonians." *Proceedings of the Literary and Philosophical Society of Liverpool,* XXIV (1869–1870), 186–244.

——. "The Origins of the Muggletonians." *Proceedings of the Literary and Philosophical Society of Liverpool,* XXIII (1868–1869), 247–279.

Gorton, Adelos. *The Life and Times of Samuel Gorton.* Philadelphia: G. S. Ferguson, 1908.

Hardwick, Charles. *A History of the Articles of Religion.* 3d ed. London, 1884.

Henry, Nathaniel H. "Milton and Hobbes: Mortalism and the Intermediate State." *Studies in Philology,* XLVIII (1951), 234–249.

Hessels, J. H. "Henrick Niclaes: The Family of Love." *Notes and Queries,* 4th Ser., IV (1869), 356–358, 404–406, 430–432.

Jessopp, Augustus. *The Coming of the Friars.* London, 1889.

John of Damascus, St. *Saint John of Damascus: Writings.* Tr. Frederic H. Chase, Jr. Fathers of the Church, Vol. 37. New York: Fathers of the Church Inc., 1958.

Jones, Rufus M. *Mysticism and Democracy in the English Commonwealth.* Cambridge, Mass.: Harvard University Press, 1932.

———. *Spiritual Reformers in the 16th and 17th Centuries.* Boston: Beacon Press, 1959.

———. *Studies in Mystical Religion.* London: Macmillan, 1909.

Jordan, W. K. *The Development of Religious Toleration in England.* 4 vols. Cambridge, Mass.: Harvard University Press, 1932–1940.

Kelley, Maurice. *This Great Argument.* Princeton Studies in English, No. 22. Princeton: Princeton University Press, 1941.

Knox, Ronald A. *Enthusiasm.* New York: Oxford University Press, 1950.

Littell, Franklin H. *The Anabaptist View of the Church.* 2d ed. Boston: Starr King Press, 1958.

McLachlan, H. John. *Socinianism in Seventeenth-Century England.* London: Oxford University Press, 1951.

Masson, David. *The Life of John Milton.* 7 vols. London, 1859–1880.

The Mennonite Encyclopedia. Ed. Harold S. Bender and C. Henry Smith. 4 vols. Scottdale, Pa.: Mennonite Publishing House, 1955–1959.

Morton, A. L. *The World of the Ranters.* London: Lawrence & Wishart, 1970.

Mosheim, Johann. *Institutes of Ecclesiastical History.* Tr. James Murdock. 12th ed. London, 1880?

Mosse, George L. "Puritan Radicalism and the Enlightenment." *Church History,* XXIX (1960), 424–439.

The Nature of Man in Theological and Psychological Perspective. Ed. Simon Doniger. New York: Harper, 1962.

Niebuhr, Reinhold. *The Self and the Dramas of History.* New York: Charles Scribner's Sons, 1955.

Nuttall, Geoffrey F. *The Holy Spirit in Puritan Faith and Experience.* Oxford: Blackwell, 1946.

Nygren, Anders. *Agape and Eros.* Tr. Philip S. Watson. Philadelphia: Westminster Press, 1953.

Origen. "Dialogue of Origen with Heraclides." *Alexandrian Christianity.* Tr. John Oulton and Henry Chadwick. Library of Christian Classics, Vol. II. Philadelphia: Westminster Press, 1954.

The Oxford English Dictionary. Ed. James A. H. Murray *et al.* 13 vols. Oxford: Clarendon Press, 1933.

Patrides, C. A. " 'Paradise Lost' and the Mortalist Heresy." *Notes and Queries,* CCII (1957), 250–251.

———. "Psychopannychism in Renaissance Europe." *Studies in Philology,* LX (1963), 227–229.

———. "The Salvation of Satan." *Journal of the History of Ideas,* XXVIII (1967), 467–478.

Pedersen, Johannes. *Israel: Its Life and Culture.* Tr. Aslaug Møller. 4 vols. in 2. 1926; reprint, Copenhagen: Branner og Korch, 1964.

Petegorsky, David W. *Left-Wing Democracy in the English Civil War.* London: Victor Gollancz, 1940.

Porter, Kenneth W. "Samuell Gorton, New England Firebrand." *New England Quarterly,* VII (1934), 405–444.

Priestley, Joseph. *Disquisitions relating to Matter and Spirit.* 2d ed. 2 vols. Birmingham, 1782.

———. *A History of the Corruptions of Christianity.* 2 vols. Birmingham, 1782.

Puritanism and Liberty. Ed. A. S. P. Woodhouse. 2d ed. Chicago: University of Chicago Press, 1951.

Robins, Harry F. *If This Be Heresy.* Illinois Studies in Language and Literature, No. 51. Urbana: University of Illinois Press, 1963.

Robinson, John A. T. *The Body: A Study in Pauline Theology.* Studies in Biblical Theology, No. 5. London: SCM Press, 1952.

Saurat, Denis. *Milton: Man and Thinker.* London: J. M. Dent, 1944.

Schenk, Wilhelm. *The Concern for Social Justice in the Puritan Revolution.* London: Longmans, Green, 1948.

Spalding, Arthur W. *Origin and History of Seventh-day Adventists.* 4 vols. Washington, D.C.: Review and Herald Publishing Association, 1961–1962.

Stace, W. T. *Mysticism and Philosophy.* Philadelphia: J. B. Lippincott, 1960.

Strype, John. *Annals of the Reformation.* 7 vols. Oxford, 1824.

———. *The Life and Acts of John Whitgift, D.D.* 3 vols. Oxford, 1822.

Theologia Germanica. Tr. Susanna Winkworth. Ed. Willard Trask. London: Victor Gollancz, 1951.

Thomas, Allen C. "The Family of Love, or the Familists." *Haverford College Studies,* No. 12 (1893), 1–46.

Tillich, Paul. *Systematic Theology.* 3 vols. Chicago: University of Chicago Press, 1951–1963.

Troeltsch, Ernst. *The Social Teaching of the Christian Churches.* Tr. Olive Wyon. 2 vols. London: Allen & Unwin, 1950.

Underwood, A. C. *A History of the English Baptists.* London: Kingsgate Press, 1947.

Walker, D. P. *The Decline of Hell.* Chicago: University of Chicago Press, 1964.

Wendel, François. *Calvin.* Tr. Philip Mairet. New York: Harper and Row, 1963.

Whiting, C. E. *Studies in English Puritanism from the Restoration to the Revolution, 1660–1688.* London: Macmillan, 1931.

Whitley, W. T. *A History of the British Baptists.* The Angus Lectureship, 9. London: C. Griffin, 1923.

Wilbur, Earl M. *A History of Unitarianism.* Cambridge, Mass.: Harvard University Press, 1947.

Willey, Basil. *The Seventeenth Century Background.* London: Chatto & Windus, 1950.

Williams, George H. "Camillo Renato (c. 1500–?1575)." Italian Reformation Studies in Honor of Laelius Socinus (1562–1962). Ed. John A. Tedeschi. *The Proceedings of the Unitarian Historical Society,* XIV (1962–1963), 103–183.

————. *The Radical Reformation.* Philadelphia: Westminster Press, 1962.

————. *Wilderness and Paradise in Christian Thought.* New York: Harper, 1962.

Williamson, George. *Seventeenth Century Contexts.* Chicago: University of Chicago Press, 1961.

Wilson, Bryan R. *Sects and Society.* Berkeley and Los Angeles: University of California Press, 1961.

Wolfe, Don M. "Unsigned Pamphlets of Richard Overton: 1641–1649." *Huntington Library Quarterly,* XXI (1957–1958), 167–201.

Wolfson, Harry A. *Religious Philosophy.* Cambridge, Mass.: Belknap Press of Harvard University Press, 1961.

Wright, Leonard N. "Christian Mortalism in England (1643–1713)," unpub. diss., University of Texas, 1939.

————. "Christian Mortalism: A Prospectus for the History of an Idea." *The Great Torch Race; Essays in Honor of Reginald Harvey Griffith.* Ed. Mary Tom Osborne. Austin: University of Texas Press, 1961.

Zagorin, P[erez]. "The Authorship of *Mans Mortallitie.*" *The Library,* 5th Ser., V (1950–1951), 179–182.

————. *A History of Political Thought in the English Revolution.* London: Routledge & Kegan Paul, 1954.

Index

Acontius, Jacobus, 91
Allegorical interpretation, 42–44, 50–54
Alley, William, 117–118
Anabaptists: defined and related to Radical Reformation, 19–20; took over Münster, 20, 96; and Zwickau prophets, 28; associated with Everard, 49; liked free discussion of Scripture, 91; source of Christian mortalism, 92–93; and literal interpretation of Scripture, 94–95; recapitulated history of heresy, 95; poor relationship with state, 96; early activity in England, 111–120; considered soul sleeping adiaphorous, 112; royal commission opposed them, 114; complaint about their increase, 117; ordered out of England, 117; and Wightman, 123–124; their Venetian synod, 125; attacked by Featley, 126; attitudes shared by Milton, 187–188, 190–191; attitudes shared by Hobbes, 187–188, 190–191; attitudes shared by Overton, 188, 190; Hobbes and Milton held one of their views of soul, 191. See also Baptists; Baptists, General; Baptists, Particular
Annihilationism: defined and distinguished from soul sleeping, 2, 13–16; followers inspired by the Holy Spirit, 4; compared with Epicurism, 35–36; associated with mysticism, 36–38; identified heaven with regeneration, 39; exposed by Rutherford and Roger Hutchinson, 39–40, 59; associated with Winstanley, 54–55; connected with Familism by Baillie, 58, 75; supported perfectionism, 67; advocated by Family of Love, 68; related to Averroism, 68; and Gorton, 71–73; denounced by Calamy, 73; five statements of, 74–75; incompatible with soul sleeping, 75; related to pantheism, 76, 86; in Randall and Webbe, 77; in Independent Churches in Somersetshire, 78–79; widespread in Army, 79; as Ranter doctrine, 83–84; disrupted Quakers, 86. See also Experimental Christianity; Familism; Family of Love; Family of the Mount; Ranters
Antinomianism: associated with experimental Christians, 46; associated with Everard, 49; associated with Webbe, 77–78; radically expressed by Ranters, 82–83
Antiscripturists, 44, 46–48, 79, 128–129
Apostles' Creed, 29, 97
Arabian mortalists: and Browne, 2, 151, 152; described by Eusebius, 16–17; condemned by St. Augustine, 17; converted by Origen, 17, 113
Archer, John, 103, 137–138
Aristotle, 4, 8, 9, 22, 28–29, 30
Attaway, Mrs., 4, 132–133, 187, 190
Augustine, Saint, 17, 173
Averroës, 8, 9, 14n, 68

Baillie, Robert, 14n, 58, 75, 137
Baptists, 67–68, 144, 145. See also Anabaptists; Baptists, General; Baptists, Particular
Baptists, General (Arminian or Freewill), 4; as church nearest the latitudinarian model, 91–92, 97–98, 121–123; not opposed to soul sleeping, 97–98; their close association with soul sleeping, 119–133; Payne warned against their soul-sleeping ideas, 119–120; first English community identified, 120; Haarlem group said soul of Christ died, 120, 180; Helwys-Murton church, 122–123; Richard Overton a member, 124–125; their numbers, 126–127; distinguished from Particular Baptists, 126–127; Crab preached mortalism, 127; identified with Edwards' Independent Churches in Somersetshire, 130; held debate on soul's immortality, 130–131; John Batty a member, 130–131;